Mindfulness and Acceptance in Couple and Family Therapy

D1431735

Diane R. Gehart

Mindfulness and Acceptance in Couple and Family Therapy

DREXEL UNIVERSITY
HEALTH SCIENCES LIBRARIES
HAHNEMANN LIBRARY

 Springer

Prof. Diane R. Gehart
California State University
Northridge
CA 91330
USA

**WM
430.5
.M3
G311m
2012**

Please note that additional material for this book can be downloaded from http://extras. springer.com

ISBN 978-1-4614-3032-2   ISBN 978-1-4614-3033-9 (eBook)
DOI 10.1007/978-1-4614-3033-9
Springer New York Heidelberg Dordrecht London

Library of Congress Control Number: 2012933752

© Springer Science+Business Media New York 2012
This work is subject to copyright. All rights are reserved by the Publisher, whether the whole or part of the material is concerned, specifically the rights of translation, reprinting, reuse of illustrations, recitation, broadcasting, reproduction on microfilms or in any other physical way, and transmission or information storage and retrieval, electronic adaptation, computer software, or by similar or dissimilar methodology now known or hereafter developed. Exempted from this legal reservation are brief excerpts in connection with reviews or scholarly analysis or material supplied specifically for the purpose of being entered and executed on a computer system, for exclusive use by the purchaser of the work. Duplication of this publication or parts thereof is permitted only under the provisions of the Copyright Law of the Publisher's location, in its current version, and permission for use must always be obtained from Springer. Permissions for use may be obtained through RightsLink at the Copyright Clearance Center. Violations are liable to prosecution under the respective Copyright Law.
The use of general descriptive names, registered names, trademarks, service marks, etc. in this publication does not imply , even in the absence of a specific statement, that such names are exempt from the relevant protective laws and regulations and therefore free for general use.
While the advice and information in this book are believed to be true and accurate at the date of publication, neither the authors nor the editors nor the publisher can accept any legal responsibility for any errors or omissions that may be made. The publisher makes no warranty, express or implied, with respect to the material contained herein.

Printed on acid-free paper

Springer is part of Springer Science+Business Media (www.springer.com)

Preface

The roots of this book go back to a hot and humid August afternoon in Williamsburg, Virginia, in 1988. My advisor had finished signing me up for the requisite first semester courses in psychology, when he told me to select an elective. As I flipped through my options, I was surprised to find that William and Mary had a department of religion; it was a state school, after all. As a native Southern Californian, the course in Buddhism caught my eye and, even though my professor was quite puzzled, I insisted he sign me up. I found the constructionist philosophy that described reality as constructed by the perceiver through language challenging but was fascinated, if not obsessed. Soon, I was speaking Chinese and majoring in both East Asian Studies and psychology. However, I was forced to keep these two worlds separate: I could not find a single professor in psychology or religion studies who was willing to supervise a senior thesis on Buddhism and psychology, all claiming the topic was inappropriate for scholarly study.

Unable to follow both passions, I decided to pursue a doctoral degree that would allow me to become a Tibetan Buddhist scholar, earning a fellowship at the University of Washington. However, when I heard most of the graduates ended up doing classified work for the CIA rather than giving boring lectures in an ivory tower, I left to go back to less adventurous study of psychology. Unfortunately, at the time, I didn't understand the nuances of the field and landed in a marriage and family therapy program instead. As often happens in life, this "mistake" turned out to be a blessing in disguise. Once I sat through my first family therapy theories course, I knew I had finally found the discipline that would allow me to follow both of my passions. The systemic and postmodern family therapy theories were nothing less than Western therapeutic versions of Eastern philosophies, allowing me to put Buddhist principles into practical action that enriched the lives of others without my having to master 11 foreign languages. I had found my academic home. Thankfully, I had an open-minded faculty that allowed me to periodically pull out some of my Buddhist resources to write about how I approached family therapy as Buddhism-in-action. After graduate school, however, I was careful to never whisper a word about the commingling of these two worlds, remembering the shameful lessons I learned earlier about subjects worthy of study in the academy.

When mindfulness began to emerge as major force in the field of psychotherapy, I was stunned. The taboo had been broken. I literally had tears of joy in my eyes. Although I know it seems a bit dramatic to those outside of academia, it was as if I were finally pardoned for my scholarly sins. I later learned that Jon Kabat-Zinn (1990) did much of the liberation by introducing the practice of mindfulness in behavioral medicine; thus, I, like so many others, am forever indebted to his pioneering spirit.

In this book, I hope to bring this journey full circle by connecting mindfully oriented therapies and their family therapy kin, to their Buddhist foundations. I will do this in three parts. In the first, I will review the research and philosophical foundations for using mindfulness, acceptance, and Buddhist psychology in couple and family therapy. The second part of the book provides a detailed and practical approach for putting these ideas into action in the therapy room, including:

- Forming and maintaining a therapeutic relationship
- Developing a case conceptualization
- Identifying goals and developing a treatment plan
- Using mindfulness and acceptance principles to approach "treatment"
- Intervening to make changes in couple and family relationships
- Instructing clients in mindfulness practices as appropriate
- Practicing therapist self-care with mindfulness

The practices in this approach are designed so that therapists can easily integrate them into their current practices, regardless of their preferred model. Finally, the last part of the book addresses using mindfulness in training and for therapist self-care. Throughout the book, I share numerous client cases, all of which are based on clients I have seen over the years; identifying information and specifics have been altered to protect their identities. I am particularly grateful to the adventurous spirit of these people who explored new territory with me as I developed the practices described in this book.

I invite you, the reader, to discover the potentials of mindfulness and acceptance in helping your clients to live fuller and richer lives and to also find ways to do the same for yourself. Enjoy the journey. Namaste.

Contents

Part III   Training and Self-Care

Part I
Introduction to Philosophical and Research Foundations

Chapter 1
Mindfulness in Therapy

Jeffery sat slumped over and quiet at the far edge of the couch in my office as his mother frantically explained that his teachers say that his behavior had become a serious problem: fighting with his classmates, yelling out in class, and not turning in the little classwork he managed to complete. The 10-year-old knew the principal's office well. They recommended the mother have him assessed for attention deficit hyperactivity disorder. Although Susana and her husband, Al, had not agreed on much since their divorce 3 years ago, they quickly came to consensus: no medication for our kid. So, Susana brought him to me in hopes that therapy may help.

During our first session, Susana's most pressing question was whether there were any treatments we could try before resorting to medication. I offered a client-friendly review of the literature and evidence base (Northey, Wells, Silverman, & Bailey, 2002) and also described mindfulness as an emerging approach that had the potential to actually address underlying neurological issues. She, more so that Jeffery, was eager to give it a whirl.

In the next session, I provided training in basic mindfulness breath meditation and worked with them to collaboratively develop a practice plan. They agreed that they would "sit and watch themselves breath" for 5 minutes before going to school was the best plan. They would do it together in the living room after breakfast and use the timer on mom's cell phone to signal the start and end of the session.

When I followed up on their experience the next week, Jeffery excitedly explained that he thought mindfulness was *very helpful*: because it put *his mom* in much better mood! He liked his "new mom" and was willing to keep practicing himself if it helped her. Susana confessed that committing to 5 minutes of quietly focusing on her breath reminded her not to rush in a crazed panic out the door each morning but to keep a sense of perspective. She also thought that Jeffery seemed calmer and more cooperative. Furthermore, she reported that her ex-husband agreed to keep up the schedule using printed instructions and online recordings to maintain consistency. Their shared value to avoiding medication enabled them to coordinate parenting around this issue better than any other in the past 3 years.

Over the next several weeks, they reported that things increasingly improved: fewer (and soon no) trips to the principal's office; fewer recesses on detention; and more classwork turned in. In session, we would discuss not only the practical elements of how mindfulness practice went each week (e.g., did you practice and how often) but more importantly the effects they saw and the *meanings* they made of these (e.g., "I am calmer"; "I am a better mother"; "Having a calm morning helps me focus more in class"). These meanings provided fertile ground for identifying new and additional actions that were consonant with being "calmer" and "better" at school and home. We also examined the effect that mindfulness had on the relationships in the family: Susana and Jeffery had significantly fewer struggles and Susana and Al were communicating the best they had since the divorce. Jeffery thought it was "cool" that he had the same routine at both homes and had the impression that his teachers and principal were more encouraging. He also liked having the special time with his dad without his stepmother present. After 3 months, not only was Jeffery rarely in trouble at school but also his relationship with his mother was the best in years, and Susana and Al were co-parenting well for the first time after the divorce.

Mindfulness had a ripple effect in the family that affected far more than their initial complaint about Jeffery's behavior. The approach helped create a positive atmosphere at home and enabled each member of the family to experience a sense of competence that spilled over into other areas of their lives. Their commitment to practice mindfulness ushered in a shared daily task that resulted in a new sense of cooperation and shared purpose. Jeffery's teachers and principal began relating to him differently, and as they did, so did his peers.

Although certainly not all families will be as cooperative or as successful as Jeffery's was with the practice of mindfulness, therapists can integrate mindfulness and related concepts such as acceptance into their work to expand options for helping couples and families. Mindfulness is quickly becoming established as a respected evidence-based treatment for adult depression, anxiety, and numerous other mental and physical issues (Baer, 2003), but increasingly its potential to help children, couples, and families is being explored. This book is designed to guide therapists with the theory, research foundation, and practical skills to apply mindfulness and acceptance to assist clients in becoming more successful in their relationships.

Mindfulness and Family Therapy

Of all the forms of suffering, perhaps the most perplexing and ubiquitous are couple and family relationships. As the saying goes: "can't live with them and can't live without them." The intensity of love relationships almost always also involves confusing moments of hurt and anger. Experienced relational therapists know that couple and family work touches the essence of what it means to be human—people learn how to trust and find safety with one another, forgive transgressions, love more fully and deeply, and discover what matters most in life. It is also hard work: often everyone leaves the session exhausted. But the work is worth the effort and investment: researchers have increasingly found that happiness and physical health are integrally tied to the quality of one's intimate relationships (Gambrel & Keeling, 2010).

This book provides therapists with a detailed and practical guide for using mindfulness, acceptance, and related practices for working with couples, children, and families in outpatient and private practice settings. A coherent, integrated approach is described that includes mindfulness approach to:

- Forming and maintaining a therapeutic relationship —
- Developing a case conceptualization
- Identifying goals and developing a treatment plan
- Using mindfulness and acceptance principles to approach "treatment"
- Intervening to make changes in couple and family relationships
- Instructing clients in mindfulness practices as appropriate ⌐
- Practicing therapist self-care with mindfulness —

Rather than prescribe a single method, a wide range of options for using these practices is described, allowing clinicians flexibility in deciding how best to integrate these ideas into their current work and skill set. But, before outlining this therapeutic approach, I will begin by defining mindfulness, exploring its philosophical foundations, and examining the current evidence base for these practices.

Defining Mindfulness

As you will soon discover, mindfulness does not have a simple, straightforward definition. Instead, as a multifaceted concept, the definition of mindfulness evolves with your experience of it. So, let's start at the beginning:

As used in therapy, mindfulness is the translation of the Pali *sati* and Sanskrit *smrti*, which are sometimes translated as *awareness* or *discernment*. Kabat-Zinn (2003), the premier pioneer of mindfulness work in behavioral health, has over the years developed the following definition:

> the awareness that emerges through paying attention on purpose, in the present moment, and non-judgmentally to the unfolding of experience moment by moment (p. 145).

The key elements of Kabat-Zinn's definition are (a) intentional awareness, (b) of present moment, and (c) without judgment. Most commonly, mindfulness practice involves the intentional awareness of one's breath in the present moment without any judgment of the breath or the thoughts and feelings that arise during the practice. Mindfulness is also applied to virtually all present-moment experiences, both internal and external, such as walking, eating, hearing, feeling emotion, and feeling physical pain.

To facilitate research on mindfulness, Bishop et al. (2004) developed a commonly used two-part operational definition that combines the first two elements of

Kabat Zinn's into one and adds further nuance and contour to the definition of mindfulness. Their definition of mindfulness is as follows:

1. The self-regulation of attention so that it is maintained on immediate experience and
2. A particular orientation toward one's experience in the present moment…that is characterized by curiosity, openness, and acceptance (p. 232).

This operational definition emphasizes that mindful attention is inherently a *self-regulated* attention, requiring continual intentional effort and a second-order process to maintain focus. Additionally, they further explicate the quality of the practitioner's relationship to present-moment experience, which is one of curiosity about and acceptance of whatever is experienced. The element of acceptance has been of particular interest to couple and family therapists (Christensen, Sevier, Simpson, & Gattis, 2004).

Brown, Ryan, and Creswell (2007) add two additional qualities to their definition of mindfulness: (a) nonconceptual and (b) empirical. They highlight that mindfulness is a *nonconceptual* state of mind: when in a mindful state, the mind does not use preconceived concepts to interpret the world (or uses them at a minimum) but instead takes on a noninterfering stance by simply noticing what is taking place. This nonconceptual approach is also empirical in that the "full facts" are sought in a manner similar to an objective scientist seeking nonbiased descriptions of phenomenon before making a judgment or determination. This nonconceptual stance integrates nicely with the numerous constructivist traditions in family therapy (Gehart & McCollum, 2007; Gehart & Pare, 2009). In addition, Brown et al. draw our attention to the bottom-up processing element of mindfulness that has also become of great interest to neuroresearchers such as Dan Siegel (see Chap. 2 for further discussion).

Perhaps one of best descriptions of the subjective experience of mindfulness comes not from a Buddhist or psychotherapy source but from Rumi, a thirteenth-century Sufi poet:

The Guest House
This being human is a guesthouse
Every morning a new arrival.
A joy, a depression, a meanness,
some momentary awareness comes
as an unexpected visitor.
Welcome and entertain them all!
Even if they are a crowd of sorrows,
who violently sweep your house
empty of its furniture,
still treat each guest honorably.
He may be clearing you out for some new delight.
The dark thought, the shame, the malice,
meet them at the door laughing,
and invite them in.
Be grateful for whoever comes,
because each has been sent
as a guide from beyond (Barks, 2003, pp. 179–180).

Rumi's description captures the subjective challenge of practicing mindfulness. "Acceptance" and "being in the moment" sound romantic, ideal, and easy enough until you sit down to do it yourself only to discover that much of what arises in the present moment is unpleasant at best and at times nearly unbearable; suddenly the "violence" Rumi speaks of becomes painfully clear. Learning to be a gracious host to whatever arises in one's consciousness is perhaps one of life's greatest challenges. Rumi's assumption of a positive benefit from greeting all that arises within with acceptance is perhaps more optimistic than many Buddhists would argue, but an extra dose of encouragement can be helpful when engaging in this challenging practice.

Multifaceted Definition of Mindfulness

Putting the behavioral, operational, and subjective descriptions of mindfulness together, we arrive at the following multifaceted definition:

> *Mindfulness*: Self-regulated, present-moment awareness that welcomes all experience without preconception or judgment, accepting "what is" with curiosity and compassion.

The most basic component of mindfulness is intentionally focusing and refocusing one's *awareness* on a single point of *present-moment* experience, such as one's breath or a physical sensation. This attention must be continually *self-regulated*, meaning effort is used to maintain the focus. Next, the spirit of this attention is a gracious *welcoming* of whatever arises without preconceived notions of what "should" be or judgment of what does arise. And, finally, a spirit of open *curiosity* and *acceptance* requires nonreactivity and an investigative yet deeply *compassionate* attitude to what is at its core, a vulnerable and humbling experience. If you are new to the practice, be forewarned it is not for the faint of heart.

State and Trait

And if this hasn't been complex enough, when reading academic literature on mindfulness an important distinction is made between the *state* of mindfulness and the *trait* of mindfulness (Didonna, 2009). As it sounds, the state of mindfulness refers to being in a state of present-moment awareness. In contrast, the trait of mindfulness refers to a person's tendency to more frequently enter into and more easily abide in mindful states; it describes a disposition. A person may demonstrate the trait of mindfulness more frequently because of regular mindfulness practice, environment, ui possibly genetics (Smalley & Winston, 2010). Most of the pen-and-paper measures for mindfulness are for the trait of mindfulness. Thus, when reviewing mindfulness research literature, clinicians should be careful to separate out these two streams of study.

Mindfulness in a Nutshell

As essentially a quality of and attitude toward awareness, mindfulness can be practiced with anything that can be the focus of awareness: an object, a bodily sensation, physical movement, an emotion, or even a thought. The all-time, cross-cultural favorite focus for mindful awareness is the breath. Always available during any conscious moment, it is the most convenient object of attention for practice. Furthermore, neurological researchers suggest that another benefit of focusing on the breath is that the back-and-forth rhythm helps bring the brain into an integrated neurological state, which promotes optimal brain functioning (Siegel, 2007; see Chap. 2 for further discussion).

In a nutshell, *mindfulness breath awareness involves observing the breath while quieting the inner chatter in the mind*. That's it. It sounds simple but takes a lifetime to master because the mind—unless trained—cannot stay focused and quiet for long. Within seconds, it is off: wondering if this is the right way to meditate; what's for dinner; what did my sister mean when she said *that*; reviewing to-do lists; reliving taunting from a bully in second grade; calculating taxes; back to dinner; etc. (and, yes, it generally is in about this much order and about this logical).

Although the basic instructions for practice are straightforward, the challenging and more critical aspect of practice is *refocusing* once the mind has started to wander: noticing that the mind has wandered off and then returning the focus *without* berating the self for losing focus. For most of us, returning the focus without judgment is the hardest part—it is also where most of the learning occurs. Returning the focus requires first accepting whatever arises without preconception or judgment and then compassionately refocusing one's attention without reprimanding the self for losing focus. Thus, *acceptance and compassion are learned primarily through the refocusing process* rather than the moments of relatively blissful nonconceptual, present-moment awareness. For this reason, I maintain that when using mindfulness to work on psychological and relational issues losing focus and refocusing are the *therapeutic moments* more so than the sustained periods of mindful awareness, which are more associated with spiritual development (see section "Is Religion or Spirituality Involved?"). I have found that when training clients in mindfulness, emphasizing this point greatly increases their willingness to try and fail and try again.

To sum up and provide a realistic picture, mindfulness practice looks something like this:

Focus—lose focus—gently refocus.
Focus—lose focus—gently refocus.

Focus—lose focus—gently refocus.
Focus—lose focus—gently refocus.
Focus—lose focus—gently refocus.

Repeat as often as necessary until the bell rings to signal you to stop.

It is much like a child learning how to walk or ride a bike, except the child actually learns and masters the task at hand. Committing to mindfulness practice involves a lifetime of falling down and picking oneself up again—and each time with more compassion for, acceptance of, and rejoicing in what it means to be oh-so fully human.

Is Religion or Spirituality Involved?

Although the question of whether religion or spirituality is involved seems like a straightforward question, again, there are many surprising answers. Most of the literature and practice around mindfulness focuses on its Buddhist roots, and indeed this was Kabat-Zinn's (1990) original source of inspiration. Most would agree that the Buddhists have the most advanced meditation practices because more so than other traditions they center their religion on such practices. However, mindfulness practices can be found in virtually all major world religions and societies. For example, Christians have a tradition *of contemplative prayer*, which has been revived and modernized as *centering prayer* in the past years as interest in mindfulness has grown (Ferguson, 2010). Interestingly, both traditions teach the same mindfulness techniques, focusing on the breath and quieting the mind, and eventually (in advanced spiritual practice) moving to having no focus, simply bare consciousness. The primary difference is that Christians use contemplate prayer as a means of having direct contact with God: as the mind quiets and settles and experiences longer periods of stillness one has greater contact with the divine. Jewish and Islamic traditions have similar contemplative meditation practices that help practitioners quiet the mind and achieve greater contact with God (Hamdan, 2010; Weiss & Levy, 2010).

Buddhism does not use mindfulness or other meditations to directly connect with God because unlike most other world religions Buddhism is technically atheistic: Buddha is not considered a god but a man. Furthermore, unlike Judeo-Christian religions, Buddhism is not faith-based; instead it is considered empirical (Levine, 2000). The Buddha encouraged his followers not to take his teachings based on faith and instead to study, explore, and experiment with his teachings and judge for themselves whether or not they are true. As the majority of its teachings addressed the sources of human suffering and their antidotes, namely moral action and managing one's state of consciousness (i.e., mindfulness and its variants), Buddhism and its empirical test-it-for-yourself tradition has many parallels with Western psychology, and in many ways is more similar to modern psychology than Judeo-Christian religions.

Furthermore, therapists should also be aware that the way mindfulness is used in therapy is different than its use for spiritual development. When practicing mindfulness for spiritual purposes, the benefits are derived primarily from the quiet moments of stillness. However, when practicing mindfulness to address psychological issues, the most important outcomes result from the *refocusing* of attention rather than the moments of sustained still awareness. Neurologically, refocusing rewires the brain so that the prefrontal cortex, the "higher" and more logical centers of the brain, is able to calm the anxious limbic system and the stress response; thus, refocusing helps develop the neuropathways to better manage stress. Additionally, it is primarily through the refocusing that a person has a chance to learn acceptance and compassion, which reduces judgment of self and other. Often clients find it helpful to reframe their "inability to focus": instead of being a sign of failure, it is absolutely necessary to provide them the opportunity to refocus and thereby derive the psychological benefits they desire most.

The Neurophysiology of Mindfulness

Many of the benefits of mindfulness are believed to be traceable to how it impacts the stress response (Badenoch, 2008; Goleman, 2003, 2005; Goleman & Schwartz, 1976; Treadway & Lazar, 2010). The stress response, also referred to as the *fight-flight-freeze response*, is comprised of the *sympathetic* and *parasympathetic nervous systems*, the former triggering stress and the latter relaxation. The stress response is carried out primarily by the limbic system in the middle regions of the brain. The stress response is triggered when the amygdala interprets an internal or external situation as dangerous; this activates the sympathetic nervous system and a cascade of neurotransmitters that prepares us to fight, flee, or freeze by increasing our heart rate, increasing muscle strength, and dilating our eyes among other things (Badenoch, 2008). In these stressful moments, the person has less access to the slower "reason" centers of the prefrontal cortex as the amygdala "highjacks" the brain for split-second survival responses necessary in life-and-death moments (Goleman, 2003, 2005). This remarkable response works quite well for physical threats, such as saber tooth tigers, an invading army, or a child in distress in need of rescue; in these cases, humans may have "superhuman" strength and stamina to defend their lives and the lives of others.

Once the situation is deemed to be safe, the parasympathetic shuts down the hyperdrive function and the body relaxes, returning to normal functioning. This stress response system is not designed to be run for long periods of time, nor is it designed to be run often as it takes a heavy physical toll on the body (digestion is shut down, blood is diverted from organs, and the heart and muscles must work overtime). Unfortunately, the body uses this same stress response for psychological threats, which often do not have the same clear signal to turn off the system when the situation is again "safe." Psychological threats can go on for hours as a person worries, ruminates, and rehearses the stressful event, greatly overtaxing a system that was designed to be used sparingly and for short bursts of time.

Mindfulness may serve to help people increase their ability to shut off the stress response and invoke the relaxation response and increase their neurological capacity to do so. In fact, emerging research suggests that brain structures may physically change to increase a person's ability to shut down the stress response. A series of studies reviewed and summarized by Treadway and Lazar (2010) have found that long-term mindfulness practice increases cortical thickness (higher centers of the brain), including in regions involved with observing internal and external sensations, decision-making, cognitive processing, memory, and sense of agency. Furthermore, in a study with new meditators who had practiced for only 8 weeks, Hölzel et al. (2010) found that mindfulness practice reduced the amount of grey matter in the amygdala (part of the limbic system) and was correlated with a reported decrease in stress. These studies provide preliminary evidence that mindfulness increases brain neuroplasticity, increasing the function of the prefrontal cortex and shrinking areas associated with the stress response and thereby physically enabling the brain to better handle stress. The profound affect that mindfulness seems to have on the stress response helps to explain the numerous and extensive psychological and relational benefits associated with this practice.

Benefits of Mindfulness

Mindfulness researchers have identified an impressive range of positive outcomes related to mindfulness, including relational and psychological benefits, which are believed to be largely attributed to its effectiveness in altering the stress response.

Relational Benefits of Mindfulness

Researchers have identified the following relational benefits of mindfulness practice and "trait" mindfulness:

- *Increased marital satisfaction*: Couples who had greater "trait" mindfulness were more happily married, the primary mediating variables being the ability to communicate one's emotions effectively and to regulate anger (Barnes, Brown, Krusemark, Campbell, & Rogge, 2007; Burpee & Langer, 2005, Wachs & Cordova, 2007).
- *Better communication*: Couples who had greater "trait" mindfulness had better quality communication, specifically less verbal aggression, negativity, and withdrawal and more positive problem-solving, communication, and support (Barnes et al., 2007).

- *Increased empathy and compassion:* Mindfulness increases a person's capacity for empathy and taking the perspective of others (Birnie, Speca, & Carlson, 2010; Block-Lerner, Adair, Plumb, Rhatigan, & Orsillo, 2007).
- *Increased acceptance of self and partner:* Mindfulness and related acceptance enhancing techniques increase acceptance of one's partner and self (Christensen et al., 2004; Harris, 2009; Peterson, Eifert, Feingold, & Davidson, 2009; Pruitt & McCollum, 2010; South, Doss, & Christensen, 2010).
- *Increased awareness of interactional patterns:* Mindfulness-based parenting programs increase parents' abilities to take a "metaperspective" and mindfully observe their problematic interaction patterns with children (Dumas, 2005).
- *Increased ability to respond with awareness:* Mindfulness-based parenting and couple programs have also been used to help participants develop mindful communication skills (Carson, Carson, Gil, & Baucom, 2004; Duncan, Coatsworth, & Greenberg, 2009a, 2009b; Pruitt & McCollum, 2010).
- *Greater sense of freedom and safety in relationships:* Experienced meditators report that consistent practice increased their ability to feel safe in relationships, allowing them to lower their defenses and reveal more of themselves (Pruitt & McCollum, 2010).
- *Greater sense of unity and separation:* Experienced meditators frequently report a deep sense of unity with all of life as well as an awareness of their experience of being a separate and independent entity; this spiritual sense of unity translates to a more holistic experience of intimacy and independence in their couple and family relationships (Pruitt & McCollum, 2010).

Psychological Benefits of Mindfulness

A rapidly growing body of evidence indicates that mindfulness may be beneficial in treating a surprisingly wide range of mental health disorders, including depressive, bipolar, anxiety, eating, attentional, conduct, personality, and substance use disorders (Baer, 2003; Shapiro & Carlson, 2009). The psychological benefits of mindfulness include:

- *Increased positive emotion and well-being:* Increasing a person's daily experience of positive emotion and overall well-being (a.k.a., happiness; Brown & Ryan, 2003; Fredrickson, Cohn, Coffey, Pek, & Finkel, 2008).
- *Reduced stress:* Reducing a person's daily experience of stress and increasing the frequency of the physiological state of relaxation (Hölzel et al., 2010).
- *Increased emotional regulation:* A greater ability to regulate negative and challenging emotions (Brown & Ryan, 2003).
- *Increased metacognitive awareness:* Improves a person's ability to view thoughts and feelings as passing mental events (Kocovski, Segal, & Battista, 2009; Pruitt & McCollum, 2010; York, 2007).

- *Decreased rumination*: Reduces the tendency to dwell on the negative emotional outcomes of events, which is associated with depression and anxiety (Kocovski et al., 2009).
- *Improved attention*: Increases a person's ability to focus and concentrate on tasks (Kocovski et al., 2009); one study found significant improvements in attention after only 5 days of 20 min/day practice (Tang et al., 2007).
- *Increased acceptance and decreased avoidance*: Enables people to better accept difficult thoughts, emotions, or situations; avoidance of such things if often viewed as the root of many mental health disorders (Kocovski et al., 2009; York, 2007).
- *Clarification of values*: By reducing the tendency to operate on automatic pilot, a person often experiences greater clarity in terms of values, goals, and life direction (Kocovski et al., 2009).
- *Increased self-compassion*: Helping people to have greater care and compassion for themselves has been associated with improved psychological health (Baer, 2010; Pruitt & McCollum, 2010).

Mindfulness, Well-Being, and Positive Psychology

As people who regularly experience mindfulness are happier and have more satisfying relationships, positive psychologists, researchers who study happiness, have become increasingly interested in mindfulness. Some have even described mindfulness as the "missing link" between therapy and positive psychology, suggesting that much of what therapists do to promote long-term happiness boils down to increasing a client's ability to be accepting of "what is" in the present moment (Hamilton, Kitzman, & Guyotte, 2006). From this perspective, therapists may benefit from exploring what is currently in their repertoire (which I will do in Chap. 2) and what they can add to their repertoire (which I will do in Chaps. 4–8) that can increase client's tendency to be mindful.

Mindfulness in Psychotherapy

Historically, mainstream psychotherapists have been suspicious of meditation practices as some form of New Age mumbo-jumbo. Images of shabbily clad groupies sitting cross-legged humming Sanskrit chants come to mind. However, Jon Kabat Zinn planted a seed over 3 decades ago that has not only sprouted but has grown beyond anyone's wildest dreams. He began offering mindfulness-based stress reduction (MBSR) workshops to patients at the University of Massachusetts hospital whose physicians believed they could benefit from techniques that would reduce anxiety. He deliberately chose to disconnect mindfulness from its Buddhists roots so that its religious origins would not become an issue in its acceptance in the realm of science and medicine (Baer, 2003, 2006; Kabat-Zinn, 1990). His remarkable success can also be attributed to careful, systematic research of his program, providing growing evidence of its efficacy with a wide range of physical and psychological concerns. The result has been nothing short of a mental health revolution. In less than a decade, the psychotherapeutic community reversed its skeptical stance to a whole-hearted embrace.

Although seemingly odd bedfellows, cognitive-behavioral therapists have most enthusiastically explored applications of mindfulness in therapy. The behavioral medicine work of Jon Kabat-Zinn's MBSR is undoubtedly the matchmaker between mindfulness and cognitive-behavioral therapists. Mindfulness revolutionizes traditional cognitive-behavioral therapies by introducing the concept of *acceptance*: acceptance of the unwanted and disturbing behaviors, thoughts, and feelings. Acceptance has been referred to as the "third wave of behavioral therapies" (Hayes, 2004). The National Institutes of Health have supported these efforts by dramatically increased funding for mindfulness-based therapies, from 0 in 1998 to 44 in 2008 (Shapiro & Carlson, 2009).

Mindfulness-Based and Mindfulness-Informed Therapies

Mindfulness therapies are typically classified as either mindfulness-based or mindfulness-informed (Shapiro & Carlson, 2009). *Mindfulness-based therapies* teach mindfulness meditation practices as primary intervention. In contrast, *mindfulness-informed therapies* incorporate mindfulness and acceptance principles into a broader therapeutic model. Several mindfulness-based and mindfulness-informed therapies have been developed in recent years.

Mindfulness-Based Stress Reduction

The first mindfulness-based approach and the template for virtually all mindfulness-based therapies, MBSR, was developed by Kabat-Zinn (1990) in 1979 at the University of Massachusetts Medical Center to serve patients with difficult-to-treat medical issues. MBSR is an intensive 8-week group program with up to 35 participants per group, making it unusually cost-effective. The MBSR curriculum includes the following key elements:

- Two to three hours of weekly group meetings over 8 weeks
- A 6-hour silent retreat in addition to the group meetings
- Daily practice of 20–45 minutes
- Mindfulness breath meditation
- Mindfulness-based body scans
- Training in simple yoga postures using mindfulness
- Loving-kindness meditation
- Experience with daily mindfulness activities

Although this is a relatively demanding program, adherence and completion rates are high, and follow-up studies indicate that 80–95% of participants continue to practice mindfulness (Baer, 2003). The teachers are carefully and extensively trained through programs offered at the Center for Mindfulness at the University of Massachusetts.

Mindfulness-Based Cognitive Therapy

Based directly on MBSR, mindfulness-based cognitive therapy (MBCT) (Segal, Williams, & Teasdale, 2002) was designed to treat depression and depression relapse. Using the same 8-week group format, MBCT is designed for smaller groups with up to 12 participants. The MBCT curriculum includes the same meditations that are in MBSR except loving-kindness meditation, which is not formally part of MBCT although kindness towards oneself is emphasized (Shapiro & Carlson, 2009). In contrast to MBSR, the didactic material focuses on depression rather than stress and the stress response. Unlike the traditional cognitive-behavioral approach of logically arguing with depressive thinking, MBCT teaches clients to become aware of the negative thought patterns and change *their relationship* to them by seeing them as "just" thoughts that will come and go if one does not "feed" into them. Thus, the emphasis is on not getting overly identified with depressive thinking rather than trying to force it to stop.

MBCT is considered the "gold standard" for depression relapse prevention (Shapiro & Carlson, 2009). Although most forms of therapy are effective in treating depression (Elkin, Shea, Watkins, & Imber, 1989), the primary challenge has been in preventing relapse, which occurs in at least half of all clients diagnosed with depression. MBCT is the first intervention that has shown significant reduction in depression relapse, from 78 to 36% for persons with three or more episodes (Ma & Teasdale, 2004).

Mindfulness-Based Relationship Enhancement

Of particular relevance for family therapists, Carson and colleagues (Carson, Carson, Gil, & Baucom, 2004, 2006, 2007) have developed and conducted initial research on a relationship enhancement program for non-distressed couples based on the MBSR model. Compared to other mindfulness-based programs, mindfulness-based relationship enhancement (MBRE) includes more loving-kindness meditation, designed to increase compassion and care for one's partner, self, and others. Loving-kindness meditation is introduced in the first session and emphasized throughout the program. In addition, the curriculum includes mindful communication and listening, yoga exercises for couples, and mindful touch exercises. MBRE is a promising approach for helping non-distressed couples develop more satisfying relationships.

Mindfulness-Based Parenting Programs

Several mindfulness-based parenting programs have been developed: mindfulness-based parent training (Dumas, 2005), mindful parenting (Duncan et al., 2009a), and mindfulness-based childbirth and parenting (Duncan & Bardacke, 2010). All integrate mindfulness into existing, well-established parenting programs, however with different foci. Dumas (2005) uses mindfulness to reduce problematic automatic interactions by helping parents bring awareness to these and then change their responses. In contrast, Duncan et al. (2009a) use mindfulness to help parents bring awareness to in-the-moment interactions with their children, increase their emotional awareness, and improve the parents' ability to self-regulate. Duncan and colleagues have conducted research with promising findings on their approach (Coatsworth, Duncan, Greenberg, & Nix, 2010). Finally, mindfulness-based childbirth and parenting is based on the MBSR format but emphasizes body scan meditations and breathing to help prepare third trimester mothers for the birthing process.

Mindfulness-Based Relapse Prevention

Modeled after MBCT, mindfulness-based relapse prevention (MBRP) is designed to reduce relapse with persons addicted to substances (Witkiewitz, Marlatt, & Walker, 2005). This approach teaches clients how to use mindfulness to effectively manage urges and cravings by compassionately and curiously observing their rise and eventual decline, using techniques similar to those used in MBCT to de-identify with depressive thinking.

Mindfulness-Based Eating Awareness

Integrating MBSR and CBT, mindfulness-based eating awareness (MBEA) is an emerging approach for working with persons with binge eating disorder and obesity using mindfulness and guided meditations that address body image, weight, and eating-related processes (Kristeller & Wolever, 2011).

Dialectical Behavior Therapy

Although mindfulness meditation is not explicitly taught as it in MBSR and MBCT, dialectical behavior therapy (DBT; Linehan, 1993) includes mindfulness techniques as one of four main strategies to help persons diagnosed with borderline personality (and increasingly other disorders). In DBT, clients use mindfulness to observe, describe, and fully attend to their emotional experiences and actions to help them choose better responses. The approach focuses on helping clients more skillfully engage opposing opposites through dialectical integration.

Acceptance and Commitment Therapy

Similar to DBT, acceptance and commitment therapy (ACT) does not teach mindfulness meditation but instead integrates elements of mindfulness and the related concept of acceptance into behavior therapy to help clients with a wide range of concerns, such as depression, anxiety, and panic. In this approach, clients are encouraged to mindfully experience thoughts and feelings that are typically avoided; they learn to accept these and then commit to choosing more effective behaviors. Central to this approach, clients are helped to avoid *cognitive fusion*, or the mistaken belief that thoughts are true, real, and a defining part of the self.

New Horizons in Family Therapy: Mindfulness and Self-Regulation

Family therapy is grounded in study of *cybernetic* and *general systems theories*, which describe systems (groups of interrelated parts that act as a whole) as having two defining elements: (a) a tendency to maintain *homeostasis*, a dynamic but stable state, and (b) *self-regulation*, the ability to use feedback to maintain homeostasis (Bateson, 1972; Gehart, 2010). Systemic self-regulation is not a conscious process but rather a process that emerges through the interaction between parts of the system. Thus, in practical terms, no one part "consciously" decides and orchestrates how the system will self-regulate, instead self-regulation processes arise out of repeated interactions that form interactional rules that organize the system. For example, early in a couple's courtship, each person's response to the other's jokes, affection, anger, sadness, etc. begins to orchestrate a dance of connection that establishes the "norms" and expected behaviors (homeostasis) of the system. No single person dictates or controls these interactions, instead they naturally and spontaneously emerge through the ceaseless and complex set of back-and-forth interactions. These interactions evolve over time, and sometimes become rigid, stuck, or problematic, creating interpersonal conflict or intrapersonal distress (e.g., depression, anxiety, etc.).

Family therapy is a process of using specific techniques to interrupt problematic systemic patterns and enable new, preferred interactional patterns to structure these relationships. For example, couples who develop the nag-withdraw pattern do so after numerous episodes of one partner requesting or demanding something and the other partner withdrawing from the other in response. The more the second withdraws, the more the first pursues; this pattern continues until the system reaches a mutually defined uncomfortable outer limit, at which point the system self-corrects to reestablish a sense of "normalcy." With each repetition of this pattern, the couple develops relational "rules" for how intimacy and distance is managed; these rules "regulate" the system, creating a sense of discomfort when interactions get too distant from the core set of behaviors that define normalcy in the relationship (i.e., homeostasis). Systemic therapists help such couples by interrupting this pattern and thereby allowing them to respond differently and thereby develop new and more productive patterns.

Mindfulness provides systemic therapists with a complementary option to systemic self-regulation: *conscious self-regulation* (Labbre, 2011). In its essence, the regular practice of mindfulness enables individuals to consciously self-regulate their emotions and thoughts. For example, mindfulness practitioners who find themselves in the nag-withdrawal cycle are better able to consciously recognize moments when they get pulled into the cycle. They are also better able to consciously self-regulate to reduce the escalation and thereby short-circuit the negative interaction cycle. In some ways, virtually all couple and family therapy approaches strive to do this. Mindfulness provides therapists with a resource that enables clients to more consciously do so.

A pioneer of systemic family approaches, Jay Haley, once explained that to change ineffective interaction patterns it is usually necessary to intervene systemically because most clients are unable to consciously self-regulate: "Giving good advice (i.e., a 'straightforward' directive in strategic therapy) means the therapist assumes that people have rational control of what they are doing. To be successful in the therapy business, it may be better to drop that idea" (Haley, 1987, p. 61). Integrating mindfulness into family therapy practice may greatly increase the number of clients who can readily self-regulate and benefit from "good advice" and straightforward directives, thus expanding the options available to therapists for helping clients and potentially speeding up the process of therapy. Furthermore, one of the key elements of change in emotionally focused therapy (EFT; Johnson, 2004) involves the therapist helping clients to identify and express present-moment emotional experiences, in a manner quite similar to mindfulness. EFT results in superior outcomes—70% recovery rate and an effect size of 1.3 (Johnson, Hunsley, Greenberg, & Schindler, 1999)—and offers a practical model for using mindful experience to improve relationships. Therapeutic applications of mindfulness may enable the next generation of couple and family therapists to more efficiently help clients in ways that prior generations had not.

Mindfulness in Everyday Family Therapy: A Down-to-Earth Approach

Upon reading some will enthusiastically insist that we begin having all clients practice mindfulness. The evidence is clear that it helps with the vast majority of problems about the numerous benefits of mindfulness for which clients seek help. I am here to temper that aspiration. Outside of highly structured group programs such as MBSR and MBCT (Imel, Baldwin, Bonus, & MacCoon, 2008), most clients are not sufficiently motivated to meditate because it does not fit well with our 24/7, always-on-the-go pace of life (which is probably why we find it so helpful). Thus, a more realistic approach for the practitioner working with individual, couples, and families in non-group contexts is to employ more mindfulness-informed practices,

practices that integrate mindfulness into the more ordinary in-session interactions, such as the relationship or interventions, and reserve mindfulness-based interventions for clients where it might be more appropriate due to their diagnosis or proclivity for meditation. Thus, in the next chapter, we will turn our attention to understanding the philosophical connections between Buddhist psychology and family therapy practice to better understand how the principles of mindfulness can be used to rethink what we do in session and why.

Chapter 2
A Mindful Re-visioning of Couple and Family Therapy Practice

All that we are is the result of what we have thought: It is founded on our thought, it is made of our thoughts (Müller, 1898, p. 3).

Humans are builders. Not just of pyramids, skyscrapers, or spaceships, but of reality. Whether in the labs of neuroresearchers, physicists studying subatomic particles, or family therapists working with distressed youth, scientists and practitioners alike are drawing the conclusion that humans actively construct their experience of reality and that these constructions dramatically shape future experiences (Gergen, 1999; Hanson, 2009; Hayward & Varela, 1992). Although most contemporary scholars draw upon postmodern literature to describe a constructionist view of how the consciousness mind interacts with environment, a constructionist perspective has a long history in both Eastern and Western philosophies (McWilliams, 2010; Sagamura, Haruki, & Koshikawa, 2007). Of these more ancient traditions, Buddhism has been the most influential and enduring constructivist tradition as well as the one with the greatest emphasis on its psychological implications. Given the dramatic rise in interest in mindfulness-informed therapy approaches, it is culturally responsible for practitioners to better understand the philosophical foundations from which they arose (Sagamura, Haruki, & Koshikawa, 2007).

This chapter outlines the Buddhist foundations of mindfulness and acceptance practice and relates these to the philosophical assumptions informing contemporary couple and family therapy approaches, exploring points of similarity and differences and the implications for practice. Finally, the chapter ends by developing a set of principles that support a mindfulness-informed approach to therapy with couples and families.

D.R. Gehart, *Mindfulness and Acceptance in Couple and Family Therapy*,
DOI 10.1007/978-1-4614-3033-9_2, © Springer Science+Business Media New York 2012

Buddhism: A Psychology or Religion?

Technically atheists, Buddhists do not consider the Buddha to be a god, but rather a man: he was born a man, died a man, and does not continue his existence as a powerful, invisible entity that has influence over the lives of humans (Dalai Lama, Benson, Thurman, Gardner, & Goleman, 1991; Hahn, 1998). However, he did (at least) one extraordinary thing: he achieved enlightenment, or freedom from suffering. What he later taught was how to re-perceive and reexperience the world to reduce one's experience of suffering; thus, some might consider him one of the first to teach the classic family therapy technique of reframing. Since his day, a set of religious practices has developed around his philosophy and teachings. But the heart of Buddhist teachings is more akin to modern psychology than religion. Buddhist psychology carefully explicates the nature of suffering, the self, consciousness, and alleviation of suffering. The major Buddhist tenants, such as the Four Noble Truths and Eightfold Path described below, outline a theory of how life problems develop and how to solve them: arguably the oldest psychotherapy model.

Buddhist Psychology and Family Therapy Theory

A Brief History of Buddhist and Family Therapy Connections

As a constructivist approach, Buddhist psychology shares a surprising number of principles and assumptions with the philosophical foundations of family systems therapy—cybernetics (construction of meaning within systemic contexts), constructivism (construction of meaning by the perceiver), and social constructionism (construction of meaning in relationship). These similarities are explained in part by an important but seldom recognized early contributor to the field of family therapy: Alan Watts. Watts was a consultant to the research teams at the Mental Research Institute in Palo Alto, where Gregory Bateson, Jay Haley, Don Jackson, Richard Fisch, Paul Watzlawick, Virginia Satir, John Weakland, and others developed many of the seminal theories of family therapy. In his landmark book, *Psychotherapy East and West*, Watts (1961) was the first to make a connection between the premises of systemic family therapy and Buddhism, both recognizing that the perceiver and perceived cannot be considered separately: the perceiver inherently is connected to and influences the perceived and vice versa. Watts encouraged the practice of family therapy, in which the individual is addressed—not alone—but in the context of relationships, society, and as Watts encouraged, the cosmos. Furthermore, Watts saw in family therapy techniques parallel to Buddhist traditions such as koans that aim to identify and dissolve life's double binds through paradox.

However, since *Psychotherapy East and West*, limited work has been done on linking Eastern philosophies and psychologies with therapy in general or family therapy theories specifically. Aside from the early work at the MRI, Jung (1927/1960; also see Meckel & Moore, 1992; Moacanin, 1988) and later Jungians have most seriously studied and integrated Buddhist psychological concepts, emphasizing spiritual elements, such as achieving enlightenment and notions of a spiritual self beyond the ego. Jung provides introductions and psychological analyses for the first translations into Western languages of many Asian texts, including *The Tibetan Book of Great Liberation* (also translated *The Tibetan Book of the Dead*). More recently, psychodynamic therapist Epstein (1995, 1999) has explored Buddhist concepts of nonself in the context of psychoanalysis, which historically has been predicated upon the assumption of a coherent self. From a Buddhist perspective, psychoanalysis analyzes a false, constructed self or ego—thus giving it a greater sense of "realness" and power—rather than seeking to realize the more profound truth of a nonself, which is also conceptualized as a socially embedded and deeply interconnected sense of self (Hahn, 1998).

In family therapy, solution-oriented therapist O'Hanlon and Weiner-Davis (1989) encourages therapists to use a Zen's "beginner's mind" when listening to clients describe their problem because this state of nonjudging, mindful awareness is more likely to enable therapists to see new possibilities in helping clients creatively and effectively address in what seem to be unsolvable problems. Similarly, Macy (1991) outlines how cybernetic systems theory and Buddhism share similar constructivist understandings of mutual causality and the interdependent nature of realty and identity. In a parallel work, Flemons (1991) identifies similarities between systemic family therapy and Taoism, a philosophy system closely related to Buddhism, including taking a both/and perspective and recognizing the contextual nature of reality. Several postmodern family therapists have also made references to the philosophical similarities (Gehart, 2004; Gehart & McCollum, 2007; Lax, 1996; Percy, 2008; Rosenbaum & Dyckman, 1996; Selekman, 1997), particularly related to the concept of "not knowing" and nonself.

Common Ground: Six Shared Constructivist Principles

Both systemic and postmodern family therapists have explored and drawn upon Buddhist psychology in the development of their therapeutic approaches. As originally outlined in Gehart (2004), six Buddhist psychological principles are particularly relevant to family therapists as they have shared and expanded upon constructivist assumptions: emptiness, interdependence, impermanence, nonself, not knowing, and compassion. These principles serve as the philosophical foundation for mindfulness and acceptance-informed family therapy. I have chosen to explore these Buddhist-systemic-postmodern parallels using Buddhist terminology because it provides therapists with fresh, new language and thereby new possibilities for understanding their work.

Emptiness

Avalokiteshvara [bodhisattva of compassion] says that all phenomena are empty. This does not mean that nothing exists. What is does mean is that all phenomena are empty of something. That 'something' is inherent, or objective, existence (Gyeltsen, 2000, p. 109).

Buddhists describe reality as "empty" (Sanskrit, *shunyata*), asserting that individuals, objects, and experiences are devoid of independent essence. Like systemic and postmodern therapists (Gergen, 1999; Watzlawick, 1984), Buddhists assert that reality is constructed and agree that language is the medium through which we construct our realities (Gudmunsen, 1977). However, more so than therapists who rely heavily on the spoken work, Buddhists view words with suspicion because they convey a "lesser" truth. Words, from a Buddhist perspective, distort lived experience because they impose sociolinguistic categories and filters upon "what is." Buddhist practice therefore "seeks to emancipate us from the grammatical fictions in which we are trapped" (Gudmunsen, p. 123); a goal similar to that of many constructivist and constructionist schools of therapy. Mindful experiencing of "what is" without language is the primary vehicle for experiencing emptiness.

Interdependence and Interbeing

[T]he subject of knowledge cannot exist independently from the object of knowledge (Hahn, 1998, p. 74).

Buddhist philosophy posits the ontological principles of interdependence (Sanskrit, *anicca*) and interdependent co-arising (Sanskrit, *pratityasamutpada*), which are the complement to emptiness. Assuming emptiness without interdependence results in nihilism, of which Buddhists are frequently accused by those who do not understand how the teachings of interdependence and emptiness work together (Hahn, 1998; Samagura & Fusako, 2007). The Buddhist principle of interdependence posits that rather than each phenomenon having independent existence, all things are interconnected: "We experience emptiness when we see…that our body, heart, and mind arise out of the changing web of life, whe[re] nothing is disconnected or separate" (Kornfield, 1993, p. 51). This description of interconnection is reminiscent of Bateson's (1979/2002) definition of "mind" as the connection between all living things through a complex series of feedback loops. Late in his career, Bateson (1991) equates the Buddhist concept of mandala, a map of this complex interconnection of the cosmos, to his concept of ecology.

Reality is viewed as an interwoven, complex, and dynamic web of relationships that is constantly changing at molecular, physiological, psychological, and societal levels. Buddhists use this idea to explain the "arising" of everything from an object like a piece of bread, which depends upon sun, earth, water, farmers' nurturance, human labor, manufactured tools, oven engineers, salt miners, millers, millers' families, irrigation, steel workers, bakers, etc., to abstract ideas such as democracy, which reflects and is embedded in thousands of years of history, philosophy, politics, and social dialogue. Hahn (1998) refers to this dynamic as "interbeing," which describes the inescapable interconnection of all things for their existence. These ideas are similar to social constructionist views that highlight how our individual realities and identities are inseparable from our social world (Gergen, 1991, 1999). However, similar to Bateson, the Buddhist concept is applied more broadly to include not only linguistic constructs but physical phenomena as well. This inherent and expansive view of interconnection is particularly important for family therapists whose work focuses on relationships and connection.

Nonself

We *are* what we perceive. This is the teaching of nonself (Hahn, 1998, p. 126; emphasis in original).

One of the earliest distinctions between Buddhism and Hinduism was the Buddhist assertion that "there is nothing that can be called a permanent 'self'" (Hahn, 1998, p. 123). Buddhists posit that the "self" is nothing more than shifting streams of consciousness, perceptions, and proclivities; the lack of essence in this stream is described as *nonself* (*Sanskrit, anatman*). This teaching essentially applies the concept of interbeing to the self. Based on the principle of interdependence, what is referred to as "self" is considered a reflection of everything and everyone else: "When we look deeply into nonself, we see that the existence of every single thing is possible only because of the existence of everything else" (p. 123). Each object we hold and each thought we think has embedded within it an infinite number of connections that stretch across time and space. For example, this book not only involves thousands of people who wrote, edited, reviewed, copied, typeset, bound, boxed, transported, and sold the book but also the thoughts and ideas that have been discussed and evolved in Western and Eastern culture for millennia.

Although more radical, the Buddhist construction of the self is similar to postmodern descriptions of the self as multifaceted, reflecting familial and social constructs of self, without a core or essential self (Gergen, 1991; Percy, 2008). Both descriptions of self share the assumption that one's identity is inextricably bound to others and context, an assumption that can be traced in all schools of family therapy. Buddhists have numerous practices designed to cultivate wisdom by helping practitioners develop a profound recognition of this insight that has potentials for use in family therapy.

Impermanence

It is not impermanence that makes us suffer. What makes us suffer is wanting things to be permanent when they are not (Hahn, 1998, p. 123).

Buddhists maintain that when one mindfully observes internal and external processes, it is quickly apparent that everything is in constant flux—emotions, thoughts, relationships, and behaviors (Hahn, 1998). Perhaps the most striking lesson from a first attempt at mindfulness meditation is that the mind constantly flits about from one thought to another like small birds before a storm. Therefore, when one becomes attached to obtaining a steady state, such as constant, unending happiness, one will inevitably experience suffering, given that life constantly changes. Systems and postmodern thinkers also describe how meanings and consequently one's experience of reality is constantly in flux depending on one's social interactions (deShazer, 1988; Gergen, 1999). Both schools of thought emphasize the fluidity of experience and meaning and assert that when we "cling" or concretize our descriptions of experience, we tend to experience problems.

The concept of impermanence is especially important in therapy where labels give rise to the perception that symptoms (e.g., depression, anger, relational tension) are constant rather than in constant flux; one fails to notice exceptions once the symptom is labeled. Milan therapists described this as the "tyranny of linguistics" and carefully adjusted their language to minimize its affects, often preferring describe client behavior using verbs (e.g., "doing" depression) to the adjective or noun (e.g., being depressed or having Major Depression; Selvini Palazzoli, Cecchin, Prata, & Boscolo, 1978). Solution-focused therapists have posited a notion similar to impermanence, asserting that things are always changing if one is open to noticing the inconsistencies and use this to direct their attention to exceptions to the problem, from which they can more easily identify potential solutions (deShazer, 1988; O'Hanlon & Weiner-Davis, 1989). Similarly, narrative therapists' assumption that unique outcomes exist for all problem-saturated narrative also reflects an understanding of impermanence (White & Epston, 1990).

Not Knowing

> Letting there be room for not knowing is the most important thing of all. We try to do what we think is going to help. But we don't know....When there's a big disappointment, we don't know if that's the end of the story. It may be just the beginning of a great adventure (Chödrön, 1997, p. 8).

Buddhists share with postmodern therapists the notion of "not knowing" (Anderson, 1997; Anderson & Gehart, 2007). Buddhists apply not knowing broadly, maintaining that we cannot "know" because life is impermanent and people continuously evolve and change. Since impermanence prevents one from determining the absolute best course of action, Buddhists view both client and therapist as "non-experts" exploring possibilities together, without overly rejoicing in "success" or overly dismaying in "failure." Buddhist wisdom encourages a tempered acceptance of joy and sorrow, tears and laughter, and triumph and failure. The idea that life constantly weaves between the extremes and that we cannot know one thing without its opposite is a concept also posited in (Bateson's 1972, 1991; Keeney, 1983) cybernetic theory. In Buddhist practice, the "wisdom" of not knowing creates a sense of *equanimity* as one moves with the ebb and flow of life, a life stance that characterizes "mental health" and wellbeing in Buddhist psychology.

Compassion

> Compassionate listening brings about healing. When someone listens to us in this way, we feel some relief right away (Hahn, 1998, pp. 79–80).

Compassion (Sanskrit, *karuna*) is the heart of Buddhist practice and the key to understanding all other concepts. Buddhist compassion implies a heart-felt concern for others that is expressed by bearing humble witness to their suffering. The bodhisattva (a highly evolved being) of compassion is known as *Avalokiteshvara* in Sanskrit and *Kuan-yin* (pronounced Guan-yin) in Chinese. The written name for Kuan-yin is composed of the Chinese characters for "seeing" and "hearing" and refers to how Kuan-yin is there to compassionately bear witness to one's suffering, having similarities to Mother Mary in Catholic traditions. Compassion is also translated as loving kindness, emphasizing that compassionate action is an intentional kindness from the heart and not the practice of decorum. In the Mahayana forms of Buddhism found in East Asia and Tibet, the cultivation of compassion is a seminal practice and informs all mindfulness practices by encouraging practitioners to develop compassion and loving acceptance of "what is."

In the field of therapy, two forms of compassion are readily identified, both of which have Buddhist parallels. The first and most common form of compassion is best embodied by humanistic therapists such as Satir, Banmen, Gerber, and Gomori (1991) and Rogers (1961, 1981), who exude palpable warmth and caring, similar to Buddhist bodhisattvas. The second form of compassion, *fierce compassion*, derives from crazy wisdom teachings that encourage a fearless and compassionate engagement with the things that we fear and dread most (Trungpa, 1991). Systemic and strategic family therapists have most clearly demonstrated this approach, viewing problems not as clinical pathology but as playing a meaningful and practical function in relational patterns that help to stabilize family homeostasis. Therefore, these therapists may engage symptoms with respect, humor, fearlessness, playfulness, or irreverence, but never in a way that imputes greater seriousness or implies an unchangeable reality (Haley, 1987; Watzlawick, Weakland, & Fisch, 1974).

More so that family therapists, Mahayana Buddhists, are vigilant in teaching compassion before teaching constructivism, which they refer to as their wisdom teachings (Dalai Lama, 1996). Novice monks are first taught to cultivate compassion for all beings before being introduced to constructivist concepts, such as nonself and emptiness to prevent a cognitive detachment that could lead to a less humane worldview. This practice is particularly relevant for the training of therapists. If a therapist intellectually understands that life is impermanent (or constructed) yet does not have a well-developed sense of compassion for clients' suffering, the therapist will logically view the clients' suffering as self-perpetuated illusions that simply need to be corrected and will lack the empathy necessary to connect with and engage the client in a helpful way.

Suffering: Origins and Remedies

One of the most valuable contributions Buddhism offers therapists is an elegant and simple definition of suffering, its origins, and remedies. For a field that's purpose is primarily to alleviate suffering, there is little direct and reflective discussion in mental health on the subject (Gehart & McCollum, 2007). At times, the field of psychotherapy feeds into the popularly held myth—or perhaps hope—that with enough therapy, money, self-help, prayer and/or love, we can avoid suffering. Instead, Buddhists propose a more moderate and realistic goal of changing our relationship with suffering, which has profound implications for therapists helping others to navigate this relationship.

Origins of Suffering

One of its most basic tenants, Buddhists use the Four Noble Truths to explain how suffering arises in this life and how best to handle it. The First Noble Truth is that there is suffering (Sanskrit, *dukkha*). From a Buddhist perspective, certain forms of suffering are inherent to the human condition: illness, change, loss, and death. However, other forms of suffering, in fact most of the suffering in life, a person creates through the desire to have things go a particular way. Rather than trying to end, avoid, or restory suffering, Buddhism encourages us to "be with" it, neither running from nor getting lost in it—but rather opening oneself to difficult experiences with curiosity and compassion. By benevolently engaging suffering, one creates a distinctively new relationship to it and thereby experiences the situation differently, typically in a less panicked and more resourceful way.

As summarized in the Second Noble Truth, the most common source of suffering is a person's *attachment* to ideas, objects, and constructs, particularly self-constructs. In a Buddhist context, attachment does not carry the positive connotation that it does in traditional psychological literature in which attachment refers to a person's relationship style formed from infancy. In contrast, in Buddhist literature, attachment has a relatively negative connotation, referring to an overinvestment and overidentification with a particular idea or desire (Hahn, 1998), such as being "attached" to idea that one should be happy all the time or to the white-picket-fence story of success.

The concept of attachment relates to cybernetic and postmodern assertions that problems are identified and sustained through language (Bateson, 1972, 1991; Gergen, 1999). Buddhists emphasize that it is not the construction itself but rather one's *attachment to* a particular construction that creates suffering. For example, it is not the "white-picket fence" story or a person's particular interpretation of it that creates suffering, but rather the strength of one's *attachment to* it that is the problem: the more invested one is in a particular story, the more one suffers in relation to it. The couple doggedly determined to have the white-picket fence, 2.2 kids, and a dog as well as the couple determined to never live such a boring, scripted life are both its prisoners. This Buddhist perspective informs a softer and less adversarial approach to dominant discourses and problems as is sometimes seen in narrative therapy (Gehart & McCollum, 2007; Monk & Gehart, 2003). From a Buddhist perspective, the person's task is simply to relax the attachment through curiosity, humor, and the insight that comes from understanding that *attachments* we create are the source of suffering far more than the situation itself; this is the Third Noble Truth.

The final Noble Truth maintains that the antidote to suffering is the Eightfold Path: right view (insight), right intention, right speech, right action, right livelihood, right effort, right mindfulness, and right concentration. Many of these are easily recognizable in most cultures and traditions. For example, having good intentions, using kind words, choosing actions beneficial to all, engaging in a livelihood that contributes to society, and applying oneself fully in endeavors are frequently cited across cultures as virtues that lead to a good life (Seligman, 2002). What is most unique about the Buddhist Eightfold Path is its emphasis on mindfulness and concentration as central to the path of liberation from suffering.

Transforming Suffering: Mindful Experience

Rather than relying on language as the medium for change, Buddhists focus on mindful experiencing to increase insight and transform problems. Mindfulness involves nonattached, engaged witnessing of internal or external phenomena in the present moment. Through mindfulness, a person can explore the richness and potential of pure experience, those brief moments when the mind is not involved in the construction of meaning. Mindfulness can be understood as the attempt to engage pure un-languaged, unstoried experience; by letting go of linguistic constructions, new space and possibilities are opened. Such moments involve awareness of body, emotions, and thoughts and require a more visceral or "bodied" knowing than is typical in therapy, except perhaps for certain forms of experiential practice. The Buddhist approach to deconstruction involves *experiential* deconstruction as well as the *linguistic* deconstruction common to Western forms of postmodernism.

Mindfulness cultivates nonattachment, which does not imply a cold, logical form of detachment. Instead, mindful nonattachment is a highly engaged, compassionate witnessing of experience without judging "what is" as good or bad, but rather acknowledging that it "is"—at least for the moment. For example, mindful nonattachment to a situation in which our partner does not call as agreed upon involves acknowledging the anger, disappointment, sadness, and other feelings that may arise as well as where these may take expression in one's body. One simultaneously feels the emotions and observes the emotions from a position of nonjudgment (of self or other) and compassion. In comparison, when mind*less*ly experiencing one's response to a partner not calling, one *becomes* angry, disappointed, and sad with very little second-order awareness that one is feeling these things. The feelings essentially overflow consciousness to such an extent that there is little awareness that this is happening. Thus, the difference is that mind*fully* experiencing emotions requires making a *conscious decision to remain fully aware* while riding the wave of difficult emotions; in contrast, mind*less*ly experiencing emotion simply involves being carried away by them without intentionally choosing to do so.

Once a person chooses to be mindful, the greatest challenge that arises is to soften one's attachment so that one can mindfully experience less-than-preferred situations. Previous life events and dominant social narratives provide endless ways to evaluate, compare, and interpret life; for most, the judgment of experience occurs almost simultaneously with the experience itself. For example, when most Americans experience sadness, they automatically sense that something is wrong and needs fixing. In contrast, nonattachment requires refraining from judging sadness as good or bad but rather experiencing all the physical, emotional, mental, and relational processes that constitute the experience.

Approach to Suffering

Similar to postmodern therapists, Buddhist-informed therapies address problems by creating space between the person and the suffering or problem. However, Buddhists do this through *experience,* while most therapists do this through *language.* The Buddhist process is most similar to what Anderson (1997) refers to as "problem dissolution," in which new understandings create new relationships with "problems." Although both approaches "loosen" a person's attachment to linguistic constructions through a curious, not-knowing stance, they use different methods. Working from a Buddhist perspective, the therapist's attention goes first to fully experiencing "what is" in the present with a minimum of interpretation as opposed to conventional therapy methods that look into the past for explanations, the present for preferred constructions, or the future for solutions. One must first fully experience and be with the problem to "know" it, allowing one to surrender the anxiety that surrounds it. From here, clients may be invited to explore the causes of their suffering and/or ways to address it.

Principles of Mindfully Oriented Couple and Family Therapy

Approaching couple and family therapy using the Buddhist psychology concepts of mindfulness and acceptance informs several unique principles that therapists can use to enhance and expand upon their current therapeutic approach:

- Cultivate compassion for self and other
- Witness experience with curiosity
- Manage the mind with kindness
- Seek insight and wisdom
- Accept the moment as teacher
- Listen deeply to the self and other
- Commit to nonaggression in word, deed, and intent

- Become mindful of mindless interaction patterns
- Move gracefully with the unending flow of relationship

Cultivate Compassion for Self and Other

From a Buddhist perspective, compassion is not a randomly assigned character trait but rather a habit that is cultivated through intentional practice (Hahn, 1997). Compassion meditations help people develop compassion for themselves, loved ones, and even strangers. It comes down to simple and clear well wishes, such as:

> May I be happy, healthy, and safe and may my heart be at peace.
> May you be happy, healthy, and safe and may your heart be at peace.
> May everyone be happy, healthy, and safe and may their hearts be at peace (see Chap. 8 for more details).

As Gottman (1999) and others have well documented, distressed couples seeking therapy typically have developed painful patterns of defensiveness, criticism, isolation, and contempt that make even such basic positive intentions difficult for some to genuinely articulate. One of the primary goals of therapy is to not only restore a sense of compassion for oneself and one's partner but to help the couple develop habits and practices to sustain and deepen their sense of compassion for themselves and each other.

The Buddhist practice of compassion is not a garden-variety compassion, but rather one that is deeply rooted in wisdom, specifically a spiritual perspective of the human condition. As outlined in the Four Noble Truths, Buddhists recognize that suffering is inherent to living and that without understanding the constructed nature of reality a person is bound to create much needless suffering. At its heart, Buddhist compassion comes from a solemn recognition of how hard it is to be human. Therapists can not only use this compassion in their relating to clients but can also use the Buddhist understanding of compassion to help couples and families learn how to love each other better.

Witness Experience with Curiosity

After compassion, the second most salient principle of mindfulness-informed therapy is learning to witness experience with curiosity. Both therapists and clients can benefit from developing a mindful approach to working with problems and difficult emotions. Therapists send a subtle but profound message when they are able to role model for clients how to mindfully engage client problems with curiosity, compassion, and fearlessness. By being at ease in exploring painful subjects, therapists help clients to become curious, look deeper, and become inquisitive about their own experience: How does the problem tend to arise? Do I do things that make it worse or better? How else does it impact my life and relationships?

Therapists can use mindfulness meditation practice as well as numerous other mindfulness-based interventions to help clients develop the capacity—and eventually the habit—of witnessing inner experience and relational interactions with curiosity and compassion. The more a person can witness their difficult inner emotions, the more likely they will be to respond effectively and transform their experience into a more desirable outcome. The habit or trait of mindfulness is correlated with greater relational satisfaction and better responses to relational stress (Barnes, Brown, Krusemark, Campbell, & Rogge, 2007). Mindfulness skills can readily be translated to help couples and families more effectively deal with potential conflict as it arises and to find better ways of resolving their issues.

Manage the Mind with Kindness

Although not always directly articulated, one of the clearest messages from mindfulness research and therapy is that humans have the capacity and responsibility to manage their minds or *self-regulate.* In most cases, using mindfulness to increase self-regulation has primarily been focused on addressing problems identified within an individual, such as depression, anxiety, or physical pain (see Chap. 3 for further discussion). Arguably, the ability to self-regulate is even more critical for improving couple and family relational concerns, which involve multiple dynamics. If even one of the parties in a couple or family is able to improve their ability to self-regulate, that effort alone is likely to reduce the frequency and severity of conflict in the relationship.

In general, few couple and family therapy approaches advocate for increasing one's capacity for self-regulation and instead the focus has been on helping couples and families to alter their behavioral interaction patterns. At some level, of course, altering behavioral patterns requires a certain amount of self-regulation. Mindfulness approaches provide therapists with more direct and efficient means of helping couples and families to improve their ability to self-regulate their thoughts and emotions to improve their relationships.

Seek Wisdom and Insight

Although most couple and family approaches are grounded in constructivist assumptions about reality, few advocate directly teaching clients about this worldview. In contrast, many mindfulness approaches advocate for educating clients about how suffering is created and encourages developing greater insight and wisdom about the nature of reality (Hayes, Strosahl, & Wilson, 1999; Segal, Williams, & Teasdale, 2002). For example, in ACT and MBCT, therapists help clients to see that their thoughts and emotions are not "facts" or "true reality" but rather momentary experiences that may or may not be helpful, accurate, or useful. Furthermore, these and other related approaches help clients to see how they construct meaning and respond to situations as if this meaning is absolute truth. Developing more tentative relationships to one's thoughts allows one to critically examine their usefulness and accuracy and also provides an opportunity to choose the most beneficial interpretation in a given situation. Thus, mindfulness-informed therapies are set as a long-term goal to increase clients' insights on the human mind and human experience.

In addition to seeking wisdom in the more traditional sense, many schools of Buddhism also espouse practicing *crazy wisdom*, using unexpected and unconventional approaches to loosen unhelpful attachments (Trungpa, 1991). Crazy wisdom plays with opposites and logic to cut through the assumptions that keep us imprisoned by our attachments and worldviews. Systemic family therapists such as Haley (1987), Keeney (1983, 1996), and Watzlawick (1984) are well known for in-session crazy wisdom, using paradox, one-down positions, and humor to "perturb" systems and promote change, such as suggesting couples set up their living room as a court room for their next argument.

In mindfulness-informed therapy, crazy wisdom is critical to keep therapists and clients alike from taking mindfulness, acceptance, and other Buddhist principles too seriously, and thus creating *further* attachments that promote suffering. Practicing crazy wisdom involves not only taking mindfulness teaching seriously but also recognizing them as "empty" in that they are simply vehicles for practice rather than the truth to which they draw our attention. Thus, I believe that mindfulness-informed therapy should have playfulness and lightheartedness at its core, even if it isn't expressed in every moment of therapy (as some moments are inappropriate for it). However, learning to laugh at life's twists and turns can be very healing for the soul and helps clients to relax into what is and connect with life's lighter side.

Become Mindful of Mindless Interaction Patterns

Helping people become more aware of their interrelational patterns is an essential element of all couple or family approaches. When using a mindfulness-informed approach, this translates to helping couples and families become more aware of their typically mind*less* interaction patterns. The term mindless highlights that if a person is able to be mindful—accepting what is with compassion and nonjudgment of self and other—it is not likely that they would be creating conflict or distressing relations. Of course, it is tempting to think that if you remain calmer than one's partner in an argument that you automatically can be considered more mindful and otherwise morally superior, but this is not what is meant by being mindful in relationships. Instead, the telltale sign of being mindful is having compassion and understanding for *both* one's own position *as well as* that of others at the same time and proceeding in such a way as to work towards positive outcomes rather than destructive ones.

Therapists have the task of helping clients become aware of their patterns and encouraging them to bring mindfulness skills to the challenging arena of interpersonal relations. For many, mindful relating is the last area of their life to which they successfully apply mindfulness. Although some mindless interaction patterns are relatively harmless—a family's busy routine for getting out of the house on a school day—some can become quite destructive: such as arguing over "small things" or avoiding the discussion of painful topics. The therapy process can extend traditional mindfulness exercises that focus on inner processes to also focusing on how one relates and interacts in normal and difficult interactions. Like all mindfulness-based practices, the challenge is to increase one's awareness without adding judgment or blame.

Accept the Moment as Teacher

A particularly relevant mindfulness teaching for working with couples and families is: this moment is the perfect teacher (Chödrön, 1997):

> feelings like disappointment, embarrassment, irritation, resentment, anger, jealousy, and fear, instead of being bad news, are actually very clear moments that teach us where it is that we're holding back. The teach us to perk up and lean in when we feel we'd rather collapse and back away. They're like messengers that show us with terrifying clarity, exactly where we're stuck (p. 12).

Intimate and family relationships are perhaps the most effective and relentless teachers of where we are stuck or in need of growth: relationships with our partners, parents, and children are often riddled with reminders of our limits, for better or worse. When therapists can help clients begin to see their tensions and conflicts with intimate others as opportunities for growth and learning—or even potential opportunities for growth and learning—this can help clients take a more proactive and effective approach to these issues.

One of the greatest struggles therapists face is helping couples and families approach their situations with a helpful attitude. By the time most seek relational help, they are deeply embroiled in bitter and long-standing conflict that they feel hopeless about. Therapists can help clients soften their positions by encouraging them to be curious as to why *they* are having a particular struggle with or reaction to their partner or family member: what does this tension reveal about their sensitivities or potential areas of growth? By bringing a gentle curiosity to what this moment is teaching can help clients to approach relational difficulties more effectively.

Listen Deeply to the Self and Other

Mindfulness practices help people learn to tune into themselves more carefully and thoughtfully. When applied to relationships, the same skills can be used to listen more deeply to partners, friends, and family. Listening deeply to another involves many of the same skills used in listening to the self: quieting inner chatter, suspending judgment, and having compassion for whatever arises (Hahn, 1997). For many, learning to listen deeply may be the most important part of the therapy process.

Therapists teach clients to listen deeply primarily by doing it in session. So often, I hear partners and parents say with surprise that they never heard a child or partner say such-and-such before our session. In some cases, when the words were spoken at home, the other really wasn't paying attention; in other cases, the thoughts and feelings were never shared because it never felt safe enough. In either case, much healing occurs by simply helping couples and families slow down enough and feel safe enough to speak and listen to each other. In many situations, the resolution is almost immediate with the deeper understanding.

Commit to Nonaggression in Word and Deed

Also part of the Eightfold Path that Buddhists follow to reduce suffering, a personal commitment to nonaggressive words and action is closely associated with mindfulness practices (Hahn, 1997). This Buddhist commitment to not use aggression should not be confused with a perfectionistic desire to have a conflict-free relationship. In marked contrast, the Buddhist version does not shy from conflict or respectfully asserting oneself, but instead is grounded in a commitment to speak the truth in a way that is respectful to all. Gottman's (1999) research supports striving for having high standards in terms of quality of communication, although his research in this area focuses primarily on women having a low tolerance for their partner's disrespectful words and using a soft start up to raising difficult issues. Based on principles of self-regulation cultivated through mindfulness practice, the mindfulness-based approach to committing to nonviolent words and actions becomes a personal code of conduct that mindfulness practitioners impose on themselves by choice.

Therapists working with couples and families using mindfulness approaches can help their clients verbalize and commit to a clearly defined code of conduct that moves them toward using less aggressive words and actions. For various reasons, many couples have relatively low standards for expression of aggression in the relationship often using examples in the media to normalize poor treatment of each other: "all couples fight"; "he/she was tired/drinking/etc."; "at least he doesn't hit me"; or "at least we are not as bad as X." Many couples and families do not have experience with how to disagree without being hostile or disrespectful.

For decades, therapists have been helping couples and families to communicate in more respectful ways but have done so primarily from an educational perspective: the expert therapist will teach the client how to communicate more respectfully. Mindfulness approaches inform a different approach: encouraging clients to make a solemn promise to themselves to avoid aggression in relationships out of principle, knowing that it does harm to *all* parties: those inside and outside of the room. Developing an understanding of interbeing—how we are all connected and how our actions affect more than the other person in the room at this moment—is a powerful force in committing to nonviolence. Thus, such clients are intrinsically motivated to do whatever it takes to have nonaggressive relationships. Therapists can work with clients to develop a commitment to nonaggressive behavior and help thcm find ways to effectively speak the truth and confront difficult issues while being respectful to self and other.

Equanimity in Relationship

Elsewhere, my colleague McCollum and I (Gehart & McCollum, 2007) have described the goal of mindfulness-informed relational therapy as creating greater *equanimity*: the ability to move gracefully with relational ups and downs. As emphasized in mindfulness practice, much of life involves accepting "what is." When applied to relationships, equanimity involves a willingness to accept the ups and downs of relationships as oneself and the other constantly grow and change. Although it is common, and partially accurate, to see relationships as stabile entities, it is perhaps more accurate and helpful to see them as constantly evolving.

As experts charged with helping people change, therapists must strike a careful balance between helping clients accept what is while also honoring clients desire for change. From a Buddhist perspective, *all change begins by accepting what is*. In some cases, accepting what is naturally translates to change. For example, helping parents begin to accept that their child is not as smart or athletically adept as they believed/hoped can begin significant shifts in the parent–child relationship that paradoxically often serve to improve a child's performance as they experience a new sense of acceptance and support from their parent. In other cases, acceptance of a child's difficulty, such as autism, may not change the child's situation but only the parent–child dynamic. In both cases, when working from a mindfulness-informed perspective, whether significant change occurs or not is a secondary issue. The primary goal is to help clients face life difficulties with greater equanimity and wisdom.

As a professional, this has been one of the most significant shifts of integrating a mindfulness perspective into my work. Before, setting client goals was more traditional and literal: what do you want to be different and then helping them achieve these ends. In fact, I was fairly good at this traditional process. However, although I still pursue such goals, I do not see my work as done until I have helped clients achieve greater levels of equanimity (a long-term goal) so that they will be more likely to successfully handle future struggles. Gottman's (1999) research with couples also supports such long-term goals: 69% of what couples argue about are the same "perpetual problems" that stem from relatively unchangeable personality differences; successful couples learn how to manage these with equanimity.

When helping clients with relational issues, developing equanimity can be especially challenging. Most of us accept our own vicissitudes and changes more readily than those in our partners, children, parents, and in-laws. When we change, it is "natural" growth; when others change (or refuse to change in ways we desire), it is a loss, burden or, worse yet, a betrayal. For better or worse, due to their greater complexity, relationships experience more up and downs than most of us do individually. For this reason, helping clients develop a strong capacity and tendency to respond to relational flux with equanimity will serve them well in all areas of life. In this way, therapists can help dissolve the culturally supported myth in places like the United States that pain-free and problem-free living is possible and sustainable and replace this myth with a more humbling and freeing insight that embraces the holistic and complex dance of life that includes good and bad, life and death, and joy and sorrow. The ultimate goal then is to shift our relationship to life itself from one of struggle to one of willingness to go for the ride.

From Philosophy to Practice

Buddhist psychology invites couple and family therapists to re-envision their work as an approach to helping clients more effectively engage the suffering in their lives rather than escape from or fix it. The process of therapy then becomes one of learning how to more skillfully embrace the unavoidable suffering in life and reduce the many forms of suffering that are self-generated. More modestly, the goal is no longer to seek problem-free living but rather to move gracefully with life's ups and downs and learn how to generate joy and happiness from within rather than seek it externally. Finally, and most salient for couple and family therapists, the Buddhist approach provide a new approach to compassion for self and others that comes from understanding the nature of suffering, a perspective that can be used to help clients deepen their love in new and unexpected ways.

Chapter 3
Mindfulness Research Foundations

Much of the excitement about mindfulness relates to the quickly expanding research foundations that include not only clinical effectiveness, but also the neurological impact of mindfulness practice. This cross-discipline, multifaceted evidence base has quickly mainstreamed mindfulness practice, moving meditation from a fringe mental health activity to a highly respected treatment option in less than a decade. Although research on specific, manualized mindfulness-based treatments with couples and families is limited, the extant research on mindfulness and its effects provides sufficient support to consider mindfulness-informed therapy an emerging *evidence-based practice* (Patterson, Miller, Carnes, & Wilson, 2004).

The research base on mindfulness includes the effects of mindfulness on:

- Physical health
- Adult mental health
- Couples: distressed and nondistressed
- Children, adolescents, and families
- The brain

Mindfulness and Physical Health

Mindfulness and Medical Disorders

Jon Kabat-Zinn began studying mindfulness-based stress reduction (MBSR) in a medical hospital, working with patients whose physician referred them due to severe and chronic medical conditions that the physicians believed were stress-related. Over the past 30 years, mindfulness has been found to improve treatment outcomes for a wide range of physical conditions, including (Baer, 2003; Shapiro & Carlson, 2009):

- Chronic pain
- Cancer: psychological, biological, and sleep outcomes

D.R. Gehart, *Mindfulness and Acceptance in Couple and Family Therapy*,
DOI 10.1007/978-1-4614-3033-9_3, © Springer Science+Business Media New York 2012

- Cardiovascular disorders
- Epilepsy
- HIV/AIDS
- Psoriasis
- Rheumatoid arthritis
- Fibromyalgia
- Organ transplant
- Type II diabetes
- Multiple sclerosis
- Sleep disturbance
- Mixed medical diagnoses

Of these, the most extensive research has been on chronic pain, the original target population of MBSR, and cancer (Shapiro & Carlson, 2009). The majority of studies in the area of physical health have focused on outcomes similar to those in mental health, such as stress levels, anxiety, and depression related to the illness. A minority of these studies uses mindfulness to directly affect disease progression or pathology; these exceptions include chronic pain, psoriasis, epilepsy, and cancer. In a meta-analysis, mindfulness used for physical disorders had relatively strong and consistent effect sizes, suggesting that mindfulness may help coping with the distress of disability and severe illness (Grossman, Niemann, Schmidt, & Walach, 2004).

Couple and Family Adjustment to Chronic Illness

A handful of studies have considered the effects of mindfulness in helping partners and caretakers of persons with a chronic or severe medical condition. In the first study on MBSR examining the impact on couples, Birnie, Garland, and Carlson (2010a) found that cancer patients and their partners both improved in terms of mood, mindfulness, and stress after jointly participating in the program. Similarly, Minor, Carlson, Mackenzie, Zernicke, and Jones (2006) found that MBSR reduced stress and mood symptoms in parents caring for children with chronic health concerns. These are encouraging findings for couples and families manage the significant levels of ongoing stress associated with providing long-term care and coping with chronic illness.

Effect on Physical Health in Healthy Adults

A handful of studies have considered the physiological effects of mindfulness in healthy adults (Shapiro & Carlson, 2009). In sum, these studies found the following:

- *Increase in melatonin*: Associated with controlling the sleep cycle; also implicated in diseases such as cancer.
- *Increased parasympathetic cardiovascular activity*: Associated with the relaxation response.

- *Improved heart rate variability*: Associated with the relaxation response.
- *Improved gas exchange in lungs*: Associated with more efficient intake of oxygen and release of toxic gases.
- *Improved immune functioning*: Associated with the ability to resist pathogens.
- *Reduced blood pressure*: Lowers systolic blood pressure (Chiesa & Serretti, 2010).

Mindfulness and Adult Mental Health

Mindfulness-based and mindfulness-informed treatments for mental health issues are quickly becoming standard, well respected, and frequently sought treatments for mild-to-severe mental health disorders. Mindfulness has been used to treat a wide range of mental health issues with adults, including:

- *Depression and depression relapse*: Mindfulness-based cognitive therapy (MBCT: Ma & Teasdale, 2004; Segal, Williams, & Teasdale, 2002) was initially designed to treat depression and prevent relapse and has a growing evidence-base documenting its effectiveness.
- *Bipolar disorder*: MBCT and DBT (dialectical behavior therapy) have been adapted for bipolar disorder (Weber et al., 2010).
- *Anxiety and panic*: ACT (acceptance and commitment therapy), MBCT, MBSR, as well as general mindfulness interventions have all been successfully used with anxiety and panic (Greeson & Brantley, 2009).
- *Substance abuse and addiction*: Patterned after MBCT, mindfulness-based relapse prevention is growing as an acceptable treatment for learning to manage cravings associated with addiction (Witkiewitz, Marlatt, & Walker, 2005).
- *Eating disorders*: The MBSR curriculum has been adapted to work with self-regulation related to binge eating, obesity, anorexia, and bulimia (Kristeller, Baer, & Quillian-Wolever, 2006; Kristeller & Wolever, 2011; Wolever & Best, 2009).
- *Borderline personality disorder*: DBT is a well-researched approach to treating borderline personality disorder that incorporates mindful awareness of emotion.
- *Attention deficit disorder*: Mindfulness has been used to help adults diagnosed with ADHD with self-regulation and self-directedness (Philipsen, et al., 2007; Smalley et al., 2009; Zylowska, Smalley, & Schwartz, 2009).
- *Trauma and PTSD*: Mindfulness is also being explored as a treatment for trauma, including experiential avoidance and other symptoms characteristic of trauma (Follette & Vijay, 2009).
- *Sexual abuse*: MBSR has recently also been adapted to work with adults abused as children with encouraging outcomes (Kimbrough, Magyari, Langenberg, Chesney, & Berman, 2010).
- *Psychosis*: Mindfulness has also been used to help increase a nonreactive acceptance of and response to psychotic symptoms as well as to decrease the sense of bodily fragmentation (Pinto, 2009).

The breadth of applications is impressive as is the growing research base, which suggests that mindfulness is a promising intervention for a surprising wide range of mental health issues. For example, in a meta-analytic study on mindfulness-based interventions, researchers found strong and robust effect sizes (0.97 and 0.95) for clients presenting with depression and/or anxiety (Hofmann, Sawyer, Witt, & Oh, 2010). Furthermore, in their study of MBSR, Carmody and Baer (2008) found that the time spent practicing mindfulness was positively related to clinical improvements, indicating that the practice of mindfulness leads to greater mindfulness, which in turn results in symptom reduction and enhanced well-being. Additionally, recent research on MBSR indicates that group dynamics account for approximately 7% of outcome variance, highlighting the importance of nurturing positive group dynamics in these approaches (Imel, Baldwin, Bonus, & MacCoon, 2008).

Mindfulness with Diverse Populations

Most of the research on mindfulness has been conducted on populations diagnosed with specific disorders, either medical or psychological, with limited focus on the diversity variables. The notable exception to this is age: several studies have been conducted exploring applications with children, teens, and older adults (Semple, Lee, & Miller, 2006). The participants in most mindfulness research studies have been educated, middle or upper class, and Caucasian. However, MBSR has been used in a handful of studies with inner city, minority youth, and adults, including Spanish-speaking populations for whom the curriculum is translated (Liehr & Diaz, 2010; Roth & Calle-Mesa, 2006). Adaptations for this population included reduced emphasis on body-focused meditation due to histories of trauma, fewer handouts and written homework assignments were used due to education levels, and the all-day retreat was not included due to logistical difficulties. In addition, the sixth class was changed from focusing on interpersonal communication to managing anger and the seventh class had a focus on loving-kindness meditation. Furthermore, certificates were distributed at the end, which had great personality significance for many of the participants. Mindfulness has also been used in case studies with gay and intercultural couples to facilitate communication and empathy (Greenan, 2010; Ting-Toomey, 2009). Clearly, more work needs to be done in identifying best practices for using mindfulness with diverse populations.

Mechanism of Change

Given the impressive range of disorders that seem to respond to mindfulness interventions, researchers have also begun trying to identify the mechanisms of change: what exactly does mindfulness do that promotes change with such a wide range of physical and emotional concerns (Baer, 2003)? The following factors have been identified as significant in the change process in mindfulness-based and mindfulness-informed therapies:

- *Trait mindfulness*: People who practice mindfulness regularly report more trait mindfulness (Baer, 2006).
- *Emotional regulation*: Mindfulness increases emotional regulation by allowing people to experience negative emotions mindfully and then enable them to choose adaptive behaviors in response (Gratz & Tull, 2010).
- *Self-compassion*: Mindfulness practices also increase one's sense of self-compassion, which is correlated with overall well-being and psychological health (Baer, 2010).
- *Decentering relationship to thoughts*: Mindfulness practices help clients "decenter" in relationship to their thoughts, meaning that thoughts are seen as transitory phenomenon rather than reflecting an essential truth about themselves or something else (Sauer & Baer, 2010).
- *Psychological flexibility*: Primarily studied in the context of ACT, people who practice mindfulness techniques increase in their psychological flexibility, which includes greater willingness to experience unpleasant or unwanted internal stimuli, such as thoughts, emotions, or physical sensations (Ciarrochi, Bilich, & Godsell, 2010).
- *Values*: Many mindfulness-informed approaches include identifying personal values and becoming more mindful of how one's choices support their values or not (Wilson, Sandoz, Flynn, Slater, & DuFrene, 2010).
- *Spirituality*: Although intentionally separated from their spiritual origin, mindfulness-based practices nonetheless seem to help people connect with their sense of spirituality, which is correlated with improved psychological functioning (Kristeller, 2010).
- *Working memory*: Mindfulness practice appears to improve working memory capacity, which in turn increases one's capacity to regulate negative affect (Jha, Stanley, & Baime, 2010).
- *Neurological changes*: Neurological studies also indicate that mindfulness has measurable effects on the brain and its structures (Treadway & Lazar, 2010; see section "Mindfulness and the Brain").

Mindfulness for Couples

Numerous couples therapists have begun exploring the potentials of mindfulness and related Buddhist principles to help both distressed and nondistressed couples (Carson, Carson, Gil, & Baucom, 2004; Christensen, Sevier, Simpson, & Gattis, 2004; Gale, 2009; Gehart, 2004; Gehart & Coffey, 2004; Gehart & McCollum, 2007; Gehart & Pare, 2009; McCollum & Gehart, 2010; Peterson, Eifert, Feingold, & Davidson, 2009; Ting-Toomey, 2009). In comparison with treatments for other adult mental health issues, the most notable difference in these mindfulness-based approaches are (a) the use of loving kindness and compassion-based exercises, and (b) the emphasis on acceptance. In addition, researchers have also begun examining the clinical implications of the relationship between adult attachment styles and mindfulness (Shaver, Lavy, Saron, & Mikulincer, 2007; Walsh, Balint, Smolira, Fredricksen, & Madsen, 2009).

Loving-Kindness Meditation

Loving-kindness meditation is derived from the later Mahayana and Vajrayana (Tibetan) Buddhist traditions, which emphasize the *bodhisattva* ideal, which is to delay one's own enlightenment out of compassion for others (Dalai Lama, 1996). With compassion as their primary if not sole motivating force, the bodhisattva chooses to accept rebirth (and the suffering it entails) in order to help all beings achieve enlightenment, which has several parallels with the Christ in Christian traditions. Loving-kindness meditation allows practitioners to develop bodhisattva-like compassion for all beings: other humans, living creatures, spiritual beings, and the most difficult, oneself.

Loving-kindness meditation typically involves sending well wishes to various others ("May all beings be free of suffering, safe, happy, and well…"; Hahn, 1997). Alternatively or in addition, it may involve breathing *in* the suffering of others and breathing *out* healing and blessings to others based on the idea that the practitioner (following the lead of bodhisattvas) transforms the negative energy into positive energy, a practice which differs significantly from many similar behavioral stress-relieving exercises in which the mediator breathes *out* the negative and takes *in* the positive. Research on loving-kindness meditations indicates that its practitioners experience an increase in daily positive emotions over time as well as increased mindfulness, sense of life purpose, social support, and overall physical health (Fredrickson, Cohn, Coffey, Pek, & Finkel, 2008). Loving-kindness meditation has clear implications for both distressed and nondistressed couples to help them develop greater compassion and goodwill toward each other.

Encouraged in many mindfulness-based approaches to working with couples (Carson et al., 2004; Gale, 2009; Gehart & McCollum, 2007), loving-kindness meditation is one of the central features of mindfulness-based relationship enhancement (MBRE). The only mindfulness-based couple approach that has been researched in a randomized trial (Carson et al., 2004; Carson, Carson, Gil, & Baucom, 2006, 2007), MBRE is directly modeled after the MBSR group format, including eight weekly 2.5 hour meetings and one full-day (7 hour) weekend retreat during the sixth week. Similar to other couple enrichment programs such as the Premarital Relationship Enhancement Program or the Minnesota Couples Communication Program, MBRE was designed to strengthen relatively happy and satisfying relationships rather than treat couples in distress and is based on the assumption that it is easier to prevent marital problems through education than fix them (Halford, Markman, Kline, & Stanley, 2002). MBRE distinguishes itself from existing couple enrichment programs by emphasizing stress coping skills in addition to communication and intimacy.

MBRE has several features to enhance couple intimacy that distinguishes it f
MBSR:

- Emphasis on loving-kindness and compassion meditations
- Mindful communication skills
- Partner versions of yoga exercises
- Mindful touch (backrub exercise)
- Eye-gazing exercise
- Mindful attention to *shared* pleasant and unpleasant activities

Carson et al. (2006) suggest that mindfulness can be helpful to couples in four specific ways:

1. Bringing nonjudgmental awareness to one's experience generates insights that are applicable to interpersonal relationships.
2. The practice of mindfulness involves acceptance of oneself as is, which facilitates acceptance with others.
3. Although not its primary goal, mindfulness induces relaxation and reduces the stress-state, which can translate to a calmer approach to difficulties in the relationship.
4. As many mindfulness practitioners report an expansion of self, this translates to a greater sense of trust, love for others, and connectedness with a greater whole.

In their 2007 analysis of data from their 2004 study, Carson et al. found that joint participation in self-expanding activities was the primary variable response for positive outcomes in MBRE, accounting for more change than acceptance and relaxation. Although these findings are preliminary, they indicate that therapists may want to emphasize shared couple activities, such as mindfulness-based yoga and meditations, that are novel and arousing, which have been correlated with positive marital satisfaction (Aron & Aron, 1997).

Acceptance-Based Couples Approaches

Two behavioral approaches emphasize promoting acceptance when working with distressed couples: integrative behavioral couples therapy (Christensen & Jacobson, 2000; Christensen et al., 2004) and acceptance and commitment therapy for couples (Harris, 2009; Peterson et al., 2009). Both approaches integrate acceptance into behavior therapy for couples, with ACT also including mindfulness-based principles. Andrew Christensen added an emphasis of acceptance of partner behavior to his and Jacobson's Behavioral Couples Therapy in the hopes of increasing long-term effectiveness of the approach, which it did, resulting in integrative behavioral couple therapy, one of the best researched couple approaches. Recent studies (South, Doss, & Christensen, 2010) found that acceptance is distinct from relationship satisfaction and mediates the link between one's partner's behavior and both (a) one's relationship satisfaction and (b) one's own behavior. As acceptance was not identified in the MBRE study with nondistressed couples, it is likely that acceptance may be a more significant issue for distressed couples.

Based on ACT (Hayes, Strosahl, & Wilson, 1999), ACT practitioners have recently begun adapting this approach for couples (Harris, 2009; Peterson et al., 2009). Among other things, interventions in ACT help clients (a) reduce their avoidance of distressing thoughts and emotions, (b) become less attached and identified with their thoughts (thought defusion), and (c) increase their commitment toward valued life directions; all of which are useful for improving distressed couple relations where partners often avoid distressing issues and/or become convinced of negative stereotyping of their partner. A preliminary case study with two couples (Peterson et al., 2009) indicates that ACT may be a useful approach for helping couples increase marital satisfaction and adjustment as well as reduce interpersonal and psychological distress.

The use of acceptance in ACT differs from IBCT (Peterson et al., 2009). In IBCT, couples are encouraged to increase their acceptance of their partner and decrease the desire to change him/her; thus, acceptance is focused *on one's partner*. On the other hand, ACT targets one's *own private reactions*. ACT encourages couples to mindfully accept their internal reactions to their partner while simultaneously recognizing that their negative internal evaluations are thoughts that may not be accurate and need not be acted upon. ACT also uses acceptance of one's internal reaction to help clients not become fused with these thoughts to increase their response flexibility.

Adult Attachment and Mindfulness

In addition to research on acceptance and couples therapy, a handful of studies have begun to explore the relationship between adult attachment patterns and mindfulness. In a study of 70 attendees of a 3-month meditation retreat, Shaver et al. found that mindfulness was negatively correlated with anxious and avoidant attachment styles. More specifically, those with anxious attachment styles had greater difficulty with the *nonjudgmental* aspects of mindfulness and those with *avoidant* attachment styles struggled more with being in the present moment compared to participants with secure attachment styles (Shaver et al., 2007).

In a study of trait mindfulness, Walsh et al. (2009) found that attachment anxiety and attachment avoidance were both negatively correlated with trait mindfulness. The authors of this study suggested that mindfulness might be useful for helping adults form more secure relationships. Similarly, Saavedra, Chapman, and Rogge (2010) found that high levels of trait mindfulness buffered relationships from the effects of high levels of attachment anxiety. These finding related to attachment and mindfulness may be of particular relevance for therapists using emotionally focused therapy (EFT; Johnson, 2004), an evidence-based couples model that integrates attachment, systems, and experiential theories. Mindfulness may be an additional resource for EFT therapists helping couples to develop more secure attachment styles and improved relations (Gambrel & Keeling, 2010).

Mindfulness with Children, Adolescents, and Parents

Jon Kabat-Zinn and his wife Myla (1997) were the first to describe how the tenants of MBSR could be translated to parenting and family life. As interest in mindfulness has grown, increasing numbers of practitioners have been eager to adapt mindfulness for working with children as young as 7, teens, and their parents (Thompson & Gauntlett-Gilbert, 2008). Although research on mindfulness-based interventions with children and adolescents is in its early stages, the current evidence provides support for the feasibility and acceptability of the approach with these populations (Burke, 2010). Furthermore, a recent analysis of 16 studies on sitting meditation with youth found only slightly smaller effect sizes than those compared to adults, ranging from 0.27 to 0.70 for behavioral/psychosocial outcomes and 0.16–0.29 for physiological outcomes (Black, Milam, & Sussman, 2009).

Work with children and their families has focused on the following issues and populations:

(a) Adapting mindfulness for work with children and adolescents
(b) Mindfulness for parents
(c) Mindfulness for children with ADHD
(d) Mindfulness for adolescents with conduct and substance abuse issues

Adapting Mindfulness for Children

One of the more recent developments in mindfulness, adapting mindfulness practices for young children and adolescents is a rapidly growing area of interest, primarily because of the potential to help with attention and behavioral issues without medication. Pioneers in this area, Goodman and Greenland (2009; Goodman, 2005; Greenland, 2010) have developed creative mindfulness practices for young children that emphasize labeling emotions, metaphor, visualization, and mindfulness-based games and playful activity. In addition, four influential mindfulness-based approaches—MBSR, MBCT, DBT, and ACT—have been adapted for use with children and adolescents (Greco & Hayes, 2008; Semple et al., 2006). In other contexts, school-based mindfulness programs have also been successfully piloted for feasibility and acceptability as well as for appropriateness with ethnically diverse children (Liehr & Diaz, 2010; Mendelson et al., 2010).

Mindfulness programs for children are taught in child-only and parent–child formats. In all cases, mindfulness practices are taught in child-friendly ways, such as mindful eating, walking, speaking, listening, body scans, and guided breathing. The group sessions are generally much shorter than with adults, 45–60 minutes, and the homework is also very brief and anchored to CD recordings and worksheets.

Research on these approaches is in its infancy, but is promising. For example, a randomized clinical trial of MBCT for children (MBCT-C; Semple et al., 2006, Semple, Lee, Rosa, & Miller, 2010) found that all children who completed the program showed significant improvements in attention and those who initially had elevated anxiety showed a reduction in anxiety and behavior symptoms as well.

Several guidelines have been proposed for using mindfulness with young children (Goodman, 2005; Goodman & Greenland, 2009; Semple et al., 2006; Thompson & Gauntlett-Gilbert, 2008):

- *Keep it fun*: To engage young children, the activities must be fun and can include adaptations of familiar childhood games and activities, such as blowing bubbles, listening to birds, or eating an apple.
- *Serve as a role model*: Even more critical with children, adults must "walk their talk," which in this case involves providing a role model for how to practice mindfulness and inspiration for doing so.
- *Include real world practices*: Traditional mindfulness practices are adapted for children and adolescents by making them more active, real world, and hands-on (e.g., having children mark down on paper each time they hear a bell ring or, or adolescents, "mindful texting").
- *Label emotions*: Mindful activities help children learn, notice, and label emotions; they can also be encouraged to see them as "visitors" rather than part of their identity.
- *Use metaphors*: Child-friendly metaphors, such as the "non-judgment" used when training a puppy, are used to help teach concepts.
- *Reinforce learning with repetition*: Even more than with adults, children benefit from repetition, such as repeating a lesson in various ways within a session and beginning each session with a review of the last.
- *Include breath awareness*: As with adults, breath awareness can be readily used in everyday life and should be included in work with children.
- *Encourage kindness meditations*: Loving-kindness meditations are a highly relevant and practical activity for children; the visualization element may make it easier for children than breath meditation.
- *Offer more explanation*: More, simpler, and entertaining explanations for mindfulness practices help engage and motivate children and adolescents to learn (e.g., habits of mindless eating).
- *Provide variety*: Child programs must balance enough variety to keep children's attention with sufficient repetition to build skills.
- *Involve parents*: Parents should be educated and involved as much as possible, especially when working with young children.
- *Adapt for classrooms*: When conducting sessions in nonclinical classroom setting, avoid practices that encourage deep states of meditation or introspection.
- *Length of practice and activities*: Rather than 25 minutes or more of practice, child programs typically use homework assignments that are 3–5 minutes long. Similarly, in-session activities should be short enough to maintain children's attention.
- *Smaller group size*: Groups of 6–8 children with two facilitators are used in MBCT-C.

Mindful Parenting

Mindfulness has been used to help parents improve their parenting both in group and family modalities. Three different structured group programs have been created by integrating mindfulness into existing, well-established behavioral parenting programs: mindful parenting, mindfulness-based parent training, and mindfulness-based childbirth and parent education. In addition, case studies with parents receiving individual mindfulness interventions offer promising directions for helping families work together to help children with developmental and externalizing behaviors.

Mindful parenting. In their Mindful Parenting program based on the behavioral Strengthening Family Program, Duncan, Coatsworth, and Greenberg (2009a, 2009b) integrate mindfulness to help parents increase their ability to intentionally bring moment-to-moment awareness to interactions with their children. The program is designed to help parents increase their emotional awareness, improve their abilities to regulate their own emotions, and bring greater acceptance and compassion to their parenting relationships. In a recent randomized pilot study, Coatsworth, Duncan, Greenberg, and Nix (2010) found that parents and youth in this program had comparable effects on child management practices and stronger effects on the parent–child relationship, which were mediated by increased parental mindfulness. These findings highlight the importance of parental emotional self-regulation and awareness in improving the parent–child relationship.

Mindfulness-based parent training. Integrating mindfulness into a traditional Behavioral Parenting Training Program (BPTP), Dumas (2005) developed Mindfulness-Based Parent Training to reduce the automatic and rigid behavior patterns that typically characterized problematic parent–child relationships. Unlike traditional behavioral parenting programs based on operant conditioning, Dumas's model assumes that the problem interactions develop through repetitive, mindless interactions that become habitual. In this program, parents learn to become mindful of these, disengage themselves through awareness, and choose more effective strategies for relating to their children.

Mindfulness-based childbirth and parenting. Based on the MBSR format, mindfulness-based childbirth and parenting is designed for pregnant women in their third trimester to help them through pregnancy, childbirth, and the transition to becoming a parent parenting (Duncan & Bardacke, 2010). This 9-week group program with a retreat and reunion (with babies) introduces a mindfulness awareness body scan (which should not be confused with progressive relaxation in which participants *try* to relax their bodies) as the first formal meditation practice to help participants more skillfully relate to the physical discomfort of the third trimester as well as develop skills for the birthing process. The course emphasizes the mind-body connection in the birthing process and how psychological stress can negatively affect labor. The program also includes mindful yoga and a pain meditation, in which participants meditate on the physical pain sensations of holding ice to learn how to skillfully work with the pain of labor. The initial pilot study on this program showed large effect sizes (>0.70) with increased mindfulness and positive affect and decreased maternal anxiety, depression, and negative effect.

Mindfulness case studies with parents. In studies with parents with clinical issues, Singh et al. (2007a, 2007b, 2010) have conducted studies with mothers of children diagnosed with developmental disabilities and ADHD. In both studies, the children's symptoms, such as aggressive behavior, social skills, and compliance, improved as a result of the mother's mindfulness parent training. In the study with ADHD, the children were taught mindfulness in the second half of the study, which resulted in further improvements. Similarly, MBSR has been found to significantly reduce stress symptoms in mothers of chronically ill children (Minor et al., 2006). Considered along with Siegel's interpersonal neurobiology and mindfulness work (see below), these findings suggest that parental ability to be mindfully in the present moment and self-regulate may be an important factor when working with childhood attentional and externalizing symptoms.

Children and Adolescents with ADHD

As mindfulness is a practice that involves sustained attention and is known to increase self-regulation, clinicians have logically begun exploring its applicability to treat ADHD, a disorder that is characterized by a lack of these abilities (Zylowska et al., 2008, 2009). Furthermore, as ADHD often involves the underfunctioning of the prefrontal cortex functions such as attention, working memory, and inhibition, then the potential for mindfulness to strengthen its functioning provides a hopeful new approach to its treatment. In fact, researchers are exploring the possibility that it may not only remediate ADHD symptoms but actually provide a potential for rehabilitation and correction (Zylowska et al., 2009). Consistent mindfulness training appears to automatize present-moment awareness, thus reducing the potential for daydreaming or spacing behaviors that are associated with ADHD. Furthermore, emerging research indicates that affect regulation is a significant issue in ADHD, thus providing additional reasons to explore the use of mindfulness for persons diagnosed with this disorder.

A handful of studies have examined the possibility of using mindfulness-based training programs based on MBSR with preteens (Singh et al., 2010) and teens (Zylowska et al., 2008). Singh et al.'s (2010) small study with two 10–12-year-olds involved teaching mother's mindfulness first, which resulted in improved child compliance to parental requests without intervention directly with the children; in the second phase of the study, the children were then taught mindfulness, which resulted in further improvement in the child's compliance, providing preliminary support for involving both parents and children. In a feasibility study that included adults and teens diagnosed with ADHD, Zylowska et al. (2008) found prepost improvements in self-reported ADHD symptoms as well as improvements on tests that measured attention, cognitive inhibition, depression, and anxiety.

Children and Adolescents with Conduct Issues

Mindfulness has also been used with children and adolescents with conduct issues to help them use awareness to increase their ability to regulate their emotions and behaviors. For example, in a small case study of three adolescents in danger of expulsion, Singh et al. (2007a, 2007b) used mindfulness to successfully enable all three to significantly decrease their aggressiveness to socially acceptable levels that enabled them to graduate. Similarly, ACT has been specifically adapted to youth with externalizing disorders, teaching them to accept their emotions, defuse (cognitively detach) from their emotions, and choose action based on personal values (Twohig, Hayes, & Berlin, 2008). Additionally, MBCT-C has been adapted for work with externalizing and internalizing disorders (e.g., depression, anxiety, etc.) in children and was successfully piloted in a feasibility and acceptability trial (Lee, Semple, Rosa, & Miller, 2008).

In the Netherlands, Bögels, Hoogstad, van Dun, de Schutter, and Restifo (2008) developed an 8-week mindfulness program for children and adolescents diagnosed with externalizing disorders (e.g., behavior and conduct issues) and simultaneously had their parents attend a mindfulness parenting training. After treatment, the children performed better than wait-list controls on sustained attention tasks and reported significant reductions in externalizing and internalizing symptoms and greater levels of happiness; their parental reports suggested similar changes. These preliminary studies suggest that mindfulness may be helpful for helping youth with severe conduct issues learn to improve their awareness of emotion, increase their ability to self-regulate, and significantly reduce their aggressive behaviors.

Mindfulness and the Brain

Studies on the Neurological Effects of Mindfulness and Meditation

Recent advances in neuroscience have allowed researchers to study the effects of mindfulness practice on brain structures and processes. In the first study of its kind, Davidson et al. (2003) found that nonclinical participants in a 8-week MBSR program had significantly increased left-sided anterior activation, a brain pattern associated with positive dispositional affect (a happy temperament and resilience under stress), as well as improved immune functioning.

Similarly, in a study of brain structure, Hölzel et al. (2010) found that nonclinical participants in an 8-week MBSR program not only reported a subjective experience of less stress but also had a decrease in right basolateral amygdala gray matter density, an area of the brain associated with the stress response. Similarly, Hölzel et al. (2011) found that MBSR participants had an increase in gray matter concentration within the left hippocampus, a region involved in learning and memory processes, emotion regulation, self-referential processing, and perspective taking. Together, these studies provide preliminary evidence that mindfulness training may improve both brain process and structures to promote greater well-being.

Several related studies conducted on experienced mediators and persons with higher levels of trait mindfulness (a person's default tendency to spontaneously engage in mindfulness) have also considered brain functioning. Vestergaard-Poulsen et al. (2009) found that experienced meditators had higher gray matter density in the lower brainstem in regions associated with cardiorespiratory control, which may account for the parasympathetic (relaxation) effects of meditation as well as some of the cognitive and emotional effects. Similarly, van den Hurk, Giommi, Gielen, Speckens, and Barendregt (2010) found that experienced meditators had more efficient attentional processing, including faster responses and fewer errors, than control subjects. In a study considering the correlation of trait mindfulness and brain activity, Modinos, Ormel, and Aleman (2010) found that persons with higher trait mindfulness had increased dorsomedial prefrontal cortex activation and decreased amygdala response to negative scenarios. These findings suggest that dispositional mindfulness may help us to exert more cognitive control over negative emotion. Researchers in China have conducted a series of studies indicating that meditation increases activity in the anterior cingulate cortex, which is believed to govern self-regulation (Fan, Tang, Ma, & Posner, 2010; Tang et al., 2007, 2010, 2009).

In sum, these neurological studies indicated that mindfulness and meditation might affect the brain to produce the following effects:

- Improved physiological ability to regulate one's stress response and emotions
- Increased brain patterns associated with a happy disposition
- Better memory and attention
- Greater ability to consider alternative perspectives

Siegel's Theory of Neural Integration and Mindfulness

Seminal interpersonal neurobiology theorist and mindfulness researcher, Siegel's (1999, 2010b) neurological models provide exciting new insight into the interconnections of mindfulness, relationships, and the brain. Siegel (2009) proposes that mindfulness promotes positive changes in the brain by increasing *neural integration* in the middle prefrontal cortex. Neural integration is a brain pattern associated with a sense of well-being: "an integrated state enables the most flexible, adaptive, and stable states to be created within a dynamical, complex system" (Siegel, 2007, p. 198). He argues that neural integration characterizes wellness and that lack of integration (either rigidity, chaos, or both) is virtually synonymous with mental disorders (Siegel, 2009). In sum, integrative brain states are described as being flexible, adaptive, coherent, energized, and stable (FACES). In addition, secure parent–child and intimate relationships are also characterized by neural integration, and Siegel proposes that future research will find that "secure adult attachment and mindfulness traits go hand-in-hand" (p. 144); indeed, emerging research is bearing this out (see section "Adult Attachment and Mindfulness").

Based on his research, Siegel (2009) identifies nine characteristics of neural integration that are also correlated with secure attachment and mindfulness practice:

1. *Body regulation*: Regulation of the sympathetic and parasympathetic nervous systems that respectively regulate the stress and relaxation responses.
2. *Attuned communication*: Communication between two people in which they become part of a resonating whole, a characteristic of secure attachment.
3. *Emotional balance*: Maintaining an optimal flow of arousal that results in a sense of emotional balance and regulation.
4. *Fear modulation*: The ability to modify a fear once an experience triggers a response, thus unlearning the anxiety and choosing a more appropriate response.
5. *Response flexibility*: The ability to pause and chose a response rather than mindlessly reacting to a situation out of habit.
6. *Insight*: An increased awareness and understanding of the self, in relation to the past, present, and future.
7. *Empathy*: The ability to accurately imagine the perspective, emotions, and inner reality of another. Combining the processes of insight and empathy, Siegel (2010a) describes the ability to map one's own and another's mental world as *mindsight*.
8. *Morality*: Identifying and choosing action for the greater relational and social good.
9. *Intuition*: Nonverbal processing of experience that is able to come into awareness.

Secure Attachment to Self and Other: Inter- and Intrapersonal Attunement

Secure attachments are characterized by integrative neural patterns. Siegel (1999) describes how parent–infant attachment in the first 3 years of life significantly affects brain development; infants need securely attached relationships with their parents in order for their brains to develop optimally. When this does not occur, children have more chaotic neural patterns and may develop emotional and behavioral disorders, such as attention deficit disorder, learning disabilities, and mood disorders. Thankfully, these childhood attachment patterns are not a life sentence. Once in a secure relationship, typically in an adult intimate relationship, the person can learn to develop a more secure attachment pattern.

Interpersonal attunement. Often correlated with secure attachment, Siegel (2009) describes how brains can become attuned with one another, resulting in changes in both parties' physiological, affective, and intentional states. Highly specialized in their functioning, *mirror neurons* map the internal states of another and provide a biological foundation for empathy. Although it is likely that mirror neurons originally developed to promote survival by identifying enemies, these neurons also enable humans to create and sustain intimate relationships.

Furthermore, mirror neurons enable a person to experience "what before may have been unbearable states of affective and bodily activation" (Siegel, 2006, p. 255).

Thus, in therapy, when a therapist and client are in relational attunement, the client is able to tolerate and "work through" difficult emotions and insights that otherwise result in emotional dysregulation. Clients can thereby increase their physiological capacity for affective and behavioral regulation.

Intrapersonal attunement. Siegel (2007) suggests that by encouraging a person to nonjudgmentally and compassionately observe one's own mental processes, mindfulness practice enables a person to develop *intrapersonal attunement*, attunement with the self, using mechanisms similar to those associated with interpersonal attunement. This self-attunement can also be characterized as having a *secure attachment with the self*. Thus, mindfulness can also be understood as one of the few concrete and specific means for increasing self-compassion and acceptance.

Not Knowing and Nonjudging: Bottom-Up Processing

Of particular interest to family therapists, Siegel (2007, 2009) suggests that many of the relational and psychological benefits of mindfulness result from an increase in *bottom-up processing*, a brain process that correlates to the *not knowing* stance frequently cited in family therapy literature (Anderson, 1997). Referring to when the bottom three cortical layers are used, *bottom-up processing* involves using one's immediate lived experience to generate new understandings, categories, and stories for what is happening; bottom-up processing, like mindfulness, embraces uncertainty with curiosity and ease. In contrast, *top-down processing* refers when the top three layers of the cortex dominate mental processes and preexisting labels are used to interpret experience in a habitual way. Although necessary for coordinating the numerous routines of daily life, top-down processing reduces response flexibility and adaptability, and thus can lead to rigidity and eventually relational and mental health problems. The bottom-up processing encourages openness, growth, and flexibility, which are required to successfully adapt to new challenges and contexts. Furthermore, bottom-up processing allows people to redefine and reshape their personal identities with new experiences rather than remain enslaved to identity narratives that no longer serve them and/or are no longer accurate. Mindfulness is essentially an intense bottom-up processing practice, in which practitioners train the mind to focus on directly experiencing the moment with minimal top-down labeling to enable fresh, new experience.

Trauma and Integration

As most therapists are well aware, trauma often results in extensive physiological, psychological, and relational problems, which Siegel theorizes is due to trauma impairing neural integration: "unresolved trauma makes a mind incoherent" (2010b, p. 190). In his model, posttraumatic stress disorder and similar trauma responses result from the brain separating implicit and explicit memory to cope with the overwhelming event. When a person experiences an extreme trauma, the stress response is triggered, impairing the ability of the hippocampus to develop *explicit memories*. Explicit memories require conscious attention for encoding so that they can then be pulled up as a coherent, past "memory." The stress response also activates the amygdala, which "sears" into implicit memory the traumatic event. Thus, traumatic events are stored primarily as *implicit memories*, which do not have the sensation of being from the past and often feel as though they are in the present; they are automatic and shape our here-and-now subjective experiences. These implicit memories result in chaotic and rigid patterns, impairing a person's brain from entering integrated neural states associated with wellness. Resolving trauma requires that the focused attention of the hippocampus to pull together the various puzzle pieces of implicit memories related to the trauma into a coherent narrative. The positive effects of mindfulness on memory, attention, and emotional regulation have the potential to facilitate this process of trauma recovery.

Reflecting on Research

Although still relatively new, the evidence base for mindfulness and its effects on physical, neurological, mental, and relational health is impressive and quickly growing. Few, if any, interventions commonly used in mental health cover such breadth or have similarly clear neurological explanations and evidence. Although much work is left to be done to better understand mindfulness and acceptance, the possibilities for more efficient and direct mechanisms of change are exciting. Mindfulness and acceptance have the potential to be highly teachable and pragmatic approaches for helping individuals, couples, and families improve their relationships by increasing their compassion for one another, developing secure attachments, becoming less reactive, and tolerating greater levels of intimacy.

Part II
The Practice of Mindfully Oriented Couple and Family Therapy

Introduction to Part II

The existing evidence base for family therapy and mindfulness-related therapies provides the foundation for a comprehensive theory of love and well-being. Therapists can use this theory when working with couples and families as well as individuals presenting with relational concerns. This model is based on the assumption that satisfying relationships and a general sense of well-being involve three core relationships that can be developed through mindfulness and acceptance practices:

1. *Self*: An accepting relationship with oneself that includes an ability to regulate difficult emotions and thoughts.
2. *Other*: The ability to develop and sustain emotionally safe and satisfying intimate relationships with partners, parents, children, and significant persons in one's life.
3. *Life*: A sense of connection with life (e.g., God, the universe) that is characterized by a sense of safety, cohesion, and benevolence (or at least non-malevolence).

Mindfulness and acceptance practices can be used to help clients develop secure and safe relationships and overall well-being at each of these levels to promote optional functioning, from the neurological level to the spiritual. These levels work in concert: the better one functions at one level the better that person can function at another.

The following chapters provide therapists with a flexible approach for helping clients improve their relationships with themselves and others based on emerging research on the mindfulness, relationships, and brain development, as well as what works in therapy. This approach includes the following:

- *A therapeutic relationship* based on mindfulness (Chap. 4).
- *A case conceptualization* approach that integrates mindfulness, acceptance, Buddhist psychology, and family therapy principles (Chap. 5).

- *Goal setting* and *treatment planning* based on research findings and Buddhist psychology principles (Chap. 5).
- Interventions for *teaching mindfulness* to individuals, couples, and families in everyday therapy settings (Chap. 6).
- Mindfulness- and acceptance-informed *intervention practices and principles* (Chap. 7).
- *Specific interventions* for special issues with couples and families (Chap. 8).

Chapter 4
Therapeutic Presence and Mindfulness

The room was quiet for what seemed an eternity, but was only a minute or two. Jane, the mother, sitting erect and neatly groomed, had a steady stream of silent tears running down her checks. Mark, her father, sat with a stare that reached to the edge of infinity. The silence was raw, touching on a pain too tremendous for words to capture. Why would a beautiful young girl choose to kill herself on her 16th birthday? Why didn't the hospital stays, medication, and therapy help her? How does a parent find the will to go on? Even the best-trained therapist does not find such a moment easy. Although professional explanations about suicide might help answer a few nagging questions, such words do not begin to fill the chasm left by such a loss. But, something does help more than reassuring words: being there, being palpably open to share in the depths of horrific sorrow. By being willing to open one's heart to the darkest of tragedies so that another must not bear it alone, therapists can help.

Mindfulness and acceptance can profoundly change the quality of therapists' presence in session by enabling them to be more fully "there" in a manner that is difficult to articulate and measure, but is generally undeniable to those in the room. After decades of research, the general professional consensus is that the therapeutic relationship is a better predictor of outcome than a therapist's specific model (Lambert & Simon, 2008; Miller, Duncan, & Hubble, 1997). Thus, the qualities that Rogers (1961) initially identified—accurate empathy, therapist genuineness, and positive regard—are readily identified in contemporary practice as key elements of successful therapeutic relationships.

Despite this widespread agreement that empathy and the quality of the therapeutic relationship are the most important variable that a therapist directly influences, few specific and quantifiable "techniques" or practices have been demonstrated to teach professionals empathy or improve the quality of the relationship (Shapiro & Izett, 2008). To fill this gap, many therapists have explored how mindfulness may provide an unusually efficient and effective method to improve therapists' ability to connect and be present with clients (Hick & Bien, 2008; Shapiro & Izett, 2008).

D.R. Gehart, *Mindfulness and Acceptance in Couple and Family Therapy*, 59
DOI 10.1007/978-1-4614-3033-9_4, © Springer Science+Business Media New York 2012

Therapeutic Presence

My colleague Eric McCollum and I have suggested that *therapeutic presence* describes the most essential element of therapeutic relationships (Gehart & McCollum, 2008; McCollum & Gehart, 2010). More a quality of *being* than state of *doing*, therapeutic presence has been described as a characteristic that therapists bring to the therapeutic encounter that includes elements of empathy, compassion, charisma, spirituality, transpersonal communication, patient responsiveness, optimism, and expectancies (McDonough-Means, Kreitzer, & Bell, 2004). Clearly, therapeutic presence is a difficult to operationalize quality, which has led many to focus on more readily observable aspects of the therapeutic relationships, such as empathetic statements, summarizing, focused listening, reflecting feelings, and refraining from advice giving (e.g., Young, 2005). Although extremely important to therapeutic relationships, these skills cannot fully capture the subtle quality of being that makes a relationship "therapeutic." Mindfulness provides a concrete means for developing therapeutic presence both in new therapists and in seasoned clinicians. Unlike the basic skills for establishing a therapeutic relationship, developing therapeutic presence is a never-ending journey that even experienced therapists can continue to advance over their careers.

To explore the potentials of mindfulness and acceptance for developing therapeutic presence, this chapter will:

- Provide a model for using mindfulness, compassion, interbeing, and related practices to conceptualize and actualize the therapeutic presence in couple and family therapy.
- Outline a neurological model for understanding how mindfulness presence enables clients to resolve trauma and work through difficult interpersonal issues.
- Describe how mindful presence can be used in a variety of challenging clinical situations.

Mindfulness and Therapeutic Presence

In recent years, numerous therapists have explored using mindfulness to develop the therapeutic relationship in a wide range of psychotherapeutic models, including psychodynamic, humanistic, cognitive-behavioral, family systems, and postmodern approaches as well as in physical medicine (Gehart & McCollum, 2007; Hick & Bien, 2008; Shapiro & Izett, 2008). Therapists regularly use mindfulness to cultivate empathy, be in the present moment, and remain calm when discussing challenging subjects. In addition to being mindfully present, mindfulness and related Buddhist psychology concepts offer three particularly useful concepts that can enhance traditional understandings of therapeutic relationships in the practice of couple and family therapy:

- Compassion
- Humanity: Humility and humor
- Interbeing

Compassion and Therapeutic Presence

Therapists have a long history of using empathy in the therapeutic encounter (Rogers, 1961). Mindfulness and Buddhist psychology provide a related but significantly different means for emotionally engaging with client suffering: *compassion*. Whereas empathy refers to accurately perceiving another's internal emotional state and reflecting back the emotion, compassion instead refers to a more spiritual and universal experience that takes the form of an engaged and emotionally present acknowledging of a person's suffering while simultaneously being able to view this suffering within its larger role of the human condition (Hahn, 1997). The therapist is not made anxious by the suffering, wanting to stop it as soon as possible, but instead maintains a calm, engaged, warm presence that embraces even the darkest forms of suffering (Gehart & McCollum, 2007).

Although not always immediately apparent, compassion is at the heart of mindfulness practice (Kabat-Zinn, 1990). For practitioners to reap the many benefits of mindfulness, the refocusing of the mind on the breath (or other focus) must be done in a compassionate, nonjudging way. Over time, this process generates increasing compassion for the human condition by acknowledging and accepting how the heart and mind work. Especially for therapists, this translates to a more profound understanding of emotions, cognitions, and behaviors and how they all work—or don't work—together. I personally believe it is critical that all people wanting to be therapists seriously dedicate themselves to "studying the mind" the way Buddhists have for centuries: by compassionately watching it. Such "in vivo" study results in a far more profound and compassionate understanding of how the mind actually functions compared to the cold, detached, third-person theories and research models generated by Western scientists. There are few things more humbling or compassion-generating than watching your own mind at work.

Developing compassion for the nature of the mind provides a foundation for developing a more spiritual form of compassion that characterizes the Mahayana (later and primarily East Asian) forms of Buddhism. In these forms of Buddhism, the "highest good" to which a human can aspire is to become a Bodhisattva, which is a being capable of becoming enlightened (and thereby end personal suffering), but instead chooses to delay enlightenment to help others who are suffering become enlightened (Hahn, 1998). The Bodhisattva has many parallels with the role of Jesus in Christianity, who also chose to endure suffering to reduce the suffering of others.

Thus, the compassion that mindfulness informs is a more spiritual—although not necessarily religious—form of compassion that comes from bearing witness to and embracing the suffering that is part of the human condition. This compassion embraces life's bittersweet qualities: there is suffering—such as loss, death, and illness—and it is because there are possibilities that life is precious. The experiences of joy and happiness seem to be meaningful and most readily accessible when experienced in a context of suffering. As numerous books, myths, and plays throughout history have illustrated and plenty of modern research has shown—living in an utopia— where no one ever dies, the weather is perfect, we never have to work, and everything is be provided for us without effort—would soon become a living nightmare. Positive psychology researchers explain that dream fulfillment does not create sustainable happiness because happiness comes from putting effort into meaningful activities and relationships that we value (Seligman, 2002).

The unique quality of this form of compassion is that it is calm and fearless in the face of suffering, sometimes referred to a *fierce compassion* (also see Chap. 2; Trungpa, 1991). Bowen (1985) intergenerational family therapists describe how they use a "non-anxious" presence to from therapeutic relationships with clients. The Buddhist addition to this would be to have a compassionate, engaged, and curious yet nonanxious presence. When the therapist can compassionately engage difficulties and suffering without fear, anger, or disgust and engage them with a spirit of open curiosity (Anderson, 1997), they enable clients to more fully experience, bear, and transform their struggles. Often, it is fear or denial of a situation that creates the greatest suffering. For example, many parents get into a panic about how their child is behaving and either become overly anxious about it or ignore it. But when therapists can help parents compassionately bear witness to, become curious about, and accept their child's behavior, there is often a remarkable calm that comes over them. Paradoxically, the calm from their acceptance often results in the child's behavior slightly or even dramatically improving. And in all cases, the parents are able to more effectively respond to the child from this place of calm rather than anxiety or denial.

Humanity: Humility and Humor

Another quality that shifts when therapists use mindfulness, acceptance, and compassion to inform their therapeutic relationship is that their humanity comes to the fore. This translates as humility, humor, and sincerity.

When I teach new therapists to practice mindfulness, there are two qualities that develop rapidly: compassion and humility. The source of compassion is obvious: it is practiced in mindfulness when the mind wanders or in loving-kindness meditation. Humility is more subtle and develops a by-product of compassion: while watching the mind do its bouncy thing—jumping from one topic to another without regard for logic or reality—one is humbled by a clearer understanding of how the human mind works. What results is not a shame-based humility, but a compassionate one that accepts what it means to fully human.

This humility also cultivates nonattachment that allows for a more relaxed sense of being as well as more humor and joy. So, yes, a mindfully informed therapist laughs and allows for joy to be shared in therapy as well as suffering and pain. Obviously, laughter and joy need to be appropriately timed and shared with clients, but it should be "allowed" and arguably encouraged in session to help clients live the fullness of their humanity. When joking with clients, whenever possible, I try to "tease up": jokes that highlight their progress and strengths rather than shortcomings. Such as, "Now that that you two are working together, your kids are going to have to follow the rules—or worse, actually do their chores," and/or "You are becoming boring parents that can't be remotely controlled by your kids." The key to mindful humor is that everyone in session has a good laugh at the fears, lessons, failures, and mess-ups that seem to characterize the journey of being human.

In most cases, therapists who develop their sense of humanity through mindfulness tend to come across to clients as being "down to earth," "real," "sincere," and "approachable." Too often, therapists (unknowingly I believe) appear smugly superior with their "answers for everything," special terms, refusal to share personal information, and habit of answering questions with questions. Even when they practice mindfulness, it is possible for therapists to become "attached" to mindfulness and/or Buddhist concepts and come across this way too, indirectly making clients who don't practice meditation as "prescribed" by the therapist feel guilty or worse. But, ideally, if practiced as intended, mindfulness should dissolve this common therapist persona as one becomes more at ease with the complexities and contradictions that make us perfectly human.

Interbeing and the Therapeutic Relationships

Family therapists have a long tradition of recognizing the interconnection of therapist and client realities. Second-order cybernetic systems theory describes how therapists are active creators of the reality they observe (Keeney, 1983). Similarly, postmodern therapists, such as collaborative and narrative therapists, view themselves as coconstructing new understandings and realities with their clients (Anderson, 1997; White & Epston, 1990). Using similar assumptions, mindfulness-informed therapists are aware of *interbeing*, a modern term for the more traditional concept of *interdependent co-arising of phenomena* (Hahn, 1997). We *are* part of the same web of life as our clients, and our actions and words directly affect their experience of themselves and vice versa.

When "viewing" clients, therapists should be mindful that what they notice and focus on says more about the *therapist* than the client: therapists' observations reveal their values and biases more than anything. Ideally, these values and biases should be useful to the client in resolving their concerns, but it is important to realize that these are nonetheless therapist biases. This is especially critical when working with clients who are different to the therapist in terms of gender, age, ethnicity, sexual orientation, social class, abilities, spirituality, etc. However, it can equally be a problem when working with clients who are similar to oneself, situations in which it is tempting to more freely make assumptions, and have more rigid expectations (Gehart, 2010).

When working with clients—whether they are notably different from or similar to oneself—the concept of interbeing reminds us that we are simultaneously interconnected and yet distinct. The awareness of interconnection reminds us of our responsibility to not harm the other and do our best to promote their welfare. It also reminds us that we are different and on unique journeys. What has worked for me—the therapist—may or may not work for you, the client. Often therapists who have benefited personally from mindfulness practices are quite eager to have their clients do the same—sometimes forcefully so. My experience has been that even when clients are interested, the stresses of modern living make it difficult for most clients to practice mindfulness with regularity for any length of time. And that is okay. One surprising (and humbling) piece of wisdom I learned from clients in a study I conducted was that most clients *don't* follow through on homework, suggestions, or ideas raised in therapy, even when they think they are good ideas (Gehart & Lyle, 1999). This isn't because they are obstinate or lazy, but because the insight they gained from the suggestion brought about enough change that following through what was discussed in therapy becomes no longer necessary. For example, introducing the practice of mindfulness may lead a client to return to church or make other forms of stress-reduction seriously so that they no longer feel the motivation to practice as discussed in session. It is important that therapist honors these alternative routes rather than force one single solution on clients.

Therapeutic Presence, Neural Integration, and Relational Resonance

Siegel's (2010b) theories about interpersonal neurobiology and attachment theory provide a new way to understand why a mindfulness-based therapeutic presence is helpful with clients. Siegel posits that therapeutic presence is characterized by neutral integration, a state of optimal neurological functioning that can be developed and enhanced through mindfulness practice (described in detail in Chap. 3). This state of integration enables therapists to become *attuned* with their clients, able to deeply perceive the subjective reality of another. When clients sense therapists' attunement, they "feel felt" by the therapist (Siegel). Attunement is more challenging than it might initially seem because the brain is in many respects an "anticipation machine": one of its primary function is to find patterns and anticipate them. In contrast, attunement requires the ability to suspend the tendency to anticipate using theory, logic, and past experience and instead tune into the actual moment-by-moment experiencing of the client. This is a shift from top-down processing that uses categories and preexisting knowledge to a bottom-up processing that is receptive to new data coming in. In the therapeutic world, postmodern therapists have been the primary supporters of relating to clients with a "not knowing" position (Anderson, 1997) that exemplifies this bottom-up processing that allows for attunement.

The therapist's ability to be fully present and attuned allows the therapist and client to enter into a state of *resonance*, in which both enter into a mutually influencing system (Siegel, 2010b). Human infants require resonance to optimally develop neurologically and emotionally, and this need continues into adult relationships to feel safe and connected. In therapy, the therapist's attunement invites the client into a state of resonance. This state of resonance changes the client and, in turn, the client's response affects the therapist, a process that opens the therapist to change as much as the client. This is an intimate communion in which two are truly one, and both directly experience interbeing in a palpable way. For example, when a sexual abuse victim shares her story for the first time, the therapist can enter into resonance with her becoming attuned to her experience and enabling the client to feel heard, understood, and most importantly, not so alone in her memory of the experience. The therapist does not and cannot control this process, but is instead on a mutual journey with the client as they co-evolve together. Siegel's theory provides a neurological description for what collaborative therapists have described as mutual inquiry and coevolutionary dialogue (Anderson, 1997).

Siegel (2010b) proposes that therapists can help clients resolve trauma and emotionally charged issues by entering into a state of resonance with them, which enables them to safely experience feelings and memories that have been too overwhelming in the past and thereby integrate the implicit and explicit memory separated during trauma. In this state of interconnected neural resonance, clients can "borrow" the stability of the therapist to help integrate traumatic memories and sensations into a cohesive narrative. Once the traumatic memories become integrated with explicit memory, clients will have an easier time entering into and maintaining an integrated neural state without needing the therapist. In session, this healing from trauma takes the shape of clients becoming increasingly able to discuss trauma with a greater sense of calm, clarity, and insight.

Although it is logical to assume that if the client and therapist are in a mutually influencing state that the therapist might be negatively impacted by the client (often referred to as secondary trauma), this has not been my experience. When in an integrated, mindful state, the therapist's resonance with the client creates a deep sense of emotional connection both with the client and humanity as a whole. This integrated state seems to reduce the potential for secondary trauma because the therapist resonates with the client's traumatic experience from a state that enables him/her to make sense of the trauma from a broader perspective. Thus, for the therapist, this moment of resonance invites a profound sense of being interconnected with the client and life more broadly, resulting in a moment of being touched by the "full catastrophe" (Kabat-Zinn, 1990) of being human.

Therapeutic Relationships with Couples and Families

Developing therapeutic relationships with couples and families requires a unique set of skills because several relationships need to be maintained in any given moment. For example, when working with a couple, therapists need to be mindful of (a) their relationship with partner A, (b) their relationship with partner B, and (c) their relationship with the couple as a unit. In general, "neutrality" or "multi-partiality" (Cecchin, 1987) has been recommended, meaning that therapist show "partiality" or understanding of each person in the room equally, without taking sides. In theory, this is easy. In practice, it is far more challenging because even the most basic empathetic reflection that is appropriate in an individual session (e.g., you seem angry right now) can quickly spiral into an alliance rupture with another person in the room (the person who person A is upset with). Similarly, simply summarizing to ensure understanding of person A's position can easily be interpreted as "agreement" to person B. In such moments, it appears that the therapist *is* taking one side over another, and this quickly results in the other party(ies) becoming defensive.

Thus, virtually every communication from the therapist must take into account the realities of person A and B (C, D, etc. for families). Family therapists have developed two primary ways of doing this:

1. *Systemic reframing*: Describing how A's reality intersects with B's (Gehart, 2010; Watzlawick, Weakland, & Fisch, 1974).
2. *Identifying primary relational emotions*: Describing the underlying relational and attachment needs, especially more vulnerable emotions (Johnson, 2004).

Systemic Reframing

When using systemic reframing, the therapist describes how each person's reality—and behaviors—are interconnected. For example, it is common for couples to experience one person pursuing connection and another as distancing, known as the pursuer distance cycle. In this case, when listening to one partner describe her experience, the therapist would be careful to respond in such a way that both the speaker and the partner listening feel as though their experiences are recognized. For example, to summarize her description of the problem, the therapist may say, "You are feeling frustrated because you keep trying to reach out to your partner and feel let down; on the other hand, you (to the other partner) experience her 'reaching out' as smothering and you begin to feel overwhelmed." This description is likely to enable both partners to feel that therapist understands their perspective and provides the foundation for clients to become mindful of their interaction patterns, an important intervention in mindfulness-informed therapy (Chap. 7).

Identifying Relational Emotions

In her emotionally focused couples therapy, Sue Johnson encourages therapists to reflect back to clients their *primary emotions*, those that relate to attachment, rather than secondary emotions, the emotions that are more readily identifiable on the surface. Primary emotions relate to feeling securely attached in a relationship, and in distressed relationships take the form of feeling vulnerable, alone, hurt, and abandoned. These are softer emotions that result from a sincere yearning for connection with the other rather than those that attack, blame, or criticize the other. As you can imagine, hearing about a partner's primary emotions is far more likely to positively engage a loved one. Thus, when working with couples and families, therapists can help them identify the softer, more vulnerable primary emotions that fuel the more obvious secondary emotions: "You are describing how angry you are that Brad forgot your anniversary; it seems that underneath that you fear that you and the relationship just don't matter that much to him." As discussed in greater detail in Chap. 7, mindfulness is an excellent tool to help clients more readily identify these primary emotions.

Being Present in Session

When most therapists think of applications for mindfulness in therapy, they assume that they will be teaching clients how to practice meditation. However, I would propose the single greatest application is for the therapeutic relationship. By changing the subtle but critical element of the therapists' presence in the room and remaining an emotionally engaged yet not anxiously reactive presence, therapists create a powerful context for promoting emotional, psychological, and relational change.

The actual practice of being present is more challenging than it sounds. Numerous issues arise with difficult clients and different issues, including:

- Being present without being weird
- Being present with difficult emotions and clients in conflict
- Being present with trauma
- Being present with mandated and "unenthusiastic" clients
- Being present with children
- Being present with adolescents

Being Present Without Being Weird

Perhaps the greatest challenge to adopting a mindful therapeutic stance is learning how to be present with clients without "trying so hard" that one comes across as being weird. We have all had conversations with a person trying to appear be "in tune" or spiritual; instead, however, the person comes across as annoying or worse. Many therapists live with the imagined pressure of trying to be perfect and beyond human suffering; learning mindfulness can exacerbate this need. If you mistakenly believe that people who meditate never have negative or strong emotions and are nearly enlightened, then you will be sorely disappointed with the outcome of sustained practice. When practiced sincerely and regularly, mindfulness will humble you. Watching your mind, emotions, and body at work is a sobering experience because you inevitably come face to face with your hypocrisy, darkest secrets, childish fears, and the painful reality that meditation does not alleviate all suffering. However, by engaging these with compassion, mindfulness helps you learn to befriend yourself and better understand what it means to be human and alive—to embrace the whole joyful catastrophe. This helps therapists then to be "real" in a very different way. This is a far cry from trying to be "perfect" or never have a human failing. Therapists who try to give off an air of enlightenment are going to have a more difficult time connecting with clients.

Paradoxically, therapists who work the hardest at cultivating mindfulness are the most likely to come across as weird. Due to their exuberant enthusiasm, their egos and identity may get overinvested in being "mindful" or "spiritual," and then they feel pressured to come across this way in session. Unfortunately, they just seem odd, and their clients have difficulty connecting with them or the practice of mindfulness. I once had a colleague mention to me that I don't "seem" like a person who would be into Buddhism and mindfulness; I interpreted that to be a high compliment. Thus, you might want to ask your friends and closest colleagues if your mindfulness practice makes you more or less accessible to others and closely monitor your clients' responses to you to ensure your enthusiasm for mindfulness hasn't created a wall rather than a window.

Being Present with Difficult Emotions and Conflict

One of the primary differences between working with couples and families vs. working with individuals is that raw and highly intense displays of painful emotion are far more frequent because interpersonal conflict takes places "in vivo" and in session. When working with couples and families, mindfulness practice on the part of the therapist enables therapists to remain emotionally present during extremely "live" difficult emotions and conflict, moments when one or more persons in the room are likely to want to "check out," either by becoming aggressive or withdrawing in some form. The more the therapist can remain fully present during these difficult moments, the more likely the couple or family will be able to engage in more meaningful and healing ways. For example, when working with couples, painful difficult issues are often lurking just below the surface. When the therapist is able to compassionately engage these issues, couples are more likely to engage them without the typical conflict or withdrawal that they experience when the therapist is not there. This ability to be fully present with difficult emotions seems to be at the heart of many interventions in emotionally focused therapy.

Conversely, if therapists do not have the ability to be present with the high-intensity emotions that frequently characterize couple and family work, they are likely to replicate the problem interaction cycle by avoiding the difficult emotions or allowing for aggression about them. Bringing a mindful presence to historically painful interactions between a couple or family enables therapists to gently and meaningfully shift the interaction process. By becoming neither fearful nor angry, but fully engaged with what is, therapists can help persons in conflict experience typical "triggers" in new ways. For example, if one partner begins to berate the other, the therapist can interrupt this cycle by having one or both reflect on what he/she is experiencing in the present moment in a nonblaming way that also honors their present experience. Being fully present in the hottest emotions moments provide fertile opportunities for couples and families to learn new ways of responding to and interacting with the other.

Being Present with Trauma

Mindfulness provides a concrete and specific way of being present with survivors of trauma that is qualitatively different from the standard empathy-based approach to forming client-therapist relationships. Rather than offering empathetic reflections of emotion, the mindfulness-informed therapy focuses on the quality of the therapist's presence and willingness of the therapist to be emotionally present with the client. When dealing with trauma, this becomes a particularly challenging task. Being fully emotionally present demands that the therapist have developed the ability to be present for emotions in a way that is rare in our society. By definition, trauma involves a situation that is so overwhelming to the person that various coping mechanisms are automatically brought into play to help the mind survive. Through sustained and regular mindfulness practice and a personal dedication to engaging trauma-inducing emotions, therapists can develop the capacity to remain emotionally present with clients when discussing trauma. As described in Chap. 3, this ability to remain emotionally present enables therapists to become attuned to traumatized clients and to resonate with them, allowing clients to borrow the therapist's "integrated" neural state to then form coherent memories that enable them to resolve the trauma. The more a therapist is able to mindfully experience difficult emotions and experience, the greater the ability to be present for clients discussing trauma and thereby help those clients integrate the trauma and heal from it.

Being Present with Mandated and "Unenthusiastic" Clients

Often new therapists ask me how I handle "mandated" clients, those referred by courts, departments of child services, frazzled parents, or disenchanted spouses. I first refer them to the work of solution-focused, narrative, and collaborative therapists, who honor clients' realities while also creating space for the concerns of others in their social world (Anderson & Gehart, 2007). What mindfulness adds to this collaborative approach—or at least ensures—is a sense of fully being present. Believe it or not, even clients mandated by courts due to violence or abuse *don't* expect therapists to take their side against the courts (although they are generally fine if we do). What they do expect and actually appreciate more is for the therapist to have integrity and to be fair (Gehart & Lyle, 1999). For example, when working with families who are required to seek therapy because they have neglected or physically abused their child, I am quite straightforward: "My job is to help you get your kids back. I am going to do all that I can to make that happen. But I will not do is lie or in any way jeopardize the welfare of your children." Bringing mindfulness presence to such conversations adds another level of trust and honesty to the conversation. Mindfulness acknowledges the good and bad—it notices "what is" without a pressure to immediately change what is not "good;" that ability to be fully present with a person's darker side and weaker moments without shaming the person—but also without ignoring their responsibility and therefore possibility to change.

Being Present with Children

Being present with children is probably the most important part of helping children resolve their issues. Our society lives at such a fast pace today that few parents are able to be emotionally present on a regular basis. Both stay-at-home parents with long daily routines of shuttling kids to school, practice, classes, and play dates as well as working parents rarely have opportunities to be present with their children. Even parents who try hard to make "quality time" with their children are finding that the daily demands of modern living make it a challenge. I would add that many children are not even present in their own lives. Earlier and earlier, children get swept into television, computers, and gaming worlds, which result in them not being immersed in their own lives. Thus, the therapeutic hour can become a place where the therapist invites children and their parents to be present with each other. For children, this is particularly important because they often do not have the emotional and cognitive abilities to fully experience difficult and challenging emotions and thoughts; they need adults to be present with them in their experience to help make sense of life's demands, limits, and injustices. Many problems are greatly reduced in their intensity and some quickly dissolve by simply bringing a compassionate, understanding presence to their situation (often leaving therapists like me wondering if all we do is offer a place for families to be present with each without the distractions of modern living). Obviously, presence does not resolve all children's issues. However, I have found that children crave this and more often than not are able to quickly transform their reality, make better choices, and resolve issues simply by having the adults in their lives be present with them.

Being Present with Adolescents

Aside from nonverbal infants, adolescents are perhaps the most honest people on the planet. They are in a transitional period between the innocence of youth and the saaviness of adulthood in which they are often capable of more sincerity than well-socialized adults who often do not allow their true thoughts and feelings to surface or be experienced. Thus, anyone who has worked with an adolescent knows that in most cases if the therapist puts on airs of adulthood or gives any indication of thinking like most adults on the planet, the adolescent is not going to trust the therapist or be particularly forthcoming. However, if the therapist communicates—most often nonverbally—that he/she is sincerely willing to listen to what the adolescent is saying, consider their perspective and concerns, and thoughtfully engage without rattling off the typical adult lines on how to behave or what to do, then things radically change. Adolescents quickly become curious, engaged, and relieved to share their journey with someone who seems to have a foot in both worlds.

Beginning with Presence

Although teaching clients how to practice mindfulness can profoundly change their lives, I have found that few do so readily and for sustain periods of time. Instead, mindfulness has most transformed my work by transforming *how* and *who* I am in session. The rest of this book will detail more glitzy and perhaps fun topics such as teaching mindfulness to families, using acceptance to conceptualize cases, and integrating mindfulness into interventions. However, I strongly believe that the therapist's practice—described in more detail in Chap. 10—and its ability to enhance therapeutic presence is the most significant and powerful contribution of mindfulness to therapy—even if it is the least visible and identifiable.

Chapter 5
Mindfulness-Informed Case Conceptualization and Treatment Planning

Case Conceptualization

What most of our professors failed to mention is that couple and family therapy is far easier to do poorly than do well. It's not until we have a "live" couple or family arguing in session that this becomes clear. Then, when faced with actual clients, most rush in with the question, "what do I do now?," perhaps vaguely recalling videos of Jay Haley or Salvador Minuchin saying something outrageous, such as "when did you divorce your husband and marry your son?" However, the magic of these masters is *not* what they said or did, but how they looked at families: how they *viewed* and *conceptualized* the problem situation.

Couple and family therapists conceptualize couple and family issues by identifying the relational patterns surrounding symptoms and problems and identifying the constructs, epistemological assumptions, intergenerational legacies, and individual realities that inform the behaviors and emotions that arise in these interactions (Gehart, 2010). When integrating mindfulness, therapists build upon these traditional methods of assessment and case conceptualization, focusing on constructions of suffering and their capacities for mindfulness and acceptance in relationships. Specifically, mindfulness-informed therapists conceptualize client issues by examining three sets of relationships, each informing distinct areas of conceptualization:

Mindfulness-Informed Areas of Case Conceptualization

1. *Self*: Having an accepting relationship with oneself that includes an ability to regulate difficult emotions and thoughts.
   Conceptualized by clients':

   - Ability to mindfully experience thoughts and emotions.
   - Ability to accept and have compassion for what is.
   - Attachment to and investment in constructions of selfhood.

(continued)

(continued)

2. *Relationships*: The ability to develop and sustain emotionally safe and satisfying intimate relationships with partners, parents, children, and significant persons in one's life.
   Conceptualized by clients':

   - Awareness of mind*less* relational patterns.
   - Ability to be mindfully present with others.
   - Ability to accept and have compassion for others.

3. *Life*: Having a sense of connection with life (e.g., God, the universe) that is characterized by a sense of safety, cohesion, and benevolence (or at least nonmalevolence).
   Conceptualized by clients':

   - Construction of their relationship to suffering.
   - Life philosophy and values.

Relationship with Self

When conceptualizing client situations using mindfulness, therapists consider clients' relationships with themselves, focusing on three areas:

- Mindful experience of emotions and thoughts
- Acceptance and compassion for self
- Attachment to constructions of selfhood

Mindful Experience of Emotions and Thoughts

Mindfulness-informed therapists are curious about how clients experience their thoughts and emotions in the present moment. Although similar to humanistic therapy practices (Rogers, 1961), mindful experiencing of inner experience is markedly different because humanist and mindfulness-informed therapists have different intentions when considering present moment experiences. The humanist sees present moment experiencing as part of a larger, goal-oriented process of self-actualization and places emphasis on the expression of emotion as it is happening. In contrast, mindful experiencing of emotion deemphasizes—or more specifically—does not even comment on the expression of emotion. Instead, the focus is on the *witnessing* of not only inner emotions but also thoughts and other internal experiences. In mindfulness-informed therapy, emphasis is placed on increasing one's ability to *observe* inner experiences—both thoughts and emotions—without acting on or necessarily expressing them in the moment. This process cultivates the ability to respond rather than react. It also involves curiosity about one's inner life without necessarily needing to change or express anything: simply acknowledging what is within the self.

When mindfulness-informed therapists are working with clients, they attend to clients' abilities to mindfully observe their inner experience without having to immediately react in conditioned ways, such as shutting down, yelling, blaming, etc. For example, if during a couples session a wife hears something that causes her to feel hurt, rather than shoot back an equally hurtful comment, she is able to verbally say in a relatively neutral and nonattacking way, "I am feeling hurt by what you just said" and then invites a respectful conversation about the issue. To further complicate matters, it is generally easier to mindfully experience one's inner life at a meditation retreat or by one's self; but when in conversation with a partner or family member, even those with years of practice can slip back into an emotionally reactive state rather than a reflective mindfulness state.

When considering clients' abilities to experience present moment functioning, therapists should consider more than just in-session interactions. In most cases, clients will be at their *least* reflective in couples and family therapy. Therapists should then ask about whether clients generally are aware of their thoughts and feelings and if they have had experiences where they are aware of a difficult emotion, such as anger and sadness, and are able to either reflect upon (notice it without immediately reacting) or mindfully experience the emotion (if they have had mindfulness training). Some clients need basic coaching and encouragement to help them simply identify emotions, while others will be capable of observing emotions and thoughts while alone and struggle with applying these skills during difficult relational moments, such as arguments or disappointment.

Questions to Explore Inner Experiencing

- To what extent is each person generally able to identify inner experiences, such as emotion and thoughts, especially difficult emotions and thoughts?
- To what extent is each person able to reflectively or mindfully experience difficult emotions and thoughts without immediately reacting or slipping into an old, problematic pattern?
- To what extent can each person identify their inner experience while in relational to significant others?
- To what extent can each person reflectively or mindfully experience inner experience without reacting when having a difficult exchange with another?

When clients have little experience with or difficulty identifying and witnessing their inner experiences, therapists will generally want to focus on developing this ability early in treatment to develop a greater capacity to experience the intense emotions associated with relational distress without having to harshly react. The ability to reflectively observe one's inner experience can be cultivated directly through mindfulness practice if clients are willing (Chap. 6) or through other in-session interventions (Chap. 7).

Acceptance of and Compassion for What Is

Accepting What Is

Similar to many humanistic, existential, and cognitive-behavioral therapists, ACT therapists posit that virtually all psychopathology stems from avoidance of reality in some form (Hayes, Strosahl, & Wilson, 1999). For example, depression often has roots in refusing to accept one's current situation, and anxiety may be an active attempt to avoid an undesirable situation. Substance abuse and addiction are perhaps the most infamous avoidance techniques, allowing one to escape large segments of everyday reality. Perhaps this is one of the reasons why mindfulness has been found to be helpful for these and so many other mental health issues: when you embrace "what is"—what you would prefer to avoid—you simply don't need these coping techniques (i.e., symptoms) as much. With the practice of acceptance, the external situation often does not immediately change, but a person's resourcefulness and ability to appropriately and skillfully respond increases dramatically, enabling them to either resolve or live with the issues in one way or another.

Although acceptance may also need to be cultivated for a difficult situation or other circumstances, mindfulness-informed therapists primarily focus on helping clients accept their own thoughts, feelings, and other internal experiences (that are typically in response to external circumstances). Because acceptance often has implications of resignation and helplessness, ACT therapists use the term *willingness* to encourage clients to open to fully experiencing their inner worlds (Hayes et al., 1999). By willingly embracing and experiencing painful internal realities— such as sadness, disappointment, failure, hurt, anger, doubt—a person does not struggle, fight, or try to flee from reality. This takes courage, because for most of us the instinct is to turn and run the other way. Acceptance of what is is about as logical as standing still as a tidal wave approaches the shore—because that is what it feels like. Paradoxically, the emotional wave is far smaller than it appears at first sight if one can bear to stand and greet it; but the more one tries to flee, the bigger it grows.

Compassion for What Is

Closely related to acceptance of what is, mindfulness-informed therapists also assess a client's ability to experience compassion for one's inner experiences, having an emotional openness for what is, not just a cognitive understanding.

Compassion for one's internal world takes the form of warmly accepting and understanding the many illogical or unreasonable thoughts, hopes, or emotions, which become clearer through meditation practice or psychotherapy. For example, meditation might make one more aware of a sense of entitlement with one's spouse or little irritations that may typically go unnoticed; often times a person is aware that these thoughts or feelings are not particularly realistic or fair. But all humans have them nonetheless. Thus, in addition to being willing to accept and experience these, it is also important to not overreact to them: either by becoming disappointed with the self or wanting to push the issue on the other. Instead, compassion for one's self and one's full humanity results in a healing acceptance that transforms the experience; it is also highly correlated with happiness and well-being (Hamilton, Kitzman, & Guyotte, 2006).

Conceptualizing Acceptance and Compassion

How does a therapist assess a person's level of acceptance of and compassion for what is? This can be tricky because in most cases clients do not overtly verbalize the inability to accept what is. Typically, a person is not consciously aware of the inability to accept that one does not have control over much, that things very rarely go according to plan, or that life dreams have fallen short. Instead, the person feels angry, frustrated, hurt, or helpless. Thus, the therapist needs to carefully listen for the reality that is being avoided. Later, this will be the target for change.

Practical Tips for Assessing Acceptance and Compassion

As you might suspect, there isn't a pen and paper test for measuring a person's ability to accept "what is" in the Buddhist sense. In fact, there are few questions that can be asked that reliably elicit useful answers to the question because most clients are not even aware that they are trying to avoid something: conscious awareness of avoidance is half the solution. However, the very act of seeking help because one feels stuck implies—from a Buddhist psychology perspective—that the person is having difficulty embracing some aspect of reality. The question simply becomes: *what unbearable reality are you afraid to let yourself experience?*

Conceptualizing Acceptance and Compassion for What Is

Some signs to look for when assessing a client's ability to be with and have compassion for what is:

- *Struggle* vs. *acceptance*: Does it feel as though the client is struggling—with an idea, person, or situation—or is there a sense of somber engagement with what is?

(continued)

(continued)

- *Analysis* vs. *compassion*: Does the client engage in an intellectual analysis of the situation or compassionate embrace?
- *Present moment* vs. *past experience*: Can the client describe what is being experienced in the moment in session or are most feelings described in a general way or in the past tense.
- *Continuous* vs. *fluid description*: Are thoughts and feelings described as "continuous" (e.g., I am depressed or I am obsessed) or is there a clear recognition that thoughts and feelings ebb and flow.

Attachment to Constructions of Selfhood

When working with clients, mindfulness-informed therapists consider the quality of their attachment to their constructions and definition of self. Historically, family therapists have viewed the interactions of the family system as mutually shaping each member's identity and sense of self: changing contexts can change identity (Watzlawick, Weakland, & Fisch, 1974). Postmodern family therapists emphasize the societal influence on self narratives and more radically propose that these identities are entirely created, sustained, and renegotiated through language and shared meaning in relationship (Anderson, 1997; White & Epston, 1990). In fact, some social constructionists have gone so far as to claim that there is no inherent or authentic self as proposed in humanistic therapies; that our experience of self is entirely dependent on relational coconstruction (Gergen, 1991). However, Buddhist teachings of no-self are more radical than anything that has been proposed by psychotherapists; they suggest that all notions of self are constructed realities that obscure the "empty," open nature of self (Percy, 2008). From this perspective, problems arise when we become attached and overly invested in our constructed identities because we try to make them consistent, coherent, and orderly when they have no inherent existence.

When working with clients, mindfulness-informed therapists, particularly in acceptance and commitment therapy (Hayes et al., 1999), consider:

(a) *Constructed identity*: the degree to which clients are fused with their *constructed identity* (i.e., their ideas of who they think they are).
(b) *Self-awareness*: clients' capacities for verbal self-awareness.
(c) *Observing self*: the degree to which clients are able to experience the *observing* or *witnessing self* (i.e., the part of the self that is able to nonjudgmentally and compassionately observe the constructed self and workings of the mind).

Constructed Identity

Most persons who come to therapy have become stuck with a limited sense of self related to the problem; the more rigid their attachment to who they think they are, generally the more difficult the client is to help. Furthermore, if a person has a rigid sense of identity, they are likely to view their partners and family members as similarly having immutable identities, thus compounding the problem. For example, the more identified a person is with being rational, the more likely he is to rigidly see a person who expresses more emotion or uses emotionally based logic as irrational. In contrast to traditional therapy practices, Buddhist-informed therapists are less concerned with the content of the identity (who clients think they are or are not) and are more concerned with increasing the fluidity and plurality of their experience of self. When clients develop a more fluid sense of self, the content—or who—of their identity also changes because it becomes multidimensional rather than one-dimensional.

Self-Awareness

The ability to verbalize an awareness of one's experiences and inner life is critical to an individual's mental health as well as the quality of their social relationships. Some clients enter therapy with very little awareness of the many thoughts and feelings that constitute their inner life; alternatively, they may have awareness, but have difficulty expressing this awareness. To develop intimate and satisfying relationships, clients must have both keen self-awareness and the ability to constructively share this awareness with the persons with whom they are in relationship. Thus, when helping couples and families, mindfulness-informed therapists assess each client's level of self-awareness and capacity for effectively communicating about their inner life.

Observing Self

Finally, a unique facet of a mindfulness-informed approach, therapists consider clients' abilities to experience their *witnessing* self: the part of the self that is able to nonjudgmentally and compassionately witness the constructed self(ves) and its (their) ongoing thoughts and feelings. Unlike constructed forms of identity or even self-awareness, the observing self is more of a lived experience than it is a thing; thus, it is referred to as nonself in Buddhism. A person who can step back and observe—even for short moments—the daily drama of inner life is better equipped to solve the types of problems for which people seek therapy, especially couple and family therapy, which most always involves honoring the realities of two or more people. This observing self is most directly cultivated through mindfulness meditation but can also be encountered through linguistic deconstruction in therapy (Gehart & McCollum, 2007).

Conceptualizing Attachment to Self-Constructions

- *Identity related to the problem*: How does each person involved define his/her identity in relationship to the problem? How does each define *others* in relation to the problem?
- *Fluidity and flexibility of self*: Is there a sense that identities are rigid and fixed or fluid and flexible?
- *Self-awareness*: Is each person involved able to (a) clearly identify his/her inner experience, and (b) constructively communicate his/her inner world to others?
- *Observing self*: Are clients able to experience the observing self, even for brief moments? May be evidenced by an ability to discuss inner life from the position of an emotionally engaged witness or observer.

Relationships with Loved Ones

Whether working with individuals, couples, or families, a mindfulness-informed case conceptualization includes consideration of how clients relate to others because it is always related to how they relate to themselves. As a person learns to have less self-judgment and more self-compassion, it becomes easier to stop judging others and accept them more; the reverse is also true. Some clients learn this more easily through relationships with others, while others experience this with the self more readily. Mindfulness-informed therapy involves three areas to consider when thinking about how clients relate with intimate others:

- *Mindless interaction patterns*: Problematic and often "stuck" patterns in couple and family relationships that cause distress for the persons involved.
- *Presence with loved ones*: The ability to be mindfully present—aware of thoughts and feelings in the present moment—while relating with significant others.
- *Acceptance and compassion with loved ones*: The ability to develop acceptance of and compassion for significant others and maintain these in moments of relational tension.

Mindless Interaction Patterns

Mindfulness-informed therapy with couples and families necessarily involves bringing a mindful awareness to the repetitive, stuck interaction patterns that bring couples and families to therapy. Assessing interaction patterns has been the hallmark of systemic therapy and is an important component of conceptualization in mindfulness-informed therapy (Gehart, 2010). This process involves identifying the pattern of behaviors and emotions that surround the problem. Essentially, the task is

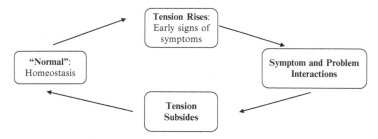

Fig. 5.1 Tracking interaction patterns

to obtain behavioral descriptions of what "normal/okay" looks like and then trace the behaviors that constitute the problem—the initial warning signs that things are getting off course and what happens when the symptoms or problems hit their peak—and then all the way back to normal or homeostasis—who apologizes or how does each party knows that it is time to act normal again in cases where there are no repair attempts. The patterns sort of look like as shown in Fig. 5.1.

Tracking the Interaction Patterns

Therapists can use mindfulness to explore and increase client awareness of self, other, and interaction at each stage of this process; client awareness, especially in the tension rising phase, can then be used to interrupt problematic interaction patterns.

Questions for Identifying Problem Interactions and Increasing Awareness

- *Normalcy*: What are things like between you when things are going "normally?" Describe common interactions, who does what, what you talk about, etc.

  - What thoughts, feelings, and interactions are you aware of during these periods in yourself and others?

- *Tension rising*: What are the first signs that tensions are starting to rise (or that the symptom/problem may start soon)?

  - Are you generally aware that things are headed in the wrong direction at this time? What are the first and smallest signs, even if they are quite brief?
  - What thoughts, feelings, and interactions are you aware of during these periods in yourself and others?

(continued)

(continued)

- *Problem interaction*: How does the problem begin? Describe it to me as if you had a video camera and were capturing who did and said what to whom; the location, time, persons in the room, and other situation factors are often important too. *Note*: If the clients use interpretation-loaded language like "she started nagging" or "he was disrespectful," then have the client go back and give a quote or example; the description of the problem must be a neutral behavioral account to allow for new understandings, labels, and interpretation.

  - What thoughts, feelings, and interactions are you aware of during these periods in yourself?
  - What thoughts, feelings, and interactions are you aware of during these periods in the others involved?
  - What do you think neutral others would notice or observe or comment on?
  - Which of these elements do you have the greatest compassion for and acceptance of?
  - Which of these elements make the relationship feel unsafe?

- *Tension subsides*: At what point does the tension start to subside? Does one person typically initiate it? How does the other respond? What is each person saying or doing to get the tension to subside?

  - What thoughts, feelings, and interactions are you aware of during these periods in yourself and others?
  - To what extent do you feel safety return?

- *Return to normal*: How do things finally get back to "normal" and everyone feels safe in the relationship?

  - What thoughts, feelings, and interactions are you aware of during these periods in yourself and others?

If clients complain of problematic interaction patterns, this tracking of the patterns is invaluable to identifying possibilities for interrupting the cycle, numerous strategies for which are discussed in Chaps. 7 and 8.

Presence with Loved Ones

One of the experiential exercises I use in teaching therapeutic presence is based on Jewish philosopher Buber's (1958) classic work, *I and Thou*, which greatly influenced the development of humanistic therapies. Buber distinguishes between I-It and I-Thou relationships. Most daily interactions require I-It interactions in which parties interact based on role; these relationships can still involve empathy and caring, but they lack the intimate quality of I-Thou relationships. Far more rare and precious, I-Thou interactions require being fully present in the moment and engaging the other as a whole being; in its fullest expression, it is an encounter of the sacred in another. I-Thou encounters include moments when two friends, lovers, or strangers share a deep moment of connection and vulnerability, both fully present and accepting to the other; the moment typically remaining clearly in one's memories years later as a moment of being heard, cared for, and valued.

In the exercise assigned to students, I ask them to engage a stranger, acquaintance, and significant other in at least one I-It encounter and one I-Thou encounter over the week. Invariably, students report it was far easier to engage the stranger or acquaintance in the I-Thou encounter. Why? Upon reflection, students report less is at risk when engaging a stranger in a brief moment of deep connection. If a stranger rejects the invitation, one is not deeply hurt. But to risk such rejection from a significant other is far more challenging. To accept such an invitation is equally risky: is this moment of softness a lead up to a complaint, sex, demand, or otherwise require vulnerability. By definition, I-Thou encounters require full exposure—of strengths, weaknesses, and vulnerabilities. Often couple and family relationships become relationships in which such safety is lost. Rebuilding this sense of safety is the focus of many relationally therapies and most explicitly in emotionally focused couples therapy (Johnson, 2004).

When working with couples and families, one of the most simple yet profound area of a mindfulness-informed case conceptualization is noticing whether clients are able to be emotionally present with the significant others in their lives. Although this is a difficult thing to quantify, it is ironically one of the easiest to identify. Most of us can "feel" when someone is present and when they are not; Siegel (2007) describes this as "feeling felt," a state of neurological interpersonal attunement. When clients are present to each other, they are engaged through eye contact, subtle nonverbal communication that indicates that they are listening, and responses that clearly reveal that they were listening, even if not agreeing. There is also greater compassion simply *because one is present.*

When working with individuals, couples, or families in therapy, the mindfully oriented therapist carefully attends to the ability of each person to be present and in the moment with the other. If this is not happening, communication will inevitably be strained and intimacy limited. Assessing presence generally does not require too many questions but rather careful or not so careful observation, depending on the level of overt conflict. Of course, culture, gender, social class, and other diversity factors inform various ways of being emotionally present to others.

Capacity for Presence

Indicators of the capacity for presence:

- Eye contact (gender and culturally appropriate)
- Open body posture (gender and culturally appropriate)
- Focused attention when the other is speaking
- Willingness to acknowledge elements of another perspective
- Expressions of empathy and compassion, even if there is disagreement
- Responses that indicate attention was paid while the other spoke
- Deliberate choice of words while speaking
- Acknowledging the other's reality while sharing one's own

Acceptance and Compassion with Loved Ones

Acceptance has been found to be a critical element in behavioral couples therapy. After carefully researching long-term outcomes of their behavioral couples therapy, Christensen and Jacobson (2000) decided to add acceptance to their approach. The new model, integrative behavioral couples therapy, which featured acceptance of one's partner, significantly improved outcomes over time, making this approach one of the two empirically supported couples treatments along with emotionally focused therapy (Johnson, 2002). In integrative behavioral couples therapy, therapists help partners to increase their acceptance of the other's feelings as understandable, of each reality as having validity, and as each partner's concern as worthy of attention (Christensen, Sevier, Simpson, & Gattis, 2004).

In mindfulness and Buddhist literature, acceptance also refers to accepting what is, which has particular implications when conceptualizing "what is" at the relationship level.

In his extensive research on couples interactions, Gottman (1999) estimates that 69% of couple's conflict surround perpetual problems, on-going areas of struggle that he surmises are attributable to personality differences that are not subject to significant change. He cautions that when you chose a life partner, you choose a particular set of perpetual problems due to personality differences that inevitably exist in all couples. According to his research, these will be the source of most conflict in the relationship. He has found that the "masters of marriage," couples who remain happy over the long haul, have found ways to stay in dialogue about these perpetual problems rather than get stuck in intractable gridlock, refusing to work with and accept these differences. The greatest fear in accepting these perpetual differences is that cherished dreams will be lost or diminished; thus Gottman recommends identifying the *dream within* (or underlying) *the conflict* and have the couple find ways to fulfill these dreams that accommodate both persons needs. For example, when couples struggle over how money is spent, the therapist invites them to articulate the dreams, hopes, and values behind spending money on a car vs. savings vs. a child's education. The conversation shifts from insisting money gets spent on certain items to finding ways to help each partner achieve as much as possible of their dreams using the available resources.

Closely related to acceptance is compassion. In general, the more easily compassion for others is expressed early in treatment, the better the prognosis because it indicates a greater sense of trust and faith in others. Much of the work that constitutes couple and family therapy is helping people better understand the suffering of others and how these play out in relational dynamics. Many times, clients have a vague sense of how the other is struggling, and in some cases there are virtually none. Therapists should take some time to get a sense of how much compassion is present to determine how best to proceed.

Similar to assessing presence, basic levels of acceptance and compassion are easily observed: harsh attacks using black-and-white language clearly indicate low levels of acceptance and compassion. Moreover, acknowledging differences—even in small ways—suggests there is some level of acceptance and a greater potential for compassion. In addition, therapists can also ask to better assess for the potential to cultivate greater acceptance and compassion.

Questions for Exploring Acceptance and Compassion

- As you describe some of these differences between you and your (partner, child, parent, etc.), are there some of these you have been more able to accept than others? How have you done this?
- As you listen to your (partner's, child's, parent's) experience of the situation, are there any elements—no matter how small—that you can empathize with or have compassion for?
- Can you share with your partner (child, parent) the story behind this characteristic/behavior that troubles them and what it means to you and your identity/dreams? (Afterwards to other): After hearing this, can you share any elements of the other's situation that make more sense to you?

Relationship with Life

The last area of case conceptualization is the subtlest and least common in traditional psychotherapy: assessing clients' relationships with life. This area brings spirituality and life philosophy into the therapy room for thoughtful reflection as to how these shape quality of life and overall wellness. Grounded in mindfulness, the areas of focus are:

- Relationship to suffering
- Life philosophy and values

As these are more difficult to identify, the conceptualization process is ongoing and evolving with each new conversation. Often, clients are becoming aware of these as the process evolves and the therapist inquires about and tries to find language that helps to describe these areas of clients' lives.

Relationship to Suffering

Unique to conceptualization in mindfulness-oriented therapy, therapists closely attend to how clients relate to the suffering in their lives. Both traditional Buddhist psychology and more modern research confirm that a person's experience of suffering has more to do with their perception of the situation than the "objective" facts. For example, when dealing with loss, a person who sees himself as cheated by another or life will suffer far more than the person who can still appreciate the good that was and acknowledging that all things in life are temporary. Thus, as therapists, when first meeting with clients, it helps to get a sense of the story the client is telling themselves about their suffering. Variations of this approach are part of systemic family therapy (understanding the family's epistemology; Cecchin, 1987) and in narrative therapy (the Problem-saturated story; White, 2007). Mindfulness-based couple and family therapy continues this tradition, adding the Buddhist insight that most suffering in life is optional.

As discussed in Chap. 2, the first noble truth is that there is suffering in life. However, the Buddha was quick to point out that life inherently includes certain forms of suffering, such as illness, death, loss, and change. However, the vast majority of suffering we experience is self-generated based on our "attachments" and beliefs about how life *should* go. Used in a very different sense from the traditional psychological sense of attachment to a primary caregiver, attachment in Buddhist psychology refers to unhelpful and rigid ideas about what we want from life: a husband who brings us flowers, a child who is successful at school, or a family that has fun together. The more rigidly we hold to these attachments—ideas about how life should go—the more we suffer in relation to them. For example, if you insist true love is only evident by extravagant gestures, you will suffer when your partner fails to perform. Realistically, we will all have preferences and cannot get away from them, but the ability to reflect upon these, distinguish what is essential and what is not, and remain flexible in meeting these preferences greatly improves coping in all facets of life.

As if lessening attachment were not hard enough, the greater relational challenge is the need to not be attached to preferences yet still maintain healthy boundaries. For example, if one partner is verbally or physically abusive, nonattachment does not mean that the abused partner should dutifully accept such treatment. In contrast, the mindful approach to handling suffering is to acknowledge that injustice has occurred, recognize the hurt and seriousness of the situation, and use skillful compassion to ensure that abuse is not reciprocated with abuse. In such cases, acceptance is the key to avoiding denial and naïve self-deception and may involve ending a relationship.

In practical terms, the assessment of client constructions of suffering happens in two ways: (a) indirectly by listening for these as clients are talking and asking them to elaborate when possible, or (b) directly asking clients.

Construction of Suffering: Indirect Assessment

Indirect assessment of client constructions of suffering spontaneously occurs with most clients to one extent or another. A client may say

- "It seems so unfair that I/we should have to deal with this."
- "I worked so hard, and now it seems my efforts were for nothing."
- "If only X... .then life would be fine."
- "I/we/she/he doesn't deserve to be treated this way."
- "This would not have happened if I/he/she/we didn't do... ."
- "I/We did everything right; it's unfair that things turned out this way."
- "I don't understand what happened."

These and long list of other comments reveal constructions of problems that are adding to rather than reducing the client's experience of suffering. The logic of the client's construction helps to identify the directions for exploring their personal logic that informs how they perceive their situation. For example, if a client expresses the belief that hard work entitles them to good outcomes, the therapist may want to encourage the client to reflect upon this assumption in the later phase of treatment and consider more realistic approaches, such as valuing the process developing integrity through sincere effort and/or being open to outcomes.

Direct Assessments of Constructions of Suffering

In some cases, it helps to directly ask clients about how they make sense of the suffering in their situation. I find this is particularly helpful when the cause of suffering is some form of loss—death, divorce, or other endings—because many assume that saying something obviously tragic—"my mother just died"—is enough to explain their suffering. In fact, there are endless ways to suffer in the face of such loss. Similarly, when clients present problems that are generally regarded as "bad" in the broader culture, it may seem like saying "I am depressed" or "I was abused" to explain their suffering. However, collaborative therapists suggest that inviting clients to describe the unique and subtle constructions of suffering—in what ways does the loss of your mother hurt or how do you experience your depression—provides numerous options for constructing new meaning related to the problem. This process is referred to as *understanding from within the dialogue* (Anderson, 1997).

By asking about the specific contours of their particular experience of loss, divorce, depression, anxiety, or other source of suffering, clients begin to put into words things that often have not been put into words before, either in their heads or aloud.

Direct Questions and Prompts for Assessing Constructions of Suffering

- Can you say more about what it like for *you* to be (angry, depressed, fighting, etc.)?
- There are many things to be (upset, angry, hurt, etc.) about in this type of situation. What in particular (upsets, angers, hurts, etc.) *you*?
- What in this situation causes *you* the greatest suffering? What in this situation causes the greatest suffering to others in this situation?

For example:

Therapist:	You say that you have been diagnosed with depression for almost 2 decades. Can you say more about what it like for *you* to be depressed, and depressed for so long? [therapist curious about unique experience of suffering to better understand client's construction of it]
Client:	Well, I have been depressed. What more is there to say? It stinks!
Therapist:	There are lots of ways being depressed "stinks": for some, it is that they cry all the time; for others, they feel like life has lost its color; and for others, say they just feel trapped in a bad movie. I am curious what it has been like for you? [The therapist rephrases the question to assist the client into a reflective position by providing a more detailed prompt]
Client:	I've never really thought about it like that before. I guess…[pause]…I guess it's like being dead inside. I don't cry. I don't get angry. It's like I have been smothered under a heavy blanket of sadness for years. Too sad to feel sad. Yeah, that's it. Too sad to even feel sad.
Therapist:	Too sad to feel sad. Can you say more about what it is like to be too sad to feel sad? [Therapist brings mindful attention to client's description of suffering, highlighting client words, and then asks for further description]
Client:	There is nothing—no life. There is quiet but no peace.
Therapist:	It sounds like you are helpless in this place [Therapist begins to outline client construction of her relationship to suffering caused by depression]

Client: Yeah. It doesn't seem like there is anything I can do. It's too big, too
                 vast. It's everywhere.

Therapist: Do you have a sense of where the sadness came from and how it got to
                 the point you were too sad to feel sad? [Therapist continues to get
                 description of how client constructs her suffering]

Client: I think it began in my senior year in college, when my high school
                 sweetheart—the one I thought I'd marry—broke up with me. I didn't
                 finish filling out my grad school applications because I didn't know
                 what I wanted after that. Instead, I just took the first good job that came
                 along....

This process will help both the client and therapist better understand the suffering and how the client understands and relates to it. This exploratory "assessment" conversation is likely to significantly reshape the client's understanding and help her develop a more proactive stance in her life.

Constructing Suffering in Relational Contexts

When working with couples and families, identifying the specifics of how the other's behavior or words create suffering in others can be particularly effective because it often promotes greater understanding and empathy: "What in particular hurts when he/she says x?" Therapists must be careful to explore these constructions when couples and families are feeling safe enough to have these more vulnerable conversations and they should help each person articulate the meanings that fuel their suffering as well as reflect upon how these constructions of suffering are interrelated. So often, each party—although taking diametrically opposed stances—is experiencing remarkably very similar feelings of rejection, loneliness, disrespect, and alienation.

Questions for Helping Couples and Families Understand Constructions of Suffering

- You have said that when your partner (parent, child) says or does X, it upsets you deeply. Can you say what it is about this that is specifically painful?
- What does it seem he/she is saying about who you are or what your relationship is that is so upsetting?
- After listening to how each of you is suffering in these interactions, do any patterns or themes become clearer?

Life Philosophy and Values

As clients begin to explore their relationship to suffering, the conversation naturally shifts to clarifying their life philosophy and values. These issues quickly come to the fore once one becomes more aware of how one relates to suffering. It becomes clear that there are choices for how to relate to, view, and construct experiences in life and that these choices directly correlate to the degree to which we suffer. Hayes et al. (1999) have placed *valuing*—making conscious choices about what we want our lives to stand for—as the centerpiece of acceptance and commitment therapy. They emphasize that values determine the actions we choose, and unlike a goal, they are never fully satisfied or achieved, but instead they inform the choices we make. For example, the choice to value emotional intimacy in marriage informs ongoing choices to nurture and deepen intimacy—even when these choices are uncomfortable or challenging—rather than being an end state or final destination. Hayes et al. highlight that virtually every choice we make is informed by our values—making the process more conscious can help clients choose behaviors that enable them to live according to their values. Developing a clear and consistent sense of commitment to these values is a central process in acceptance and commitment therapy.

Gottman (1999) has concluded from his almost 4 decades of research that a fundamental element of successful marriages is that they create a microculture of two that enable both parties to pursue their hopes and dreams. He explains that they do this by creating shared meaning, emphasizing that in this regard "*everyone* is an existential philosopher" (p. 109, emphasis in original). Humans cannot *not* have a philosophy of life that informs how they interpret the events of their lives and the choices they make in response to these events. Thus, couples and families can greatly benefit by having overt conversations about these values, hopes, dreams, and philosophies that shape the "culture" of their relationships and are often a part of both the struggles and bond that define who they are together.

These issues ultimately lead to questions of spirituality, which I define broadly as how clients conceptualize their relationship with life, God, the universe, the divine, or that which is larger than the self (Gehart, 2010); this is distinct from religion, which is a more formalized set of beliefs and practices to which a person ascribes. When asking a person to describe his or her spirituality—the relationship between self and life—clients very quickly reveal their personal existential philosophy: Is there are greater context for one's personal life? What is the meaning of life? Although these questions are often mocked in modern media, each person's answers to these questions are clearly revealed in their emotional responses to life, the choices they make, and how they relate to others. Although generally not first on the agenda in therapy, identifying and reflecting upon a client's, couple's, or family's unspoken life philosophy at some point in the therapy process opens the door to transformation at a fundamental level.

Questions to Reflect on Life Philosophy

Therapists can use some of the following questions to assess a client's life philosophy spirituality, whether traditional or nontraditional:

- Do you believe there is a God or some form of intelligence that organizes the universe? If so, what types of things does that being/force have control over?
- If there is not a God, by what rules does the universe operate? Why do things happen? Or is life entirely random?
- What is the purpose and/or meaning of human existence? How does this inform how a person should approach life?
- Is there any reason to be kind to others? To one's self?
- What is the ideal vs. realistic way to approach life?
- Why do "bad" things happen to "good" people?
- Do you believe things happen for a reason? If so, what reason?
- Does the person belong to a religious community or spiritual circle of friends that provides spiritual support, inspiration, and/or guidance in some way? (Gehart, 2010, p. 24)

Identifying a general life philosophy can help clarify client values that can then be used to inform client action. Acceptance and Commitment Therapists (Hayes et al., 1999) help clients identify their values in nine areas of life and guide clients through a process of identifying, operationalizing, and ranking these values. The heart of their approach is to help clients work through barriers that keep them from regularly making choices in accord with their values.

Value Identification

1. *Marriage/couple/intimate relations*: Describe the type of person you want to be in your intimate relationships? What do you stand for in these relationships?
2. *Family relations*: Describe the qualities you want to demonstrate as a sibling, child, and/or parent?
3. *Friendship/social relations*: Describe what you stand for in terms of being a good friend?
4. *Career/employment*: Describe your ideal work and why it appeals to you. How does your chosen work express your values? What type of professional, worker, colleague, and/or boss do you want to be?

(continued)

(continued)

5. *Education and personal growth and development*: Describe the type of education and/or specialized training you want to pursue and why this has meaning to you?
6. *Recreation/leisure*: Describe the type of recreational life you would like to have and why these activities have particular meaning to you.
7. *Spirituality*: Describe how you would like to relate to that which is larger than you—whether a formal religion or personal set of beliefs. What are the values that are most important to you in this realm of life?
8. *Citizenship*: Describe how you would like to participate in your community and the contributions you would like to make, no matter how small.
9. *Heath and well-being*: What are your values related to maintaining your health and well-being, including sleep, diet, exercise, substance use, meditation, etc.

Once clients have identified values related to their life philosophy, they can identify one or two priority areas to target for change. The focus is not on achieving a particular end state (e.g., forever after love romance) but rather to consistently make choices in accordance with these values by learning how to skillfully handle barriers to making these choices (e.g., choosing convenience and short cuts or giving into perceived expectations of others).

Goal Setting and Treatment Planning

Redefining Mental Health

One of the most significant shifts when integrating mindfulness and acceptance in therapy is that the overall goal of the therapy processes shifts away from symptom reduction and towards developing a life philosophy and concordant actions that support wellness. Specifically, a mindfulness-informed approach defines mental health as simultaneously possessing:

(a) *Mindfully present equanimity*: the ability to mindfully embrace "what is" and move gracefully with the ups and downs of life
(b) *Compassion*: the ability to open one's heart to life's inherent suffering (Gehart & McCollum, 2007)

At the outset, these may not sound like radically new ideas, but when put into practice, these can significantly alter the overarching goals and tone of therapy. When mental health is defined as possessing greater levels of equanimity and compassion, the therapy process no longer engages problems as things to be solved or eradicated or otherwise ousted as quickly as possible from the client's life. To this end, mindfulness-informed therapists also debunk the popularly held hope that with enough therapy, self-help books, beauty treatments, and cool stuff, a state of near perfection and constant happiness can be achieved—that one can somehow escape life's inherent suffering. In many ways, the therapy profession has colluded in perpetuating this myth with its implicit promise to "fix" and "cure" suffering; if we claim to "treat" emotional and relational problems, it logically follows that clients can expect they will not experience such suffering once they "successfully" complete treatment (Gehart & McCollum, 2007).

Ironically, much suffering today is created by the widely held illusion that others—those with intact families, more money, cool jobs, nifty gadgets, successful kids, beautiful bodies, big houses, or otherwise on the other side of the fence from where we currently stand—suffer less or not at all. So many of the rigid attachments to how life should go are informed by misperceptions about what is to be reasonably expected from life. Unfortunately, many mistake fairytale and Hollywood happy endings as a realistic template for what to expect out of life. Most would adamantly deny that they strive for perfection, but if you watch closely they then torture themselves for years trying to achieve what they know to be impossible. For example, I have worked with numerous people whose hearts were broken in their youth and they never dare to fully trust again, terrified that such vulnerability would crush them. Similarly, many adults still harbor resentment for parents who favored a sibling or were not there for one reason or another. In such cases suffering could have been avoided "if only" someone did something different. Equanimity is the ability to gracefully accept what is even if it is not perfect or ideal, because little in life is. Compassion is the ability to keep one's heart open and embrace the humanity and imperfection in us all.

Equanimity

Equanimity refers to the ability to move gracefully with the ups and downs of life. Translated into therapeutic goals, this means that once clients have successfully addressed, managed, and/or somehow resolved a particular issue, the work is not done. Instead, the goal is to help clients develop a greater capacity for gracefully responding to life's next challenge, while remaining emotionally present and engaged. Ultimately, developing equanimity involves developing a life philosophy based on the assumption that life will involve an ongoing stream of ups and downs that respond primarily to one's attitude and perception rather than trying to create a problem-free life (or some equivalent). In addition to contributing less enthusiastically to foundational myth of consumer-driven societies that enough money *will* buy happiness, such a philosophy has fallout in virtually all areas of person's life—from relationships to career choice to recreational activities—and ultimately informs lifestyles pursued by a relative minority of people in industrial societies.

Compassion

Buddhist psychologists would say that compassion is central to mental health; their claim is supported by the increasing research on the importance of secure attachment in adults for both their personal and relational well-being (Johnson, 2008; Siegel, 2010b). Compassion opens the heart and connects one to life and others; without it, life quickly becomes hollow. Thus, the ability to remain emotionally engaged with others and life when things get difficult is an extension of equanimity that becomes the long-term goal of the process.

Treatment Planning

Therapy—like most things in life—rarely if ever goes according to plan. Nonetheless, treatment planning can be helpful in therapy because sometimes things *do* go somewhat according to plan. More importantly, treatment planning helps clinicians to more fully think through a client's situation to develop a coherent proposal for most expediently and effectively helping clients. Whether or not therapy goes according to plan, the thought process in developing a plan is *always helpful* in negotiating the unexpected.

Below you will find three sample treatment plan templates for working with couples, families, and individuals using the mindfulness-informed approach described in this book. As these are templates, they are designed to be modified as needed to meet individual client goals. If you are new to integrating case conceptualization and treatment planning, you may want to do further reading (Gehart, 2010, 2012).

Treatment Plan Template for Couples

The majority of couples seek treatment for unsatisfying couple interactions, which most frequently take the form of arguing or other form of "lack of communication." The following treatment plan is a template to get you started in customizing a plan for working with couples wanting to improve how they relate with each other on a daily basis.

Initial Phase

Initial phase treatment tasks

1. Develop a strong therapeutic relationship with both members of the couple.
   Interventions

   (a) Using *mindful therapeutic presence* to create a sense of safety and nonjudgment.

   (b) Demonstrating *compassion* for both partner's perspectives and experiences.

   (c) Inquire about and respect each partner's *values*, especially those related to gender, sexual orientation, religious, and cultural dynamics and differences.

2. Develop a case conceptualization to guide treatment.
Interventions

   (a) Identify each partner's *relationship to themselves and capacity for mindful experience*.

   (b) Identify the *mindless interaction patterns* between the couple that relate to their presenting concerns.

   (c) Identify *life philosophy and* habitual patterns of *relating to suffering*.

Initial phase client goals

1. Increase capacity for *mindful experiencing* and *acceptance/compassion* for "what is" in the relationship and life.
Interventions

   (a) Introduce couple *loving-kindness practices* in session and at home.

   (b) Use *facilitated mindful awareness* to when discussing problem interactions in session.

2. Increase awareness of *mindless interaction patterns* with partner and compassion for how each partner experiences this pattern.
Interventions

   (a) *Mindful observing* and *facilitated mindful conversations* and tracing of systemic interaction patterns through entire cycle.

   (b) *Listening deeply* to help couple work through gridlock issues.

   (c) Homework assignments to track cycle and their experiences of the cycle between sessions.

Working Phase

Working phase treatment tasks

1. Monitor therapeutic alliance with each partner to ensure a balanced alliance.

   (a) Inquire directly and observe for signs of each partner feeling safe in session and equally connected to the therapist.

Working phase client goals

1. Interrupt and restructure *mindless interaction patterns* using mindfulness to consciously choose more effective responses.
Interventions

   (a) *Mindful* "walk through" *enactments* of problem interaction cycle to identify emotions, expectations, and interpretations that are generally unspoken yet fuel the cycle.

(b) Introduce *mindful pauses* during difficult conversations.
(c) Collaboratively work with couple to choose and integrate *mindful communication strategies* that alter the problem pattern and are a realistic "fit" for them.

2. Increase ability to be emotionally present and *compassionate* with partner.
   Interventions

   (a) Help couple develop regular *loving-kindness meditation practice* at home (5 minutes 5 days per week to start).
   (b) In session *compassionate life review* guided meditation.
   (c) *Listening deeply* to help partners understand and support each other.
   (d) *Mindful sex and intimacy* to promote greater physical and emotional closeness.

3. Decrease rigid *attachments* to individual identity and relational constructs and increase role flexibility and *fluid, evolving sense of self*.
   Interventions

   (a) *Mindful observation* of one's own thoughts and feelings as well as learning about a partner's lived experience of relational interactions.
   (b) *Embracing* "who" and "what is" with self and partner.
   (c) Developing "not knowing expertise" and an increased ability to tolerate ambiguity.
   (d) Exploring commitment to *nonviolent speech*.

Closing phase

Closing phase treatment tasks

1. Develop aftercare and maintenance plan.
   Intervention

   (a) Discuss realistic *mindfulness* and acceptance techniques that both partners are motivated to continue that can be used to continue to infuse compassion in the relationship and identify potential problems.

Closing phase client goals

1. Reduce "unnecessary suffering" by learning to reduce attachment to outcomes and increase *equanimity* and openness to what is.
   Interventions

   (a) Increase ability to "befriend" *relationship challenges* as a means to deepen love for who each partner is become and to embrace what is in their lives at any given moment.
   (b) Help couple to *cultivate wisdom and compassion* based on the struggles they came to therapy to resolve.

2. Increase relational cohesiveness by articulating shared *life philosophy and values* to provide foundation for relationship.
   Interventions

   (a) Facilitate *love dialogues* with couple to explore and redefine their definition of love, its purpose, and how it is shown.
   (b) Develop a set of easy-to-maintain practices and rituals that will encourage ongoing *compassion for and emotional presence* with one another.

Treatment Plan Template for Families

The vast majority of families who come to therapy are seeking assistance with problem interaction patterns: parents and children arguing or complaints that the kids "just don't mind." Mindfulness and acceptance practices can be helpful to create greater harmony, and the potential for mindfulness to increase attentiveness and compassion is of particular benefit for families with children diagnosed with ADHD or other conduct issues (Zylowska, Smalley, & Schwartz, 2009). The following treatment plan is designed for families wanting to improve their interaction patterns at home.

Initial Phase

Initial phase treatment tasks

1. Develop a therapeutic relationship with all members of the family.
   Interventions

   (a) Using *mindful therapeutic presence* to create a sense of safety and nonjudgment, using playfulness to connect with children.
   (b) Demonstrating *compassion* for the perspectives and experiences of all family members, including the often illogical constructions of young children.
   (c) Inquire about and respect *values*, especially those based in culture, gender roles, religious beliefs, and other diversity dynamics that may be central to family dynamics.
   (d) Respect age- and culture-based generational boundaries in the family.

2. Develop a case conceptualization to guide treatment.
   Interventions

   (a) Identify each family member's *relationship to him/herself* and *capacity for mindful experience* of thought and emotions.
   (b) Identify the *mindless interaction patterns* in the family that relate to presenting concerns, with particular attention to *emotional attunement* between parents and each child as well as age-appropriate parent–child hierarchy.
   (c) Identify *life philosophy* and habitual patterns of *relating to suffering*.

Initial phase client goals

1. Increase each member's capacity for *mindful experiencing and acceptance/compassion* for "what is."
   Interventions

   (a) Introduce entire family to *out-the-door mindfulness* and *loving-kindness* practices in session and at home.
   (b) Facilitate *emotional attunement* between parent and children in session.
   (c) When discussing their experiences in session, invite members to describe their experiences using *mindfulness awareness*.

2. Increase each member's awareness of *mindless interaction patterns* between family members and compassion for how each experiences this pattern.
   Interventions

   (a) *Facilitated mindful communication* to trace mindless interaction patterns through entire cycle.
   (b) Homework assignments to track cycle and their experiences of the cycle between sessions.
   (c) With younger children, use *puppets enactments*, switching roles with other family members to increase.

Working Phase

Working phase treatment tasks

1. Monitor therapeutic alliance with each member of the family to ensure a balanced alliance.

   (a) Inquire directly and observe for signs of each family member feeling safe in session and equally connected to the therapist.

Working phase client goals

1. Interrupt and restructure *mindless interaction patterns* using mindfulness to consciously choose more effective responses.
   Interventions

   (a) *Mindful* "walk through" *enactments* of problem interaction cycle to identify emotions, expectations, and interpretations that are generally unspoken yet fuel the cycle; use puppets with younger children—or just to add fun.
   (b) Introduce *mindful pauses* during difficult conversations; parents will need to initiate with smaller children.
   (c) Collaboratively work with family to choose and integrate *mindful communication strategies* that alter the problem pattern and are a realistic "fit" for them.

2. Increase ability of family members to be emotionally present with and have compassion for each other.
   Interventions

   (a) Help family regular *loving-kindness meditation* and/or *rocking mindfulness* practice at home (5 minutes 5 days per week to start).
   (b) Introduce *slowing to the present moment practices to increase* family time without outside distractions and allow parents and children to be more fully present with each other.
   (c) *Listening deeply* to help family members understand and support each other's needs.
   (d) *Mini-mindfulness practices* to create regular periods of attunement and connection.

3. Decrease rigid *attachments* to individual identities, stereotypes, and relational constructs; increase role flexibility; and develop *fluid, evolving sense of selves*.
   Interventions

   (a) *Narrating* "what is" to help children develop greater emotional awareness and communication with parents.
   (b) *Mindful observation of one's own thoughts and feelings* as well as learning about each member's lived experience of relational interactions; children can illustrate in art.
   (c) *Embracing* "who" *and* "what is" for each person and role in the family; for small children, use art to illustrate different "identities."
   (d) Developing "not knowing expertise" and an increased ability to tolerate ambiguity; for children, illustrate with art.

Closing Phase

Closing phase treatment tasks

1. Develop aftercare and maintenance plan.
   Intervention

   (a) Discuss realistic *mindfulness and acceptance* techniques that family is motivated to continue that can be used to continue to infuse compassion in the family and identify potential problems.

Closing phase client goals

1. Reduce "unnecessary suffering" by learning to reduce attachment to outcomes and increase *equanimity* and openness to what is.
   Interventions

   (a) Increase ability to "befriend" *relational challenges* in the family as a means to deepen love for each member and to embrace what is in their lives at any given moment.
   (b) Help family to cultivate *wisdom and compassion* based on the struggles they came to therapy to resolve.

2. Increase family cohesiveness by articulating shared *family philosophy and values*.
   Interventions

   (a) Help family to explore and redefine their definition of love, its purpose, and how it is shown.
   (b) Develop a set of easy-to-maintain, *mini-mindfulness practices* and rituals that will encourage ongoing compassion for and emotional presence with one another.

Treatment Plan Template for Individuals

According to the 2008 US National Survey on Drug Use and Health conducted by the Substance Abuse and Mental Health Services Administration, 74% of women, 65% of men, and 86% of persons over 50 years old seeking mental health treatment are diagnosed with depression, making it by far the most commonly treated mental health issue in the United States. The majority of people experiencing depression report related relational concerns, either as triggers and resulting from the depression: it is hard to experience depression without it affecting one's relationships. The following treatment plan is designed to help you design customized treatment plans for clients expressing depression, anxiety, and related symptoms using a mindfulness and acceptance-informed approach.

Initial Phase

Initial phase treatment tasks

1. Develop a warm, working therapeutic relationship.
   Interventions

   (a) Using *mindful therapeutic presence* to create a sense of safety and nonjudgment.
   (b) Demonstrating *compassion* for the client's experiences.
   (c) Inquire about and respect *client values* related to culture, gender, sexual orientation, religion, socioeconomic class, and other aspects of diversity.

2. Develop a case conceptualization to guide treatment.
   Interventions

   (a) Explore quality of client's *relationship to him/herself* and capacity for *mindful experience.*
   (b) Identify the *mindless interaction patterns* between client and significant others in his/her life.
   (c) Identify *life philosophy* and habitual patterns *of relating to suffering.*

Initial phase client goals

1. Increase *awareness* of how (symptom) enables them to avoid (specific experiences, thoughts, or emotions).
   Interventions

   (a) In session *mindful experiencing of thoughts and emotions* that client has been avoiding through symptoms.
   (b) Homework assignments to track ups and downs of symptoms to better understand how they function to *avoid distressing experiences*.

2. Increase basic capacity for *mindful experiencing* and *acceptance/compassion* for "what is."
   Interventions

   (a) Introduce client to *breath meditation* in session and at home.
   (b) When discussing problems in daily living, invite client to describe experiences using *mindfulness awareness*.

Working Phase

Working phase treatment tasks

1. Monitor therapeutic alliance to ensure an ongoing alliance.

   (a) Inquire directly and observe for signs of feeling safe in session.

Working phase client goals

1. Increase *mindful experiencing* of previously avoided (thoughts, emotions, feelings, interactions, etc.) related to (symptom).
   Interventions

   (a) In session *guided mindfulness experiencing* of avoided thoughts, emotions, and experiences related to symptom.
   (b) *Befriending problem* dialogues to develop curious relationship with distressing thoughts and feelings.
   (c) Develop a regular, *at-home mindfulness* practice.
   (d) *Journal* related to mindfulness practice.

2. Increase *acceptance* of and *compassion* for others in client's life.
   Interventions

   (a) Alternate loving-kindness meditation with at-home mindfulness meditations.
   (b) In session, explore interactional patterns with others to identify areas where greater compassion and acceptance are needed.

3. Decrease rigid *attachments* to individual identity and increase *fluid, evolving sense of self.*
   Interventions

   (a) *Mindful observation of one's own thoughts and feelings.*
   (b) *Embracing* "who" *and* "what is" with self and life.
   (c) Developing "not knowing expertise" and an increased ability to tolerate ambiguity.

Closing Phase

Closing phase treatment tasks

1. Develop aftercare and maintenance plan.
   Intervention

   (a) Discuss realistic *mindfulness and acceptance techniques* that client is motivated to continue that can be used to identify potential problems as they start to arise.

Closing phase client goals

1. Reduce "unnecessary suffering" by learning to reduce attachment to outcomes and increase equanimity and openness to what is.
   Interventions

   (a) Increase ability to "befriend" *challenges* and to embrace what is at any given moment.
   (b) Help client to cultivate *wisdom and compassion* based on the struggles he/she came to therapy to resolve.

2. Increase clarity and *commitment to life philosophy and values.*
   Interventions

   (a) Help client to define and *commit to life philosophy and values* that are culturally and personally relevant.
   (b) Develop a set of easy-to-maintain practices and rituals that will encourage *mindfulness and acceptance in daily life.*

Putting It All Together

Mindfulness-informed therapists are relational therapists who focus their attention on the three core relationships that uniquely defines each person's life: the relationship with self, significant others, and Life. By attending to all three relationships, therapists conceptualize clients' situations at multiple levels and can more readily identify how best to assist them. Most often, the same patterns and themes can be found at each level. For example, the pursuit of perfection is frequently sought in relationship to the self as well as in relationships with others and in what one gets from life. This process of case conceptualization naturally leads to developing holistic and coherent treatment plans that attend to the personal, relational, and spiritual/philosophical aspects of a person's life. Although rarely a straightforward roadmap for therapy, these plans help therapists to keep the big picture and end goal in mind so that process of therapy has momentum and leads in the right direction.

Chapter 6
Teaching Mindfulness Practice in Therapy

The Hard Part

When most people hear of mindfulness-informed therapy, they assume that a lot of meditation is going on. That may or may not be the case. I have found that getting my average client (or student) to practice mindfulness regularly for any length of time is challenging. In fact, I selectively introduce it only: (a) to clients who likely be able to practice regularly without too much added stress, and (b) at a time when they are likely to be motivated to do so. For most of us, the greatest challenge to mindfulness is making the time to do it consistently, an obstacle that is insurmountable for many, especially those seeking professional mental health services. Thankfully, there are many other ways that clients can benefit from mindfulness aside from a regular practice. However, this chapter is for those clients who are near ready and mostly willing to try mindfulness.

Mindfulness Practice with Couples and Families

Compared to working with individual clients, getting couples and families to develop a regular meditation practice is generally easier (perhaps the *only* thing easier in couple and family work). Why? Simply put: peer pressure. The most successful programs for teaching mindfulness, such as Mindfulness-Based Stress Reduction and Mindfulness-Based Cognitive Therapy, are *group* therapy approaches. When I started trying to teach mindfulness to individual clients, I quickly realized why these successful programs used a group model. Not only is it more cost-effective, but it also creates a strong motivation and bond that helps clients to practice. For most, mindfulness meditation is a solitary pursuit with few tangible or immediate benefits, especially when first starting out. Such solitude is not valued and in some cases even ridiculed in our modern always-on-the-go and ever-connected culture. Even with the benefits are immediate and quite obvious, many students and clients

D.R. Gehart, *Mindfulness and Acceptance in Couple and Family Therapy*,
DOI 10.1007/978-1-4614-3033-9_6, © Springer Science+Business Media New York 2012

that I have worked with still say they struggle to create the time or motivation to do it because there are so many other priorities competing for space in the daily routine. However, when you have to report to a group each week about progress and know that there is a class of similarly minded people practicing during the week, many find it far easier to make practice a priority.

Practicing mindfulness with a partner or family member actually creates motivation and accountability for practice, similar to but with different dynamics than a group. Thus, many families and couples are more successful at creating a regular practice routine than individuals practicing alone. Having an in-home practice group ensures greater regularity for most people. The unique challenge when practicing with those you love is that relational dynamics come into play. For example, with couples generally one partner is more invested in practice than the other, resulting in the second partner feeling "pressured." Similarly, parents who use aversive motivation strategies rather than making mindfulness practice fun run the risk of losing children's interest. However, in my experience, if the therapist sets up the practice agreement well and develops a modest, realistic plan that all members of the couple or family believe doable, then generally the practice goes well.

Introducing Clients to Mindfulness

How a therapist introduces mindfulness to clients makes a significant difference as to whether or not they will actually practice it. There are several steps that precede and follow the technical introduction of mindfulness practices when working with clients who are not in a group context (e.g., individual, couples, or family therapy). The following overview will focus on working with couples and families, but can be easily applied to individual clients. The steps to inviting clients to practice include:

1. Identifying need and interest
2. Strengthening motivation
3. Introducing the practice
4. Developing a practice plan
5. Anticipating barriers to practice
6. Fine-tuning and follow-up

Identifying Readiness and Interest

Identifying Readiness

"Only fools rush in" is an aphorism that is true in love as well as mindfulness training. One of the telling signs of how long someone has been practicing mindfulness is the eagerness with which they assume others will enjoy doing it too. I have to caution my students to not rush out and try it out on every client who experiences one of the many issues for which mindfulness has shown to be helpful. For better or worse, ongoing practice generally tempers that urge. It is not an easy practice and has a discipline to benefit ratio that is less satisfying than many activities in modern life, such as television, ice cream, a glass of wine, or popping a pill. So, therapists need to approach the introduction of mindfulness practices with a heavy dose of humility and lowered expectations.

First of all, mindfulness practice is *not* for everyone or every issue. Thus, therapists should avoid recommending it to everyone who walks in the door. Instead, it is important to establish a potential and specific need and/or benefit for mindfulness for a specific client, couple, or family. For example, *starting* mindfulness practice during a period of crisis generally does not help—it mostly frustrates and adds to a sense of helplessness. If a couple or family are having intense conflict and have a chronic pattern of viewing everything the other says or does as an attack, then they will likely fight about mindfulness too. Here are some common indications and counter-indications of readiness for mindfulness practices; these are not a list of absolutes and can vary dramatically across clients, but they should get you started.

Common Indications of Readiness for Mindfulness Practices

- Have struggled with presenting problem long enough to be annoyed or frustrated with it and/or a strong desire to address the problem.
- Asking "what-should-I-do" questions in therapy.
- Strong desire to avoid psychiatric medications.
- Couple or family able to agree on common goal of wanting to improve their relationships.
- Couple or family able to generally acknowledge positive feelings for each other in session.
- A current spiritual practice or positive history of one.

Common counter-indications for readiness for mindfulness practices

- Current crisis or chaotic situation.
- Lacking sense of ownership of problem and/or solution.
- High conflict in couple or family relationships.
- Extreme exhaustion or feelings of being overwhelmed.
- Active psychosis, mania, or trauma symptoms (although clients with such symptoms *can* benefit from mindfulness, therapists should be well trained before using it with these populations and proceed with caution).

Inquire About Interest and Willingness

Once the therapist identifies a potential readiness for mindfulness, I recommend a collaborative approach in which clients are *invited* to consider the idea (Anderson & Gehart, 2007). The invitation to learn or return to mindfulness practice needs to be a genuine invitation that clients feel free to decline. Creating pressure will *never* help anyone start a meaningful practice. I always respond with a mild sense of surprise when clients say they want to learn, such as, "Wow. Okay. I can certainly help you learn to meditate if you are interested. Is now a good time?" to provide an additional opportunity for them to ask questions, defer, or back out.

Assessing honest interest and willingness is one of the challenging parts for therapists because any therapist who has the background to teach clients mindfulness generally is invested in them doing so and may inadvertently push too hard. Thus, I highly recommend a somewhat skeptical or pessimistic stance, at least internally, so that therapists are less likely to project their enthusiasm for mindfulness onto their clients. Therapists need to also be aware that interest waxes and wanes and that clients may change their minds over time.

Strengthening Motivation

The primary difference between learning mindfulness in a mindfulness-based group and learning mindfulness in one-on-one sessions is motivation and support. Clients in a mindfulness-based group pretty much know what they are signing up for: M-I-N-D-F-U-L-L-N-E-S-S. From day 1, there is a clear expectation that meditation is involved and there is a strong community to support this. However, learning mindfulness in outpatient therapy—whether individual, couple, or family—requires that therapists solidify the motivation to practice, especially with individuals who have no support other than the therapist, but even with families and couples who have some support but often less than in a group setting.

I recommend that once clients have indicated a sincere interest and desire to learn mindfulness to help with their presenting concerns, therapists take time to strengthen this motivation before rushing to teach them actual mindfulness skills. Generally, *the primary impediment to benefiting from mindfulness is not improper technique but rather irregular practice.* So, I find it best to start there. As mindfulness practices go against most of what Western culture values and espouses, significant motivation rather than casual curiosity is needed to benefit from mindfulness practice. In essence, asking clients to practice mindfulness regularly for any length of time is—at its core—is asking for a significant change in lifestyle, one that is at odds with the mores of modern life. Thus, the conversations therapists have with clients about this practice should duly recognize and reflect this.

I actually begin by telling clients that the practice itself is not hard, but consistently taking 5–10 minutes per day (let alone the recommended 20 or more) to do it is. By highlighting that the challenge is to take time to do it, therapists shift clients' anxieties from whether they are "good" at it to whether it is done at all, which, in my humble estimation, is a more productive anxiety to have in the early phases of learning (I am a realist and believe there will be some anxiety in any case). Thus, the motivation I try to generate is not whether to practice but rather generating greater motivation that essentially develops a commitment on the client's part to do the practice fairly regularly for a period of time. Although all people are different, I generally use one or both of two primary motivators: science and metaphors.

Science that Moves People

I always try to start with positive forms of motivation based on moving-toward values rather than fear-based tactics; research generally indicates that such goals work best in the long run. Thankfully, mindfulness research has identified many positive benefits, so it is easy to find ample positive motivations for doing mindfulness. For many of my clients, reviewing the encouraging research findings for so many issues along with a clear biological model for what it does helps motivate them to commit to the practice. The following information can be shared with clients—either verbally in session or on a handout—to increase their motivation to practice mindfulness by reviewing a wide range of findings in the research literature, a summary of which is listed below and you can develop your own based on the information in Chaps. 1–3 and your other favorite readings.

Reasons to Bother Meditating

Sharing one or more of these may be helpful to strengthening interested clients' motivation to sustain regular practice.

- *General stress reduction*: Emerging neurological studies indicate that mindfulness may physically increase a person's ability to consciously manage and interrupt their stress reaction, thus reducing depression, anxiety, and other stress-related symptoms.
- *Specific health and mental health disorders*: Research has demonstrated that mindfulness can be effective to help clients with a wide range of physical and mental health issues including:

  - Mood disorders: Depression, bipolar, and depression relapse
  - Anxiety disorders: General anxiety, trauma, panic, and PTSD
  - ADHD in children, teens, and adults
  - Substance abuse relapse
  - Eating disorders
  - Personality disorders
  - Couple and relational functioning
  - Chronic stress
  - Chronic pain
  - Immune functioning
  - Sleep disorders
  - Cancer treatment side effects

(continued)

(continued)

> - Fibromyalgia
> - Type II diabetes
> - General health: Improves immune functioning, cardiovascular health, and lowers blood pressure
>
> - *"Rewire" brain for happier disposition, possibly necessitating less medication use*: Neurological research indicates that mindfulness practice may actually help to "rewire" the brain and develop a more consistently positive and happy disposition.
>
>   - Mindfulness practice increases one's ability to manage stress because when redirecting one's attention during practice (i.e., when distracted with a thought, noise, sensation, etc.), the prefrontal cortex sends a signal to the limbic system; with repetition, this ability to redirect one's thoughts increases the neural connections between the higher centers of the prefrontal cortex and limbic system, thereby increasing one's ability to interrupt the stress response.
>   - This ability to invoke the relaxation response is related to a greater ability to develop a "secure" emotional bond with partners and children.
>   - This ability may also reduce the need for medications for anxiety, depression, and ADHD.
>
> - *Observing the mind for relapse prevention*: Mindfulness practice also increases one's ability to watch and witness one's own mental process; combined with the increased ability to interrupt thinking, this enables a person to more quickly notice depressed, anxious, addictive, or other problem thoughts and interrupt them and choose more realistic alternatives.
> - *Statistics from practice*: Many of my clients and students have also been very motivated to practice when I share with them that 98% of people I have worked in the year 2008 (unpublished study; approximately 100 people) who practiced roughly 5 minutes a day 5 days per week reported *some* form of improvement in the first 2 weeks; 90% reported a noticeable improvement in stress management in the first month; and 70% spontaneously listed significantly improved sleep in the first 2 weeks. I highly recommend that each practitioner conduct similar research to learn more about how their clients benefit from and struggle with practice.

Metaphors that Reframe and Motivate

In addition to using the evidence base to increase motivation, therapists can offer various metaphors to help clients recategorize mindfulness in their minds in such a way that they will be more likely to practice regularly. Clinicians should try to identify metaphors that fit with a client's personal values, worldview, values, and sense of humor, generally offering more than one over the course of therapy.

Metaphors and Images that Motivate

Flossing

- *Metaphor*: I often compare mindfulness to flossing or brushing one's teeth: although essential to our health and doesn't take *that* much time, it is easy to find excuses not to make the time to do it.
- This metaphor is good for practical people who already have some basic health routines established; I recommend that they connect their mindfulness practice to one of these.

The "real deal" snake oil

- After reviewing the list of the conditions it helps, I often jokingly say it at first sounds like the snake oil of the twenty-first century; and if there weren't research to support the claims, it would be.
- I explain that because it is so effective in reducing stress, it really does benefit the majority of ailments of the twenty-first century, which are either caused or greatly exacerbated by stress, a physiological state that the body is not designed to experience frequently but only in case of emergency.
- This metaphor is often helpful to clients who have a range of issues and/or describe "stress" as a main contributor to their issues.

Rebooting the brain

- Practicing mindfulness is often experienced as "rebooting" the brain, just as you would reboot your computer when it goes haywire; it gets everything working smoothly again.
- This metaphor may be useful to clients who have technologically oriented minds or are struggling with a sense of being overwhelmed.

Rewiring the brain

- The most current neurological research and theories suggest that regular and sustained mindfulness actually rewires and restructures the physical brain for optimal functioning, increasing our disposition towards happiness.
- This image can be very motivating for persons diagnosed with ADHD, depression, bipolar, substance abuse, and other disorders that are often chronic.

Core health regimen

- The research on mindfulness is so consistent that many professionals are categorizing it as a core health regimen, along with eating a whole food diet and exercising regularly.
- For clients who are already exercising and eating well, putting mindfulness into this category may help them.

(continued)

(continued)

> *Quintessential spiritual practice*
>
> - Mindfulness breath meditation is one of the most ubiquitous spiritual practices with some form of it found in virtually all religions, including Christianity, Judaism, Islam, and Buddhism.
> - This framing motivates clients who have existing religious or spiritual beliefs that have connections to mindfulness or contemplative practices.

Introducing Mindfulness Breath Mediation

Introducing the actual practice of mindfulness breath meditation in session is relatively straightforward: describe the practice, how to deal with common distractions, and then do a practice round to illustrate and answer questions. In mindfulness groups, eating meditation may be taught first, but with individual clients in one-on-one sessions, I typically begin with breath meditation. With couples and families, a guided loving-kindness meditation is generally the most appropriate, but mindfulness breath meditation or walking meditation may also be appropriate, especially with families who have children diagnosed with ADHD. In the end, I believe whichever form of mindfulness or contemplative practice a client is most interested and willing to practice is the one with which to start.

Teaching Mindfulness with Breath Focus in Session

Mindfulness can be taught in one-on-one sessions with individuals, couples, and families. After spending several minutes to an entire session generating motivation in clients (depending on the specific client and level of motivation), I reserve at least 20 minutes for teaching the techniques of mindfulness breath meditation. With most clients, I begin teaching breath meditation by summarizing the simplicity of the task:

> **Mindfulness Breath Meditation in a Nutshell**
>
> - Focus on your breath while quieting your mind.
>
> or more simply put…
>
> - Focus—Lose Focus—Refocus

After this brief summary, I go through how to do each part in detail:

- *Focus on breath*: The focusing part of mindfulness practice: Focus on your breath while quieting your mind.

    - I suggest that clients begin by focusing on the most noticeable experience of their breath, often the rise and fall of the stomach or the sensation of cool/warm air going in and out of the nostrils.

- *Refocus when distracted*: The refocusing element of mindfulness: When the mind gets distracted and wanders off (which it will numerous times per minute), gently and compassionately return your focus.

    - Examples of distractions: Thoughts, feelings, physical sensations, external noise, temperature, or wind: any internal or external stimuli that the mind begins to think about.
    - Emphasize: the key for mental health benefits is to *refocus* without berating the self and instead be patient, understanding, and compassionate.
    - Provide options for compassionately refocusing:

        Labeling thoughts (e.g., worry, planning, etc.); then return to the focus of the meditation

        Visualizing thoughts as clouds or bubbles that drift away; then return to focus

        Thinking "ah, yes, that too" ("not surprised you showed up today") then return to focus

- *Focusing aids*

    - Many people find focusing on the breath hard in the beginning, so I let them know they have other options:

        *Cou*nting: Count each breath up to ten and then go back and begin at one again.

        Mantra: A repeated phrase or word, such as peace in/peace out or breathe in/breath out.

        Visual: A candle, flower.

        Sound: Periodic ringing of bell to remind one to focus or chanting a mantra such as "om" or "amen."

- *Acceptance of distraction*: Emphasize importance of *losing focus* for psychological benefits to be realized:

    - Provide an acceptance-oriented framework for mindfulness practice by emphasizing that unless you are a full-time, ordained monk or nun who spends all day meditating, the practice of mindfulness should be a gentle back and forth between focus-and-distraction.
    - I often move my hand back and forth and repeat several times: focus-distraction-refocus-distraction-refocus-distraction so that clients get the rhythm and feel of what it is like. If I suspect a client to be a perfectionist who wants to get meditation "right," I will add that it is not like a straight line (and, again, demonstrate with my hand). Many report that emphasizing this difference and highlighting that they have permission to not be perfect is one of the most helpful parts of the instructions.
    - Framing in terms of psychological/relational vs. spiritual goals: The back-and-forth of refocusing is the key to "rewiring" the brain to reduce stress, depression, and anxiety and address other psychological and relational gains that are associated with mindfulness. In contrast, if a person is meditating

for spiritual development, then they would want a more steady state of focus to achieve greater oneness with God (for Christians, Jews, etc.) or other spiritual goals.

- *Addressing practicalities*
    - Eyes: I let clients know that they may choose to close their eyes or keep them partially open with a soft gaze a few feet ahead of them. If a client has unresolved trauma or psychosis in their history, I encourage them to try it with their eyes open with a soft gaze.
    - Posture: It is best to sit with a relaxed yet erect posture, ideally without resting one's back against a chair. I also let clients know that they may choose to sit back in the chair or lie on a couch at home if that works better for them.
    - Hands: I recommend that their hands rest comfortably on their laps or knees.
- *Practice in session*
    - In session, I either do a guided mindfulness meditation, in which I describe the focus and refocusing process or an unguided one in which I practice with the client, depending on what they prefer. When doing an unguided meditation, I use a timer and practice with clients for 1–5 minutes, assuring them I will keep my eyes closed and meditate too.
    - Afterwards, I answer questions the client may have about the practice, and if there are no questions, specifically ask about how they refocused and what helped them to do so nonjudgmentally.

Teaching Loving-Kindness Meditation in Session

Teaching loving-kindness meditation (discussed in more detail in Chap. 8) involves a similar process, but loving-kindness phrases are used instead, and the therapist most often guides this process during the practice session. Using a collaborative approach (Anderson & Gehart, 2007), I work with each client to identify a personally meaningful set of 4–5 phrases that fits best for them. I offer some classics as an example to get us started:

The Makings of Loving-Kindness Meditation

Loving-kindness meditation involves (a) selection persons to whom to direct good intentions, and (b) phrases that constitute the meditation itself. Therapists and clients can decide together (or the therapist may simply offer suggestions) of whom to direct the intentions and then determine which phrases and terms are most significant to the practitioner. Generally, the practice involves beginning with one person and going through the entire list of intentions and the going back to the beginning and going the list focusing on the next person.

(continued)

(continued)

Potential persons to whom to direct loving-kindness

- A neutral other (e.g., acquaintance, coworker)
- Significant others (e.g., partner, family)
- Difficult other (e.g., someone with whom there is conflict)
- Self
- All beings (e.g., everyone)

Potential phrases for loving-kindness meditation

- May X be happy (joyful, mentally happy, loving, etc.).
- May X be free from suffering (pain, harm, illness, etc.).
- May X be physically well (healthy, in radiant health, healed, etc.).
- May X have ease of well-being (a sense of well-being, live with ease, etc.).
- May X be deeply at peace (dwell in peace, live with peace, etc.).
- May X be at peace with people in his/her life.

The minimal list I recommend for couples and families is (a) significant others, and (b) self. In session, I generally guide them through all five possibilities so they have the experience to compare and develop a firmer understanding of the practice. At home, I let them decide whether to do it silently, with a recording, or take turns doing it aloud.

In Session Follow-Up

Because this meditation can bring up a wide range of emotions, I spend extra time discussing their experiences to address potential feelings of guilt, confusion, or surprise that came up. This follow-up can be a difficult discussion especially for couples if one or both have trouble sending well wishes to the other; in such cases, I use this as an opportunity to practice acceptance of self and other, encouraging the realization that feelings for our loves naturally wax and wane to a certain degree. The practice of loving-kindness meditation generally makes it easier to experience positive emotions for them, and that is precisely why they are practicing in the first place.

Developing a Practice Plan

After completing a short practice session, I spend a significant amount of time helping clients develop a realistic and doable practice plan using the following series of steps:

1. Identify an existing daily, routine activity.

    (a) Have clients identify a routine activity that they do virtually every day to which they can "attach" their practice routine. Activities such as brushing one's teeth, showering, reading the newspaper, prayer, arriving at work, lunch time, arriving home, or going to bed can all serve this purpose.

2. Attach mindfulness practice to the selected routine.

   (a) After identifying a few possible candidate activities, help clients then select the most realistic choice to serve as a time for practice. Factors to consider are:

      i. Client's level of wakefulness (e.g., if client is usually totally exhausted upon going to bed, a daytime option may work better).
      ii. Possible interruptions (e.g., if client chooses a time when other family members or office duties may interrupt, find a better time).
      iii. Level of control over this time period (e.g., if client does not always have full control over what happens during this window of time because work, family, or other duties may take priority, consider alternatives).
      iv. Appropriateness of the time and space (e.g., if client does not have a private office space and/or must go outside, this is not an ideal situation).

3. Set realistic length of time for practice

   (a) I recommend starting clients off with a 2-minute time limit and tell them to increase to 5 minutes only after they start feeling like 2 minutes is too short. Similarly, I tell them to wait to increase to their practice from 7 to 10 and eventually 20 minutes only after they feel like an increment is too short and they want to do more.

4. Identify a potential timing device

   (a) I always recommend a timer (that does not tick) because it better enables one to focus on the practice rather than be distracted by wondering when the time is up and generally reduces the temptation to check a clock. I suggest the following for timers:

      i. Meditation Apps for iPhone, iPads, and other smartphones/devices
      ii. Cell phone alarms
      iii. A digital egg timer that does not tick
      iv. Computer meditation timers (Widgets for Apple; apps for PCs)
      v. A formal meditation timer

5. Use a practice log or diary

   (a) I encourage all clients to use a practice log in the first few months that they begin practicing. Mindfulness practice does not have the obvious effects that dieting or exercise may have and so it can be hard to keep motivated. For many, being able to check off the log or write in a dairy helps them see their progress and the effects of practice more clearly. I use a solution-oriented log to help clients identify what works, what does not, and help them to set small, achievable goals for the next week's practice (example at end of chapter and available for free download at www.dianegehart.com).

Anticipating and Planning for Barriers

Finally, I work with clients to identify potential barriers: what is likely to get in their way with the plan we have? I have clients try to identify what are the most likely scenarios that would lead them not to practice.

- What things are likely to "come up" in their schedule that would lead to not practicing at all one day?
- Are certain people, sounds, noises, phones, etc. likely to interrupt practice sessions?
- What internal thoughts or feelings might come up that would lead to not practicing?
- If a couple or family, how are they going to handle varying levels of motivation or priority-making each day? How will they handle if one person wants to do it one day and the other does not and/or if their practice timeline gets off? How will they handle it if one person is consistently more motivated than another to practice?

These questions often get to the nitty-gritty of practice issues and more often than not lead to a serious revision of the practice plans. Clients who already lead relatively structured, goal-oriented lives often do a better job at anticipating potential problems than those who do not. In any case, most people require several weeks of fine-tuning to find practice times and schedules that work.

Fine-Tuning and Follow-Up

When clients return from their first week or two of practice, therapists should take time to follow up with what worked and what didn't. Areas to explore:

- Clarifications about how to practice, focus, refocus, etc.
- Exploring blocks and resistance to practice.
- Fine-tuning realistic practice schedule.
- Discussing differences in motivation for couples and families.
- Exploring insights, thoughts, and emotions that may have arose during or from practice.
- Identifying changes, positive or negative, in daily life that the client attributes to practice.
- Deciding whether to continue.

Having frank and open conversations about these common issues that arise for several weeks following the introduction of mindfulness can help clients develop a practice that is useful and realistic for their busy lives.

Mindfulness for Two (or More)

Getting Started Together

When working with couples and families learning mindfulness, I typically suggest that they commit to 2–3 weeks of regular "synchronized" practice in which all parties meditate together, or at least at the same time. As recommended above, I have them practice loving-kindness meditation for 2–3 minutes for the first few days until they "feel the urge" to go longer. I have found that setting a very doable goal combined with the restraint "don't add more time until you feel the urge to do more" generally helps most clients actually sit down, practice, and learn how to successfully integrate mindfulness into their schedules.

With couples and families, I build up practice with a schedule similar to this:

- *Week 1*: 2–5 minutes (with a timer) 5 days per week at a time jointly agreed upon by the couple (and sounds realistic and workable to the therapist) in session. I have them do 2 minutes for the first couple days and then work up to 5 if they both agree.
- *Week 2*: 5 minutes 5–7 days per week at a mutually agreed upon time. If one or more have a typical 5-day per week job, I generally suggest they resist the urge to say "let's do Saturday and Sunday" because more often than not they do not use these days to practice because life interrupts. Most people have greatest control of their time on the weekdays. They can then use the weekend for longer practice if they'd like or to rest.
- *Week 3*: 5–10 minutes 5–7 days per week. I encourage couples who are enjoying their practice to try to work up to 10 minutes if it is comfortable. Others who are struggling "making the time" or enjoying the practice, I encourage them to stay with 5 minutes. If clients would like to add mindfulness breath meditation, this is a good time to do so.
- *Week 4 and beyond*: At this point, I have couples and families discuss and decide what might work best for them, both in the short term related to therapeutic goals and longer term, after their work in therapy is done. I also discuss other potential practices, including mindful touch (Chap. 8), the body scan (see end of chapter), or daily experiences (see end of chapter).

Maintenance Together and Apart: Second-Order Acceptance

Once the couple and family have established a basic routine and are comfortable with practicing, the next big question is maintenance, which has many levels of complexity for couples and families. *In all cases*, one person will be more motivated than another, at least on a given day. *In many cases*, the couple and family are in therapy to begin with because one or more person tends to be more disciplined, more organized, etc. and sees the others as "not so" organized, disciplined, etc. Very quickly, mindfulness practice becomes a source of struggle and "a thorn," especially for couples or families with this dynamic. Thus, when couples and families practice together, there is a much greater need to cultivate *a second-order practice of acceptance* of the ebb and flow of the other person's mindfulness practice.

To facilitate a second-order acceptance, I discuss the mindfulness-informed principle of *acceptance* as it relates to one's partner's or family member's practicing or not practicing mindfulness. I encourage clients to openly discuss how they want to handle variations in motivation to practice, length of practice, timing of practice, and style of practice. In most cases, with couples and families in therapy for relational distress, therapists need to work carefully in-session to help them cultivate this second-order acceptance of their differences in practice habits. If successful, this learning to accept the "differentness" of the other can be transferred to other areas of distress.

The Practice of No Practice

I certainly have worked with a number of clients who—after 1, 2, 3 weeks, months, or years—decide not to practice. In some cases, their symptoms are better and in other cases mindfulness has less relevance for one reason or another. I enthusiastically honor their right to practice based on the belief that accepting the ebb and flow of dedicating oneself to practice *is* part of the big picture of practicing mindfulness. In fact, the people I know who never miss a practice are often overly identified or anxiously attached to their practice and do not benefit as much as they would otherwise.

As mentioned earlier (but it is so counterintuitive I will repeat it), in one research study I conducted, I was surprised to discover that many clients report that they find the ideas therapists offer them—such as practicing mindfulness—helpful *even when they do not follow the suggestion* (Gehart & Lyle, 1999). One client in this study reported that even though she did not follow through on her therapist's suggestions to do slow, deep breathing when stressed, *just the thought* that she could do *something* other than freak out when stressed was enough to dramatically change her behavior when stressed—so much so, she never felt the need to actually do the suggested relaxation exercise. Similarly, *many clients to whom you introduce mindfulness will not practice much or at all.* And that is okay. They will likely still benefit greatly from the idea of knowing that they are not helpless or powerless against the feeling of stress.

"Mini-Meds" and Their Unexpected Benefits

More so than many meditation teachers, I am a fan of practicing "mini-meditations" or "mini-meds" (sessions that last 5 minutes or less). At first, I thought these were somehow a "lessor" form of practice, but over time I have begun to see them as powerful interventions. As a therapist, I am particularly interested in mini-meds because (a) most clients readily agree to work these into their schedule, and (b) there are many unexpected benefits that function similarly to other therapeutic interventions. Much of the mindfulness literature seems to imply that longer is better, and for certain issues that may be true. But I would also like to propose that for many issues commonly brought to therapy, shorter, frequent sessions work well and may even work better.

The Obvious Benefit of Mini-Meditations

Practicing "mini-meds" has the most obvious effect of serving as a short meditation session that results in an immediate sense of calm and a more focused mind. In these situations, it feels similar to meditating for a longer period, with perhaps less profound states of inner quiet being reached. When I initially began, I assumed this was the primary benefit of mini-meds. But over the years, I have learned that there are many other benefits.

The Not-So-Obvious Benefits of Mini-Meds

Perturbing the System: Interrupting Negative Cycles

All systemically trained family therapists are experts in "perturbing" relational systems as a means of reducing negative interaction cycles between people. This is one of the original systemic/family therapy interventions, developed at the Mental Research Institute and clearly demonstrated in the work of Paul Watzlawick, Richard Fisch, Jay Haley, and the Milan Team among others (Cecchin, 1987; Watzlawick, Weakland, & Fisch, 1974). Thus, family therapists can readily appreciate how mini-meds can serve the same type of "system perturbing" interventions, at the level of the individual mind as well as the relational system.

In traditional systems therapy, the therapist "perturbs" a system by introducing something new to alter the habitual interactional sequence. This "perturbation" requires that the system do something *different* because the habitual response no longer "fits" or has the same meaning. In most cases, the system reorganizes in a more effective way. For example, a classic family therapy intervention is to have a couple schedule arguments at appointed times and/or hold them in an unusual context (e.g., fully clothed in the bathtub). By interrupting the systems normal problematic sequence of events (e.g., spontaneous responses), the couple is free to (or forced to, depending on your perspective) *choose* their response in the new situation because they can no longer function on automatic pilot (i.e., they don't have a default behavior for how to argue on command or in the bathtub fully clothed so they have to *think* about it). In most cases, when given the choice, the couple will choose to interact in more desirable and preferred ways.

Mini-mindfulness practices can have the effect of perturbing a problematic pattern, whether at the individual, couple, or family level. For example, if a mother typically gets stressed when one of her children refuses to do homework, inserting a mini-meditation into that interaction cycle can greatly increase her ability to respond more effectively to the same old problem. Similarly, couples can use mini-meditations before or during typically stressful events to help them alter their interaction cycle. However, if using the meditation as a type of timeout, couples should be encouraged to consider (not necessarily strictly follow) the findings of Gottman's (1999) research that indicates that if one partner's heart rate rose above 100 beats per minute, they need at least 20 minutes before a time out can be effective; many couples, men in particular, require even longer.

Reconnecting with Preferred Identity (a.k.a. Your Better Self)

Narrative, solution-focused, collaborative, and other postmodern therapists encourage clients to find ways to enact their preferred identity narratives: the actions, thoughts, and behaviors they associate with their "best selves" (Anderson, 1997; O'Hanlon & Weiner-Davis, 1989; White & Epston, 1990). Often by enacting even small behaviors associated with the best or preferred self, a person very quickly resumes this identity rather than a problem-saturated identity.

One of the common side effects of mini-meds is that they can quickly get you in touch with your better or preferred self. For example, when a mother is at her wits end with a child's misbehavior, taking 2 minute out for a mini-med can quickly reconnect with her preferred parenting self and enable her to respond more gracefully. Thus, therapists using postmodern approaches may find it particularly helpful to encourage clients to do mini-meds not only for the known mindfulness benefits, but also to help them reconnect with their preferred self.

Reframing a Problem

Another unexpected outcome of mini-meds is that they often reframe the problem as an emotion or thought one is having rather than the *only possible* means of interpreting the situation, which is generally how problematic emotions, thoughts, and interactions are experienced, especially in intimate relationships. Often in the 1–5 minutes that a person does a mini-med, the process of quieting the mind and observing the thoughts and emotions that arise serves to highlight that the current "problem" is only one way to view what is happening. Although many times this may not make everything magically better, it generally significantly softens one's response allowing one to at least minimize destructive choices and perhaps begin to move toward more resourceful responding. For example, if during a tense time between a couple, one is able to take a short mindfulness break and realize that their interpretation of their partner is not the only way to look at the situation and that other frames are available; this partner will more likely begin to cool down and move toward actions that resolve rather than exacerbate the tension. If both partners have this experience, even better.

"Rebooting" the Brain

One of my students once described mindfulness as "rebooting" the brain; Siegel's research (see Chap. 3) that indicates mindfulness promotes integration brain states may help explain my student's experience, and the experience of many others. Even brief mindfulness sessions can help the brain rebalance itself and get into more effective states that facilitate emotional regulation and improved stress response.

Handouts and Online Resources for Clients

I generally provide my clients with several resources to support them in their at-home practice:

- A brief *handout* reviewing how to do mindfulness or loving-kindness meditation.
- A *practice log* to increase a sense of accomplishment, help them track their practice, and identify what works and doesn't work.
- Free guided meditations for download, some fully guided and some with just a bell that rings to time their practices; a recent randomized control study provided initial support has for web-based mindfulness instruction (Glück & Maercker, 2011).
- Suggested readings and online resources to support them in their practice.
- Local mindfulness groups.

Getting Start with Mindfulness Practice

What is Mindfulness?

- Mindfulness is a non-judgmental, sustained attention to your immediate experience. Most cultures have some form of mindfulness practice, the most common of which is mindfulness breath meditation.
- Mindfulness breath meditation involves non-judgmentally observing your breath by redirecting your mind to refocus each time it wanders off to other thoughts. Typically, your mind will wander off numerous times per minute.
- Each time you redirect your focus back to your breath, you are improving your ability to regulate your emotions and stress response and increasing your tendency for positive moods and overall positive disposition.

Why Bother Practicing Mindfulness?

- Recent research studies indicate that regular mindfulness practice can be helpful for a number of physical and mental problems, including chronic pain, skin conditions, cancer treatment, immunity, depression, anxiety, ADHD, bipolar, panic, eating disorders, substance abuse, and other stress related disorders.
- Preliminary brain research indicates that after as little as 8 weeks of mindfulness practice, there was a sustained increase in activity in centers of the brain associated with positive mood and disposition as well as immune system functioning. Thus, after a relatively short period of time, there are measurable changes in brain and body functioning.
- Current theories and brain research indicate that regular mindfulness practice can increase compassion for others and oneself, resulting in improved self-esteem and relational functioning.

Making Time for Mindfulness Practice

- A good way to start making mindfulness part of daily practice is to set aside 2–10 minutes per day for 5–7 days per week. Short frequent sessions are better than long but infrequent practices for mental health benefits. Start with 2 minutes and build up to 10.
- The best way to do this is to identify your most regular habits (meal times, working out, work schedule, television shows, bedtime, etc.) and find time before, during, or after one of these activities during which you can fit in mindfulness.
  - Ex: Add 5 minutes of mindfulness before or after breakfast/lunch/dinner.
  - Ex: Before watching TV at night, meditate for 5–10 minutes.
  - Ex: Meditate during the first/last 5 minutes of your lunch hour; or 10 minutes before work starts; or 10 minutes at end of workday.

Mindfulness Techniques and Strategies

- **Focus**: Ideally "watch" your breath by focusing on the nostrils or belly movement. You can also try counting each breath up to ten and then repeating from the beginning. Others find it help to use a mantra or focusing words attached to the in-and exhalation, such "peace in, peace out," "be peace," or any simple phrase that focuses you.

- **Refocusing**: There are many options for refocusing when your mind wanders off, which it will do several times a minute in most cases. The most important part is to choose a refocusing technique that reminds you to be patient and nonjudgmental with yourself (e.g., not beat yourself up or put yourself down) when you find that your mind has wandered off.

Some of options for redirecting your focus:

  - "Yes, that too": Ah, yes, that too; I expected this thought to show up today.
  - Labeling: When you catch mind wandering, you can label each thought, e.g. "worry," "planning," "anger," "feeling," "thought" and then return to focus.
  - Clouds Image: You can imagine the distraction as a cloud or bubble that floats away.

- **Posture:** It is generally considered best to sit in an upright yet relaxed posture on the edge of a hard chair or cushion. If this is uncomfortable, you may also lie down or sit back in a chair.
- **Eyes:** You may close your eyes or keep them slightly opened with soft gaze a few feet ahead.
- **Timer:** It is often very helpful and motivating to set a timer to set boundaries on your practice. You may use an egg timer, a timer on your mobile phone, buy a meditation timer (www.zenclocks.com), or download one on your computer (Mac: meditation timer widget; PC: Buddha bell softpedia. com) or iPhone/smart phone/tablets: meditation apps.
- **Environment:** It may be easiest at the beginning to meditate in a quiet location, but it is not necessary. Distractions can be helpful in improving your focus.

Overcoming Barriers to Regular Practice

- **No Time:** If you are motivated, you can always find 2–5 minutes a day to practice. The easiest way to find the time is to "attach" mindfulness to another daily or regular activity. Then it will quickly become a habit.
- **I Can't Focus:** Be patient and kind to yourself! Over time, mindfulness helps you improve your focus. Each time you lose focus and then refocus, you are increasing your brain's ability to maintain focus and regulate emotion.

Cultivating Acceptance

- At its core, mindfulness practice is about cultivating acceptance of self, others, and life. Acceptance is cultivated by your *attitude* when refocusing your attention.

- You will lose your attention frequently and often: what you do to ɪ cus is key. You should work towards accepting with kindness and c... passion whatever thought, feeling, or distraction has captured your mind's attention while also accepting that your mind has wandered without berating yourself for having lost focus.
- The more you can learn to accept whatever the mind is doing as well as the fact that the mind has wandered, the greater your acceptance will be of self and other.

Online Instruction

On my website, www.dianegehart.com, you will online instruction and guided meditations to help you get started.

Additional Resources

www.meditateinthousandoaks.org: **Tushita Kadampa Buddhist Center**, Local Buddhist mindfulness groups

www.marc.ucla.edu: Mindful Awareness Research Center at UCLA; MBSR classes and Podcasts

www.mbsr.mass.edu: Mindfulness Based Stress Reduction; Research and Info

www.contemplativeprayer.org: Christian Based Contemplative Prayer Information

http://jewish-meditation.co.tv: Jewish meditation traditions and history.

© 2011. Diane R. Gehart, Ph.D. All rights reserved. www.dianegehart.com

Please note: Feel free to distribute this handout or a close version of it to your clients. I simply request that acknowledge credit and include my name and web address: www.dianegehart.com. You may download a copy from the mindfulness page on my website. Thank you.

Mindfulness Practice Log

I encourage clients new to mindfulness to try using a practice log because it helps them "see" progress and have a greater sense of accomplishment and accountability. In addition, the reflection section on the bottom allows them to improve their practice as well as develop a feasible and realistic practice schedule the fits with their routines. I have both a weekly and daily version that I make available to clients.

Mindfulness Practice Log: **Weekly Version**						
Week of:_____ Target # of Days/Time:_____						
Monday	**Tuesday**	**Wednesday**	**Thursday**	**Friday**	**Saturday**	**Sunday**
❑ 5 min ❑ 10 min ❑ 20 min ❑ _____ ❑Day off	❑ 5 min ❑ 10 min ❑ 20 min ❑ _____ ❑ Day off	❑ 5 min ❑ 10 min ❑ 20 min ❑ _____ ❑ Day off	❑ 5 min ❑ 10 min ❑ 20 min ❑ _____ ❑ Day off	❑ 5 min ❑ 10 min ❑ 20 min ❑ _____ ❑ Day off	❑ 5 min ❑ 10 min ❑ 20 min ❑ _____ ❑ Day off	❑ 5 min ❑ 10 min ❑ 20 min ❑ _____ ❑ Day off
Notes:	Notes:	Notes:	Notes:	Notes:	Notes:	Notes:

Doing It: What strategies (i.e., time of day, place, timers, etc.) made it easiest to practice this week?

Quality: What strategies (i.e., type of focus, refocus technique, etc.) helped to improve the quality of practice?

Changes: Did I notice any benefits in daily life (patience, calmness, etc.) that seemed to come from my practice?

Plans for Next Week: What is one thing I can do next week to improve practice and maximize these benefits?

©2007. Diane R. Gehart, Ph.D. All rights reserved. www.dianegehart.com

Daily Mindfulness Practice Log

Date:_____ Day of Week: M T W Th F S Su Time:_____ Length of practice: _____
General Notes:
Doing It: What strategies (i.e., time of day, place, timers, etc.) made it easiest to practice today?
Quality: What strategies (i.e., type of focus, refocus technique, etc.) helped to improve the quality of practice today?
Changes What positive changes have I noticed recently in my life related to practicing mindfulness?
Plans for Next Time: What is one thing I can do between now and my next practice to improve the frequency and quality of practice and/or maximize the benefits?

Please note: Feel free to distribute these logs or close versions of them to your clients. I simply request that acknowledge credit and include my name and web address: www.dianegehart.com. You may download a copy from the mindfulness page on my website. Thank you.

Additional Mindfulness Practices

In addition to mindfulness breath meditation and loving-kindness meditation, therapists can also introduce clients a variety of mindfulness practices, depending on client need and preferences. The three more common are:

- Mindful body scan

  - Particularly good for clients with physical complaints, sleep difficulties, or frustrated with lack of concentration in breath meditation

- Walking meditation

  - Particularly good for clients with active trauma or psychotic symptoms or who have difficulty with sitting meditations

- Mindfulness in daily activities

  - Particularly good for those who "don't have time" for more formal techniques or for those with high levels of stress

- 3-minute breathing space

  - A quick mindfulness "first aid" for stressful moments or to recenter oneself during a busy day

These are described below. In addition, additional mindfulness activities and meditations described later in this book that can be taught to clients include:

- Loving-kindness for couples and families: compassion and caring meditation (Chap. 8)
- Compassionate life review: guided compassion meditation (Chap. 8)
- Mindful eating: a guided exercise using all the senses (Chap. 9)
- Mindful walking: standing and walking mindfulness (Chap. 9)
- Ice meditation: an exercise for mindful awareness of pain (Chap. 9)
- Mindful yoga: mindful awareness with very simple stretches (Chap. 9)
- Mindful listening: a sound awareness exercise (Chap. 9)
- Vipassana: a more advanced mindfulness meditation with open focus (Chap. 10)

Meditation: Mindful Body Scan

Ideal for clients with physical pain or other ailments, the mindful body scan differs from traditional body scans in that it emphasizes *observation* of various parts of the body rather than an intention to "relax" each part. Many clients find it easier to focus on the body scan rather than the breath because the focus continually moves from one body part to another and is, to be frank, more interesting. It can be practiced as a guided meditation or done alone. Many clients find it easy to integrate into their routine before bed, often preferring a recording (I have a free version available at www. dianegehart.com and several versions are available from other sources for purchase).

Basic outline for mindfulness body scan:

- *Introduction*: Sit or lie down in a position that is comfortable for you. Take a few deep breaths to turn your attention inward. You may want to close your eyes or lower your eyelids and soften your gaze. We are going to do a mindful scan of the body, which requires no effort on your part. You do not need to try to relax any part of your body. You need only simply observe sensations—such as the touch of fabric, warmth, coolness, pain, tingling, or numbness—or the lack of sensation without judgment or evaluation. Simply notice and quiet the mind.

Meditation

- *Left toe*: Begin by noticing your left big toe. Notice any sensations in your toe: the feel of the shoe, feel of the ground underneath, warmth or coolness, or pain. You may feel nothing at all, and that is perfectly fine too. Simply notice what sensations are there in this moment, trying not to judge them as good or bad, simply notice.
- *Left foot*: Now expand your awareness to your entire left foot. Again, notice any sensations in your left foot. If there is pain, notice the qualities of the pain: is it sharp or dull? Pulsing, moving, or constant? Is it hot, cold, or neither? Become curious about the pain.
- *Right foot*: Now shift your awareness to your right foot. Notice what sensations are there: coolness, warmth, the feel of your shoe, the floor, any discomfort. Simply notice what is there.
- *Legs*: Move your attention to your ankles and calves on both legs. Notice any sensations you may feel. You may not feel much or anything at all. That is okay too. Or you may feel an article of clothing, the air in the room, or pain. Simply notice. Simply notice what is there without judgment.

   – Repeat with *knees and thighs*.

- *Hips and pelvis*: Now move your attention to your hips and pelvic region. Notice what sensations are there. There may be heat, numbness, pain, or nothing at all. Simply notice what is there, without judging it as good or bad. Simply notice.
- *Back and shoulders*: Move your attention up your back, an area where many people experience pain. You may or may not feel anything. Simply notice. If there is pain here, become curious about it. Notice whether it is hot or cold; sharp or dull; pulsing, moving, or relatively constant. Be curious—and just notice its subtle qualities without judging it as good or bad.

   – Repeat with shoulders

- *Belly and chest*: Now move your attention to your belly and notice what is going on in this area of your body. You may feel pressure or openness, a sense of fullness or lightness, pain or discomfort. Simply notice what is there.

  - Repeat with chest.

- *Neck and head*: Now move your attention to your neck and the base of your skull. Notice if you have any sensations in this area: tightness, coolness, heat, tingling. Simply notice.

  - *Scalp*: Now see if you have any sensations in your scalp. You may or may not feel anything. Simply notice: perhaps you experience a sense of tightness or coolness.
  - *Forehead*: Now move your awareness to your forehead. See if you notice any sensation in the small muscle of your forehead or if you feel your hair or the air. Simply notice what is there.
  - *Eyes*: Now move your attention to your eyes and eye sockets. You may experience a sense of tightness in the tiny muscles around your eyes; you may feel the eyes as they sit in their sockets. Or you may not feel much at all. Simply notice what is there.
  - *Nose*: Now turn your attention to your nose. What sensations are you experiencing there? Can you feel your breath move in and out? Is there discomfort or other sensations. Simply notice.
  - *Mouth and jaw*: Next, notice what you are feeling in your mouth and jaw. Notice any tightness, the feel of the tongue in the mouth, warmth or coolness. Simply notice what is there without judgment.
  - *Checks*: Now notice your checks and notice what sensations are there. The feel of the air, any tightness, or maybe not much at all.

- *Closing*: Now take a moment to scan the entire body and notice what stands out. Are there areas that feel different than others? Is there noticeable pain? Are there parts that have little feeling at all? Are some parts warmer than others? Simply notice. You may also want to take a moment to notice how the body feels now compared to when you started. When you are ready, take a few deep breaths and open your eyes.

Meditation: Walking Meditation

Ideal for clients who have trouble with sitting meditation, mindful walking exercises apply mindfulness to the everyday bodily experiences of standing and walking. This is a great guided introductory mindfulness exercise and can also be used as formal practice. This exercise requires more room than most other forms of mindfulness, as each participant needs about a 10-foot space to do the walking portion of the exercise. If doing it with a couple, family, or group, it is ideal to have an area with no furniture to allow the participants to be in a large circle when doing the standing parts of the practice.

There are many variations of this practice, but my colleague Eric McCollum and I tend to start with the experience of standing, move to the experience of shifting weight from foot to foot without walking, and then moving to the walking part of the exercise. This is also one mindfulness exercise that is done with *eyes wide open*, which is often important for clients currently working on trauma or with psychotic symptoms.

- *Introduction*: In this exercise, we are going to focus on the bodily sensations of standing and walking, things we do hundreds of times each day without much notice. We are going to take a few moments to just notice what is going on in our bodies during these activities.
- *Standing*: If you want to close your eyes, you may for this part, or you may want to keep your eyes slightly open with a soft gaze about 3 ft ahead of you. If you have trouble with balance, it is a good idea to keep your eyes open. Take a few deep breaths to settle your mind and bring your focus inwards. And then turn your attention to the sensation of standing. Notice what it feels like to have your feet supporting your weight and touching the ground. Notice the sensation of your feet on the ground. Notice the strength in your legs holding you up. Notice your back, your head, your whole body: how it supports you as you stand. Notice what it feels like to simply stand erect and tall. If you notice thoughts or emotions floating through your mind or start to wonder if you are doing this right, let those thoughts to simply float away, like a cloud or soap bubble. Spend a few moments in silence, simply experiencing what it is like for your body to stand.

  - *Shifting weight*: If your eyes have been closed, *please open them now*. Allow a soft gaze a few feet ahead of you. In a moment, I am going to ask you to slightly shift your weight to your left foot, but I want you to know that this movement is so small that no one on the outside is likely to notice. Now, start to very, very slowly shift your weight to your left foot, without leaning to one side or another or lifting your foot. Simply remain standing, shifting your weight to the left foot. Experience what it is like to have one foot supporting most of the weight of your body. Just notice the sensations in the foot and rest of the body. Now, very slowly, shift most of your weight to your right foot, without necessarily leaning to one side or the other. Experience the sensations of standing on your right foot. They may be the same or different from the left foot; either way, it is fine. Simply notice. Now take a minute or two to slowly shift the weight from one foot to another, simply experiencing the sensations in your feet and body, quieting any emerging narrative or other thought emerging from your mind. Remember to keep your eyes open.

- *One step*: Now we are going to take one mindful step. Please keep your eyes open for this exercise too. Begin by shifting your weight to your left foot. Now slowly lift your right foot—very slowly move it one step ahead. Notice the sensations of moving your foot through the air and having it touch the earth again. Shift the weight to your right foot. Then slowly and mindfully bring your left foot to meet the right. Then take a moment to experience standing on both feet. Now go ahead and take a slow mindful step with your right foot, bringing your left to meet it. (If done in a group, this is a good time to allow for questions before moving into extended walking meditation).

- *Walking meditation*: Now, please find about 10 uninterrupted feet of space to do your own walking meditation. After walking to the end of your 10-foot space. Pause. Stand mindfully for a moment or two. Then do a quarter turn step. And then another slow quarter turn step. Then return back on the line you walked up. Silently and mindfully walk back and forth for the next 10 min.

Meditation: Daily Activities

A famous Zen teaching goes: "Before enlightenment, chop wood and carry water; after enlightenment, chop wood and carry water." Not very motivating for the goal-oriented practitioner. What is perhaps not immediately clear is that the quality of mind that is brought to these daily activities changes everything. Being present while chopping wood and carrying water is entirely different from mind*less*ly completing the same tasks.

The ultimate practice for pragmatists, applying mindfulness to daily activities involves being fully present to and mindfully aware of any one of the many daily experiences for which our minds are typically not in attendance, such as filling a glass of water or turning on the stove (the modern equivalent of the Zen classic). Therapists can help clients learn how to bring mindful presence to any of their many routine daily tasks by quieting the mind and simply focusing on the task at hand.

Common activities include:

- Washing dishes
- Washing one's hands
- Feeling the water in the shower or bath
- Listening to the first two rings of the phone
- Drinking the first few sips of coffee or tea in the morning
- Eating first three bites of a meal
- Mindful sitting at a traffic light
- Feeling the breeze through a car window
- Listening to sounds outside
- Taking a sip of water
- Smelling a flower
- Touching a fabric

Just about any experience in one's day can be done mindfully. The simpler, the better.

Meditation: Three-Minute Breathing Space

A cornerstone of Mindfulness-Based Cognitive Therapy (Segal, Williams, & Teasdale, 2002), the 3-min breathing space can be used on a scheduled, regular basis throughout the day and/or it can be used whenever an unpleasant thought, emotion, or sensation arises. I like to think of it as a form of *mindfulness first aid* or crisis response. The purpose is to interrupt the automatic pilot response we are prone to under stress, slow down, and allow for an alternative response. As you might imagine, it only takes 3 minute and involves three parts:

1. *Mindful awareness and acceptance*

   • Assume an erect and dignified posture, closing your eyes if it is comfortable. Take a minute to answer the following question: "What am I experiencing right now: in my thoughts…feelings…and body?"
   • Simply notice and acknowledge your experience even if it is unwanted or undesirable. Accept what is for the moment.

2. *Gathering*: *mindful breathing*

   • Then, take a minute to breath mindfully: allowing your attention to follow your breath in and out; redirecting it as many times as necessary during that minute. Take a moment to be fully in the present moment.

3. *Expanding mindful awareness*

   • Expand your mindful awareness to your entire body, posture, and facial expression. Notice and be present to what is happening in your entire body. Be in this moment as it is.

I like to think of this as having a mindfulness sandwich: Experience-Mindful Breath-(re)Experience. Mindful breathing is the "meat" served between two slices of experience: one before the breath and one after. Each time it tastes a bit different, and the challenge is to simply experience each for what it is.

Chapter 7
Foundational Mindfulness- and Acceptance-Informed Interventions and Practices

With many clients, mindfully oriented therapists will never whisper the word mindfulness or meditation. Nor will they ask them to practice meditation at home or encourage them to do anything that looks much different than most other forms of therapy. But something will be noticeably different. Because mindfulness and acceptance practices are far more than a set of meditation techniques: they are a *philosophy*, *attitude*, and *stance* toward life and the challenges it presents. Without adopting the philosophy and attitude of mindfulness and acceptance, the practice quickly becomes hollow. In fact, this philosophy can be used to inform practices from other theoretical orientations, allowing therapists to build upon and reconfigure their existing knowledge.

This chapter describes foundational practices based on the principles of mindfulness and acceptance that are designed for regular use with a wide variety of clients and problems, including individuals, couples, and families dealing issues such as depression or anxiety. I prefer the term practices to interventions, because it implies a less hierarchical relationship between therapist and client and a less conflictual relationship with the "problem." Chapter 8 describes practices and activities specifically for use with couples and families addressing relationship issues.

The foundational mindfulness and acceptance practices described in this chapter are divided into three groups:

- *Philosophy-in-action practices*: These are the primary practices that provide a means for putting the philosophical principles behind mindfulness and acceptance into action.
- *Practices for cultivating equanimity*: This set of practices specifically helps clients develop a greater sense of calm and equanimity in the face of life challenges.
- *In-dialogue mindful experience*: This set of practices uses mindfulness-based questions to help clients identify, reflect upon, and transform their inner and relational experiences.

D.R. Gehart, *Mindfulness and Acceptance in Couple and Family Therapy*,
DOI 10.1007/978-1-4614-3033-9_7, © Springer Science+Business Media New York 2012

Philosophy-in-Action Practices

The philosophy-in-action practices are subtlety woven throughout the therapeutic process and are primarily an attitude and set of assumptions that shape how the therapist discusses and relates to suffering and problems, inviting clients to subsequently experience their situation from a new perspective. Rather than directly advocating for an alternative perspective, these practices gently introduce new possibilities for relating to difficulties into the conversation. For example, the practice of *befriending problems* most always fails if it is offered as a reframe or more realistic way to think about a situation. For it to be meaningful, the therapist must exude a clear and consistent commitment to befriending the client's problems by not flinching in the face of what seems unbearable or being unflustered by setbacks and disappointments.

Befriending Problems

Befriending problems entail mindfully accepting what is. Chödrön (1997) has been a long-time teacher and advocate for mindfully engaging one's most painful life challenges, which she summarizes as: "This very moment is the perfect teacher" (p. 6). And, yes, she recommends getting "intimate" with fear, which goes against our modern sensibilities, and to be fair, our physiological hard wiring, making it a life-long lesson that is never entirely mastered. And just when you master it in one area of your life, it seems another problem appears in another sphere of living that invites you to learn the lessons in a new context.

Most simply stated, befriending problems involves *shifting one's relationship* to the problem from one of resistance to one of willing engagement of "what is." This stance naturally follows from mindfulness practice in which one nonjudgmentally and compassionately accepts whatever arises rather than become overly fixated on it or rejecting it. This willingness to stay engaged with but not overwhelmed by what is—to maintain a sense of equanimity—enables more resourceful in responding to difficulties.

When most therapists hear that "befriending problems" can be used as an intervention, they often assume the client is the one befriending their problems. While that is a possibility, McCollum and I (Gehart & McCollum, 2007) have suggested that it is primarily the *therapist* who needs to befriend the problem. Therapists who haven't gotten "chummy" with problems will not be able to help clients learn how to do the same. So, this intervention begins with the therapist.

Befriending Problems for Therapists

Most therapists are good at befriending problems in the first few sessions, but as therapy progresses it becomes increasingly difficult because the therapist's job is to "oust," solve, or otherwise resolve the problem. Not only is this characteristic of traditional forms of therapy, but even more recent therapies, such as narrative, have employed an adversarial stance with problems, encouraging clients to "take a stand against" their problems (although a combative stance is not the only option used by narrative therapists; Monk & Gehart, 2003; White, 2007).

For therapists, their struggle with problems really begins when the problems become persistent, resist change, or return after subsiding. At this point, many therapists become more perturbed by the problem in one way or another and may see the client as "resistant," blame others for undermining the therapy process, blame themselves for making a mistake, or simply not look forward to the client coming to session. Instead, therapists who have learned how to befriend problems soften, become curious, and accept that such setbacks are not only part of the process but generally are the most valuable learning opportunities. In most cases, they reveal exactly where and how a person is stuck (Chödrön, 1997).

Befriending the problem involves gracefully moving with the ups and downs of therapy even if they are "preventable," "a sign of resistance," or otherwise indicate that the client, therapist, or someone else could/should do something differently. Befriending offers therapists a refreshing sense of "yes, this too can be compassionately addressed" rather than a mild-to-moderate panicked feeling that things are not going according to plan and I need to do something to fix it fast. Befriending problems is not a skill that is learned once and then forever mastered; instead, much like the practice of mindfulness, it is a continually evolving lesson that emerges in new forms even after years of practicing. Over time, therapists become more adept at knowing when befriending is necessary and how to do so expediently.

To illustrate the point, I will share a recent situation in which I had to consciously practice befriending problems in session. A couple months ago, I met with Al, a client who has had a severe and chronic depression for 15 years and it has not been responsive to psychotropic medications or mood stabilizers. He also has several severe endocrine disorders, including thyroid disorder, which he does not believe are being properly treated by his physicians. Typically, I expect to see significant progress with depression in the first two to three sessions; with him there was none. When he reported this on the third session, I was quite surprised. Part of me wanted to quickly rush to blame medical explanations for the lack of progress; no part of me wanted to assume culpability for the lack of improvement, but it didn't take long for my mind to wander there too.

After all of these thoughts and more ran through my head in a nanosecond, I caught myself and—paused. That second nanosecond of quietude almost made me laugh aloud. I had slipped into adversarial mode, but caught myself mid-slide. At that point, I simply had to acknowledge that there were no wise words to say or magical thing to do: nothing other than surrender and befriend this painful situation—for him and me. I was then able to use mindfulness and equanimity to be curious and open to learn more about the client's experience and to also be open in discussing how I could be more helpful to him and/or someone else might be more useful to him. We had a more candid discussion about what might be beneficial and over the next few weeks we began to see some improvements, which I freely admit were also correlated with changes in medications. Although it is hard to directly pinpoint the cause of the improvements, my ability to befriend the problem was critical to my being useful to Al, who is now doing far better than when we first began.

Shifting the Relationship to the Problem for Clients

In many respects, the therapist's primary job has always been to shift clients' relationships to their problems. However, in mindfulness-informed therapy, a highly unlikely relationship is formed with problems: that of curiosity, openness, and willingness to engage. This shift *allows for* change and alternative action to emerge. In contrast, if a client remains in gridlock with a problem—either fighting it or avoiding it—there is virtually no other option than to keep doing what they have been doing. In contrast, as soon as their relationships to problems begin to shift, new options for responding to them become immediately available and feel natural to pursue. For example, when working with a couple in which they struggle with feeling as though the household chores are not evenly divided, helping them move to a place where they "accept" that neither is satisfied and that this is an area of struggle for them generally enables both to soften.

Although I believe it goes without saying, I will say it anyway: directly suggesting clients befriend their problems rarely works. It generally only irritates. Or worse, leaves clients feeling belittled and misunderstood. Thus, much of helping clients learn how to befriend problems comes from the therapist's nonverbal cues, such as a fearless willingness to get a detailed description of suicidal or other dark thoughts or an unflappable response to a report of hallucinations. When the therapist shows a sincere curiosity and willingness to explore and learn about a client's greatest fear or pain, it generally makes the fear less frightening or the pain less painful. There are also a few specific things that therapists can do to invite clients to befriend problems when the moment is right:

> #### Inviting Clients to Befriend Their Problems
>
> *Indirect invitations*
>   The two most simple and indirect ways to cultivate a friendlier relationship with problems are to point out (a) what clients are learning or (b) what benefits they are getting from the problem whenever the chance arises.
>
> - *Learning*: This really has been a frustrating (sad, disappointing, etc.) situation. Do you think there is anything you are learning from it?
> - *Benefits*: Although this has not been a fun situation, from what you are saying, it does sound like you have found a silver lining: (describe the exception or unexpected benefit client has shared).

(continued)

(continued)

Direct invitations

Some clients—due to their spiritual beliefs, resiliency, or optimism—seem to be more open to direct invitations to befriend problems. I generally do this after the therapeutic relationship is *well* established and the client is in a position to be more reflective. I most always preface and/or follow up with a comment that they do not need to see things this way.

- *Potential lessons*: This has been such a painful experience for you. Do you think there is anything positive you could learn from it?
- *Spiritual*: You have mentioned several times that you believe in God. I am curious if your belief in God is somehow involved here. Can you imagine any way in which how grace may come from this?
- *Things happen for a reason*: You've said, "Things happen for a reason." Have you ever thought about what the reason might be for you to be experiencing this, now, in your life?
- *"Go with it"*: Okay. So there is nothing you can do to control this situation. So what would happen if you just "went with it?" If this is the hand life has dealt you, how are you going to play it?
- *Humor*: So, now that the universe has totally dismantled your life in the most elegant fashion, I am guessing it is now crystal clear why you had learn some life lesson. Have you figured out what it is yet?

Whether or not a client seems to accept any of these invitations in session, simply asking them has the powerful effect of introducing the alternative line of thinking into the repertoire of repetitive thoughts that go through their head related to the issue. Thus, they may come around to it weeks, months, or even years later. In fact, many clients report "noodling" one of these strange questions for weeks after it is asked.

Whether or not any of the specific techniques above are used, clients can still learn to befriend problems. Below is a list of the common signs that clients are becoming chummy with their problems.

Telltale Signs of Befriending Problems

- *Humor*: The ability to laugh if not "at" then at least "with" one's situation; perhaps the best indicator of a friendly relationship with problems.
- *Appreciation of the good*: The ability to appreciate the good things that are still in one's life.
- *Appreciation of the lesson*: Feeling appreciation for the ultimate good that comes from learning a life lesson associated with the challenge.
- *Mystery*: A sense of awe and reverence for the mystery of life, even if it is not unfolding like one expected.

(continued)

(continued)

> • *Spirituality*: Using spirituality to cope, generate hope, or find strength.
> • *Absence of blame*: No one, including the self or a particular situation, is blamed for the problem.
> • *No "what ifs" or "if onlys"*: Avoiding the temptation to wonder "what if" or "if only."

Embracing "What" and "Who" Is

Most clients come to therapy hoping for change: to change who they are, what they do, or how they feel. In the case of couples and families, they typically want change too, but namely for *others*: their partner, children, or parents. Most therapists are tempted to rush in and try to achieve the desired change as fast as possible: in fact, clients, insurance companies, and third-party payers often advocate for this as do many popular therapy approaches to some degree, such as cognitive-behavioral, systems theory, and solution-focused. *Mindfulness-informed therapy paradoxically proposes that the first step to change is to accept what is.* A person does not have to spend a long time in the process of acceptance, but one needs to do it fully, which may take a session or several months depending on the issue. For example, accepting that a dating relationship is not a good fit may take only a session; accepting the loss of child takes years if not a lifetime.

Embracing what is comes directly from mindfulness practices in which practitioners "accept" whatever arises in their consciousness: neither trying to push it out of consciousness or become overly identified with it. When dealing with emotional and psychological issues, acceptance of what is requires *leaning into* the unwanted feelings, thoughts, or actions by being fully present with them rather than denying them or somehow psychologically detaching, either through objectification, substance use, or distraction. This acceptance often feels like a type of *surrender* because one finally stops "fighting" what is; although the moment is difficult, overwhelming, and humbling (because you finally experience what you have been avoiding), at the same time it brings a certain form of relief.

In relationships, embracing what is involves an acceptance of who the person is at this moment in time, knowing that each person is doing the best that he/she can in that particular instant. This is challenging when the person's behavior or attitude creates significant or even moderate suffering for us. In relationships, accepting what is in another is especially difficult because "what is" affects one's own happiness, life options, daily comfort, and dream fulfillment. Surrender in relational contexts is often far more difficult than dealing with thoughts in one's own head because it seems far more hopeless and can make one feel helpless. Yet, it is important to remember that surrender in relationships does *not* mean that one must forever accept ill or abusive treatment by another; it simply means opening oneself up to fully experience what is rather than frantically trying to fix or change it with force or avoidance.

Obviously (I hope), simply telling someone to accept their problem situation is rarely if ever helpful. Forcefully trying to get clients to embrace their situation in their most vulnerable moment of seeking help is futile. However, gently inviting them to become curious about their experiences in ways that feel safe often quickly leads to openness to what is. In a surprising number of cases, a sincere moment of acceptance of what is significantly shrinks the problem into a size that suddenly seems manageable and/or the path of action is clear.

For example, John, a client who had not seen me in years, called me in a panic, saying things had never been worse and that his life was falling apart. His wife had decided to leave him, his oldest daughter was recently caught smoking pot and spending time with older boys, and his youngest son revealed that he was gay; at least, things at work were going well, it was his safe haven. In our session, I began curiously exploring these developments using the questions below. When I asked about the marriage—whether this was a surprise, does he understand why she feels this way—he quickly confessed "no" because he had stopped trying years ago and was just trying to hang on until the kids graduated. In exploring what was going on with his daughter, he shared that both his and his wife's family have substance abuse issues, that he had struggled with them when he was younger, and that he had always had great concern for his children. Finally, in sharing about his youngest son, he admitted he always suspected that there might be a problem when he was young because he preferred playing with his sister's toys, hated sports, and never really fit in with other boys.

Our discussion was *slow*, with many silent *pauses* to let the words he spoke to *linger* in the air. As the words lingered, I would listen to them with *curiosity* and openness, allowing them to reverberate in me; as I did this, John seemed to naturally do the same. The realities of each statement washed over us during the quiet pauses. Each thought shared was treated as if sacred, worthy of deep reflection and engagement. At the end of our 50-min session, John was no longer in a panic, but was rather quiet and somber. Somber, but in a place of greater peace. As he was better able to accept what was going on with each member of the family, he became clearer as to what need to happen. With his wife, he believed divorce was inevitable; he had hoped for later but was willing to do it now if needed. In regard to his daughter, he felt guilty about the problem marriage possibly fueling her desire to use substances, but he also believed that she needs his involvement in her life to help keep her on a good path. As for his son, his coming out was a loss—he admitted that he felt disappointment—but not shock. In fact, he was eager to let go of his hopes for his son and move toward greater acceptance because he knew his son would need support through the many challenges of being a gay teen. My helping him to accept what is did not "solve" his problems, but instead enabled John to find greater peace in relation to the issues and also consciously choose courses of action that fit with his personal values and ideals.

Acceptance-Generating Dialogue

In their collaborative therapy approach, Anderson and Goolishian (1992) describe their approach to *problem-dissolving* conversations in which they invite clients to become curious about the various definitions of the "problem." Although not initially conceived of as an "acceptance" technique, I have found that engaging clients in a mutual process of becoming curious about their problems results in a near effortless process of accepting what is: because to be curious about something, you have to acknowledge rather than deny or avoid it. A curious conversation about a painful issue feels far safer and more engaging than a practical problem-solving one or a "get real" approach. For such a conversation to occur, therapists need to create a context that is secure, open, and even playful.

Setting the Stage for Acceptance-Generating Conversations

The following characteristics set the stage for acceptance-generating conversations.

- *Slow*: The conversational pace should be slow to allow all participants to hear themselves speak and have time to let it "sink in."
- *Reflective pauses*: Allow for pauses between talk turns to encourage reflection about what was just said by oneself, the therapist, or another in the session. These should not be forced but rather a natural expression of sincere curiosity, perhaps accompanied by "hmmm" or encouragement for reflection: "that is an interesting thought." Although only a few seconds in duration, these pauses can significantly increase a client's ability to be present with what is in the room.
- *Lingering*: When clients say something that seems to have great significance for them, the therapist allows those words to linger in the air, by repeating the "charged" words with the greatest meaning and allowing a pause for the words to echo in the minds of everyone present.
- *Sincerity and presence*. As already described in Chap. 4, therapeutic presence—the deeply felt sense that the therapist is present as another human being—is also key to setting the stage for accepting what is.

Inviting Acceptance into the Conversation

The key to acceptance-generating conversations is a good old-fashioned honest curiosity, which is extraordinarily difficult for well-trained professionals who, by definition, are expected to have a better-than-average sense of what is going on. Contrary to what might be expected, it requires remarkable discipline for a mental health professional to engage clients from a stance of true, not-knowing curiosity. To do this, they must suspend technical knowledge while conversation with clients in order to understand the world from their perspectives (Anderson, 1997).

In essence, therapeutic curiosity involves an enthusiastic willingness to learn about the logic that makes the client's world "make sense." From the constructionist perspective, which both Buddhist psychologists and postmodernists embrace, there is no taken-for-granted or inherent meaning; these are always imputed by the observer (see Chap. 2 for full discussion). Thus, rather than go with one's personal logic or the logic of a particular therapy theory, the constructionist recognizes that in the client's world only one logic system works: *the client's*. The therapist's job is be a respectful but curious visitor who inquires about why things appear the way they do, the sensibility that connects the events, and meanings that are made of the events.

Each person creates this logic system from the various cultural worlds that they inhabit, which include their families, friends, ethnic and religious traditions, media sources, social class, neighborhoods, etc. Thus, each new client reveals a new world and logic system to the therapist. Certainly, there are themes across many people's worlds of logic—ideals of beauty, wealth, womanhood, etc.—but each person has incorporated these larger social discourses in a unique manner. By becoming sincerely curious about the logic of the client's world, the client not only more easily embraces what is, but also quickly learns that the experience as "what is" actually isn't anything "real" at all, but rather a construction.

Curiosity Questions for Inviting Acceptance

Rather than directly encourage acceptance of what is, curiosity quietly invites it using questions below. In answering these questions, clients innately engage with "what is" in their world in a manner that is safe and tolerable.

- You say you have been feeling X (e.g., depressed). There are many ways to feel X; can you share what this is like for you specifically?
- Hmmm. That is interesting. (I have never thought about it quite like that). Can you say more about how all of that fits together for you?
- What meanings have you made from the situation you just described? (Continue exploring numerous possibilities without necessarily trying to reconcile inconsistencies and contradictions).
- Can you say more about the logic behind how you arrived at that decision/ meaning?

Acceptance and Harm

Given that the small things are difficult enough to accept, more gross violations are even more ethically and personally challenging. How do you accept "what is" when another has committed acts of violence against you, betrayed you, or consciously set out to do harm? In these cases, accepting what is takes the form of fully acknowledging that these things have actually happened rather than avoiding the painful reality. In fact, some would argue that the cycle of violence perpetuates in part because the person being abused fails to accept and thereby avoids what is by making excuses or diminishing what is happening. "Accepting" what is does not mean that one tolerates abuse or unhealthy relationships; instead, it involves acknowledging that indeed something is not working, that trust has been breached, and that something is wrong. When there is betrayal, the most difficult part is emotionally accepting that it has happened. The process of "accepting what is" requires cognitively and emotionally acknowledging what has happened and then taking responsibility for responding thoughtfully rather than out of passion or avoidance. In cases where trust has been betrayed, "accepting what is" may involve taking reasonable action to protect oneself or removing oneself from the situation. In other cases, it may involve working towards reconciliation and forgiveness. The process of mindfulness helps clients bring a centered and reflective presence to the situation that allows clients to avoid automatic, knee-jerk responses and instead enables them to make proactive choices.

Cultivating Wisdom and Compassion

One of the distinguishing features of mindfully oriented therapy is that there is an emphasis on not simply ending troubling symptoms or conflict, but also an imperative to help clients develop wisdom: or, more simply put, help clients develop philosophies for living that are more effective than what they initially possessed. The purpose of cultivating wisdom is to prevent problems from resurfacing in the future and is based in the Buddhist assumption that suffering is primarily caused by *ignorance* (Hahn, 1998): not illness, bad genes, thoughtless partners, damaged kids, or an insecure attachment. Because ignorance is not casually remedied, a person must consciously become a seeker of wisdom. In fact, it almost seems as though the human mind's default means of perception naturally generates the illusions that create ignorance (i.e., seeing separateness, scanning for safety, not seeing one's own part in creating meaning, etc.), and thus on-going concerted effort is needed to overcome this tendency and achieve a greater sense of freedom and peace. Thus, mindfulness-informed therapy includes the pursuit of wisdom as part of its late phase goals.

To clarify from the outset, *the therapist is not the source of wisdom*: simply the one who encourages clients to seek it. I would not dare to consider myself wise enough to teach wisdom but have been humbled enough in life to know that seeking it is an important part of being human and reducing suffering. So, the therapist's role in this case is to be a midwife and also a fellow traveler in the journey of life. Seeking wisdom begins by simply reflecting with clients about how their current life struggles are teaching them about "what is" in life.

Some of the more common life insights that arise in couple and family therapy include:

- You cannot change another person.
- You are usually a large part of the problem you attribute to your partner or kids.
- The things that bother you most about another person are things that you have an issue with yourself (either you do it too or go to an ridiculous extreme to not do it).

- Most things that seem to be fixed qualities of a person are generally only a quality that is demonstrated in certain contexts, situations, and relationships; if the behavior is undesirable, change the context.
- Inconsistent reinforcement of and responses to a particular behavior tend to reinforce it.
- Love heals most things.
- Love is the most precious thing in life.
- It's more important to show someone you care than to have a clean house.
- The only moment for living one's dream is now.
- Life is not fair or logical; it just is.

Wisdom can easily be cultivated in session by helping clients notice what life lessons they are learning from the struggle they are having. By bringing the client's attention to these themes and putting them into words that are meaningful to the client can help them glean important life lessons and increase in their sense of wisdom. For example, when working with many of today's busy families—even when one parent stays home with the children—they often arrive in my office because they are learning that *being fully and mindfully present* with one another is more important than all the other wonderful things we can do for our children: private schools, soccer leagues, music lessons, language schools, and play dates. Helping families to reorganize their priorities and connect this to a transformed understanding of what life is truly about is how we help our clients cultivate wisdom that is meaningful in their lives.

Questions for Wise Reflection

Questions such as these can be used as progress is being made and in the later phase of therapy to help clients reflect in ways that cultivate wisdom:

- In learning how to better handle X, what type of lessons have you learned or insights have you had?
- How did you feel about or see yourself for having acted according to this principle?
- Where else in your life or someone else's have you also seen this lesson/ life principle in action?
- Is this insight about life something you want to incorporate into your personal philosophy for living and have it affect future decisions? If so, then how might you do this?
- Are there others in your life with whom you share this value or belief? If so, are there ways the two of you can support each other in living from this perspective?
- If you were able to live from this principle, how might that change your life, relationships, sense of self, etc.?

In addition to gleaning wisdom from "what is," therapists can help clients cultivate wisdom through reading, talking with people they respect or find "wiser" than themselves, and tapping into their religious traditions or the religious traditions of others. When clients are going through a difficult life struggle, I often encourage them to find inspirational readings that help with keeping perspective or developing a new perspective on this problem. When they have a spiritual tradition or even the faintest interest in spiritual traditions, I encourage them to connect with people, communities, and/or readings that can deepen their understanding. One way to think of religions and spiritual practices is that they are sources of wisdom and commonly useful reframes for difficult life situations.

If clients are already practicing mindfulness, they are more likely to "stumble" on wisdom and insight than in other circumstances. The practice of beginning to compassionately watch one's own mind in operation and also quieting the mind seems to allow a person's innate or latent wisdom emerge and/or makes such wisdom more readily accessible. For example, one client I once worked with had been attending temple regularly for years while struggling with a severe and chronic depression. After beginning to practice mindfulness in session, she soon discovered that her temple also had a meditation class based on Jewish meditative traditions. She started attending these during which time her rabbi also offer brief talks related to the practice. She began to find that even though she had know this rabbi for years and heard him speak hundreds of times, she somehow found his words far more profound and inspiring in the meditation groups. Although the exact reason for this may be difficult to determine—the primary differences were the small group format, meditating before listening to him speak, and her changing life circumstances—but some combination of these resulted in an insight so profound (life may end at any moment, so you need to savor this very moment) that it essentially ended her 2-year depression in one afternoon and transformed her attitude about a lackluster marriage and empty nest. After this episode, our sessions began focusing on ways to implement her insight and learn how to more regularly and consistently live in the moment.

Practices for Cultivating Equanimity

Not-Knowing Expertise

Buddhist psychology defines mental health as equanimity (Gehart & McCollum, 2007), which is not easy to do in the face of life challenges. Therapists can help clients do so by "planting seeds of equanimity" when the opportunity presents itself, which includes when times are good, bad, and anywhere in between. So, yes, that means the seeds of equanimity can be planted throughout the course of therapy because the key to equanimity is realizing that life will move between these three states—good, bad, and in between—in a regular but unpredictable flow. Because the lesson is a tough one, help in all three phases enables clients to better master it.

Planting Seeds of Equinity in Good Times

Strategic family therapists have been known to caution clients to "go slow" when they start to make progress as a paradoxical technique that will either inspire rebellion to progress faster or buffer them if there are setbacks; either way, it's a win (Haley, 1987; Segal, 1991). Mindfulness-informed therapists do something similar but for different reasons. When clients are making progress or have made progress, drawing clients' attention to the larger picture that encompasses the ebb and flow of their lives can help them develop a greater sense of equanimity. Rather than dampen their excitement about their success, noticing the ebb and flow during good times should be framed in such a way as to help clients savor and mindfully experience the good times in their lives, while remaining cognizant of the fact that the good times too shall pass. For example, when a couple or family that had been struggling with conflict finds themselves in a period of harmony, the therapist can draw their attention to this while planting seeds of equanimity: "It seems as though your attention to patterns of communication, you have been able to better resolve your differences. Hopefully, you can use the process you used this time for the next time you encounter a period in which you experience conflict. Chances are that there will be a time of more conflict again, but hopefully the next time you will be better able to recognize it when it arises and know how better to respond. What will be some of the warning signs and how might you respond based on what we have learned together?"

Mindfulness-informed therapists may want to consider lessons from positive psychologists in relation to this topic. Positive psychologists would add to this Buddhist practice by encouraging clients to see or story the good times and their good qualities as *stable* and the bad times as exceptions or *temporary* (Seligman, 2002). This recommendation is based on research of people who are happier than average. In the example above, clients would be encouraged to see the good times as typical and generally expect them, also knowing that setbacks and challenges inevitably arise along the way, but they can be dealt with.

Cultivating Equanimity in the Good Times

Questions and comments such as these can be used to help cultivate equanimity when progress has been made toward client goals:

- *Future applications*: How have you learned to deal with (the problem)? How can you use this knowledge to better manage it going forward, knowing that it is possible that it will occur again?
- *Preparing for setback*: On a scale from 1 to 10 with 10 being very confident, how confident are you that the problem might resurface again? How might you better handle it then?

(continued)

(continued)

> • *Ebb-and-flow perspective*: When you consider that your life may involve an ebb-and-flow of this problem arising and then fading way—hopefully at less of severe degree than it was when you first came here—what thoughts do you have?
> • *Expand the context*: Can you savor the good times you are experiencing now and still keep in mind the bigger picture that includes more difficult times down the road?
> • *Life perspective*: While in these good times, can you step back and look at the whole of your life? What type of mosaic do you see of good, bad, and somewhere in between?
> • *Spiritual view*: From your perspective, what role might the good times play in a person's entire life?

These types of questions can be very helpful in undoing the commonly held myths and fantasies that with enough therapy, effort, or money, one can live a problem-free life. Although such thoughts are alluring to virtually all of us and, ironically, to a large extent drive a person to do things such as mindfulness, these are nonetheless naïve and misleading. Therapists should avoid harshly bursting clients' "bubbles of hope" related to the issue, but they should be willing to gently contextualize good times with their inescapable counterpart, times of challenge.

Planting Seeds of Equanimity in Difficult Times

During periods when clients are experiencing difficulties—generally the reason they are seeking therapy thus it is in the early and middle phases of therapy—therapists can help develop equanimity by *enlarging* client's current view of life. Therapists can help clients expand their view of the current situation—which often seems unresolvable and likely to be permanent, which they rarely are—as a temporary fluctuation that happens in life. Several options are possible for expanding clients' view of their situations, such as asking questions, inviting reflections, or considering hypothetical situations. These can be used to help clients keep perspective on their situation.

> **Expanding Perspectives in Difficult Times**
>
> Therapists have numerous options for helping clients remember the larger context of the problem, and the most appropriate option varies based on the particular client and problem. These should be explored only *after* the client feels heard and accepted by the therapist and is in a place to consider the larger context. Some options include:

(continued)

(continued)

- *Separate actual experience of problem from worry*: For most of us, when we experience problems, it seems as though they consume every waking moment, when in reality it is mostly that we think about them day-and-night and that their actual impact on our daily life is quite minimal (e.g., fretting and stewing over a fight vs. the time it takes to fight). Can you estimate how many minutes (or what percentage) of your day/week are spent actually experiencing the problem? How does that compare to the time you spend thinking or worrying about it?
- *Contextualizing with current good*: Are there any areas of your life that are going well right now? If so, then what percentage of your life (day/week) is problem-filled vs. going okay?
- *Future retrospective*: How much do you think you will still be worrying about this issue in 5, 10, 20 years?
- *Entire life perspective*: If you took a step back and looked at the situation, what percentage of your whole life would this issue consume/take up?
- *Spiritual view*: How might the problem fit with your spiritual and religious views? Why do you believe people experience problems as part of their life journeys? Can good come from them? Can good come from what you are experiencing now?

When working with clients who tend toward pessimism or hopelessness, therapists sometimes must work harder and get behavioral or more objective descriptions to develop accurate and fair answers. In some situations, such as a history of severe trauma or abuse, equanimity may be cultivated by drawing clients' attention to the future and highlighting that the traumatic period of their life will end (with the help of therapy) and that their life will get to a better place.

Planting Seeds of Equanimity in the In-Between Periods

In addition to the "good" and "bad" times, there are times in life that are somewhere in between. These unexceptional periods are part of the constant ebb and flow of life. For many in modern cultures, being in an in-between period is often *more* frightening than a truly difficult time because they feel adrift, aimless, or even bored. I've had clients who are so accustomed to drama that when life settles down, they feel anxious and report conscious attempts to stir up excitement or trouble. Therapists can help clients such as these learn to just allow themselves to float and "be" in the in-between times, knowing that it may get better or worse, but it will keep moving and that they will continue to experience ups and downs.

Ironically, the more a person accepts that there will be ups and downs, the fewer ups and downs there seem to be. Becoming comfortable with the ambiguity of the in-between periods can be particularly beneficial because in many ways the more equanimity one cultivates, the more life always seems to be neither good nor bad—it just simply is—and it is beautiful.

Questions for the In-Between Times

When clients report being neither up nor down, questions such as the ones below can help with cultivating equanimity:

- *Mindful experiencing of the in-between*: That is interesting. You are saying you really don't feel as though you have reached your goal but you also are better off than when you began. You are in in-between place right now. Can you describe what it is like for you to be here now? What types of thoughts and feelings do you have about being here?
- *Mindful experiencing of progress*: You've said you have not quite reached your goals yet but feel like you are making progress. Can you describe what it is like to be in place in-between the worst and best of times? What do you like? What do you find challenging?
- *Mindful experiencing setbacks*: Things are a little worse this week than last. Can you say what it is like to be not as bad off as when you started by not as good as last week? What types of thoughts and feelings do you have about this?
- *Mindful reflection on ups-and-downs*: You say that you are neither really up or down. If you take a step back and look over the whole of your life up to this point and imagining out into the future, what percentage of your life do you think will be spent in these "mundane" times? Given that you might spend a lot of time being "in between," how would you like to approach such times?
- *Spiritual view*: From your view, what role might these "in between times" play in the spiritual journey?

In-Session Mindful Experience

Mindful Experience of Thoughts and Feelings

Whether working with individuals, couples, or families, helping clients learn how to observe their thoughts and feelings can be helpful for a wide range of concerns. Clients who practice mindfulness meditation generally have significant experience with mindful observation and therefore respond with minimal prompting. However, most clients do not have a well-developed practice and need a little more structure and encouragement, especially when in difficult dialogue with loved ones.

Within the field of family therapy, there are several therapists who have developed established models and approaches for accessing present moment experience. For example, in emotionally focused therapy, Johnson (2004) intervenes with couples to help them identify their primary attachment emotions underlying secondary emotions and needs, such as helping a client who is angry at her spouse who forgot an anniversary pause and explore the deeper fears and feelings that fuel the expressed anger. Johnson uses evocative responding and empathic conjecture to help clients tune into their inner experiences.

Similarly, when Andersen (2007) heard a word or saw a significant nonverbal expression (that the person was not trying to hide) that seemed to be particularly pregnant with meaning, he would ask clients to identify what is "in" the word or expression, often asking about what it would say if it could speak. For example, "if your tight fist could speak right now, what would it say?" or "When you look into the word 'alone,' what do you see?" Such questions are invitations for clients to become more mindfully aware of their experience. Andersen invited clients to lean into their meaning they are making with eyes and hearts wide open.

In addition to these and other conversational approaches, therapists can also use basic mindfulness observational principles used in meditation practice to encourage clients to more mindfully encounter their inner worlds. All of these approaches to helping clients to observe their present moment thoughts and feelings in session help them to create new relationships with these experiences. This alternative perspective on problem thoughts and feelings transforms client's lived experience and allows for more resourceful handling of these issues.

Guided Mindful Observation

If clients are willing, you can invite them to spend a few moments mindfully experiencing troubling thoughts or emotions in session.

"You said you felt/thought X. Can you take a moment to just watch and notice the thought/feeling—notice the details about it":

- Is it one thought/emotion or many?
- Does it dominate your mind or flitter in and out?
- Is it familiar or unfamiliar? Do you have secondary thoughts or feelings about it?
- Is it strong or weak?
- Do you experience it anywhere in your body?
- Are there colors or images associated with it?
- What other thoughts and feelings seem to be associated with it?
- Does it make you feel tired, wired, or some other way?
- How does it affect your sense of self? Your feelings about the day? Your feelings about life?

After a period of mindful experiencing, the therapist and client can discuss the implications of these observations for how to relate to these thoughts and feelings outside of session.

In addition to the above direct and guided approach to mindful observations related to the problem, therapists can also use more subtle questions to encourage clients to relate to their present moment experience in new ways.

Conversational Invitations for Mindful Observation of Thoughts and Feelings

- *Observing in an imaginary room*: Imagine you could put this troubling feeling/thought in a room, then shut the door, and go to a safe place outside and observe it through a window. Describe what you see and notice as you watch it in the room? (Adapted from internal family system; Schwartz, 1995).
- *If it could speak*: If that (symbol, word, metaphor mentioned by client, e.g., knot or little girl inside) could speak, what would it say?
- *What is happening*: What is happening for you inside right now? (For couples): What is happening for you inside right now as your partner is speaking?
- *A look inside*: If someone could look inside you right now, what would they see?

After inviting the client to either directly or indirectly experience thoughts and feelings mindfully in session, therapists should then invite clients to reflect on what they noticed and consider how they may use this to improve their situation.

Reflecting on Mindful Experience

After one of the above exercises, therapists can invite clients to reflect on what they learned:

"It sounds like you were able to experience your thoughts and feelings from a slightly new perspective. May I ask you more about this?"

- Do you have any new thoughts or feelings about the situation?
- Did anything surprise you? What didn't surprise you?
- Did you gain any insight or wisdom from this experience?
- Did you gain even a little more compassion for you and others in the situation?
- Did anything you experience give you ideas about how to handle this situation in the upcoming week?
- How do you think the stories you tell yourself about this situation may slightly change based on what you just described?

Mindful Awareness of Relational Patterns

When you get down to the nuts and bolts, one of the distinguishing features of couple and family therapy vs. individual therapy is the focus on relational interaction patterns (Sprenkle, Davis, & Lebow, 2009). Most professionals who identify themselves as couple and family therapists maintain this relational perspective whether there are one or more people in the room. In fact, I would argue that when helping an individual, it is even more critical to maintain a relational perspective— carefully attending to the client's interaction patterns with others—otherwise it is difficult to avoid colluding with clients against the significant others in their lives because you only have half of the story.

Most often, people are only vaguely aware of how their problematic interaction patterns unfold because they are in a highly emotional state when they occur. This difficulty with remembering these patterns may be related to impaired memory functioning when in the stress response or experiencing trauma (and for many fighting with loved ones either triggers past trauma or is experienced as a new one; Siegel, 2010b). Thus, helping clients clearly identify these patterns, especially their personal half of the interaction, is a very important first step to changing them. Once the problem interaction pattern is identified, then the therapist can help the clients slow down the sequence to bring mindful awareness to each person's emotions, fears, and thoughts that fuel the painful interactions. By bringing compassion to one's own and others' emotions in this process, greater understanding and new potentials for action are possible.

A mindful approach to observing relational patterns builds on common practices for observing interactional patterns while adding a curious, mindful approach. Traditional systemic approaches aim to interrupt problem interaction sequence and allow the system to naturally reorganize (Watzlawick, Weakland, & Fisch, 1974). In contrast, cognitive-behavioral therapists educate their clients on better ways to interact (Gottman, 1999). A mindful approach uses present moment awareness of and reflection on being in the interaction to invite clients to identify for themselves better options for relating.

Questions for Bringing Initial Awareness to Problem Interaction Patterns

Therapists can help clients bring awareness to their patterns by adapting various family therapy techniques, most notably systemic circular questions and narrative mapping of the landscapes of action and consciousness. Circular questions used in Milan systemic therapy (Selvini-Palazzoli, Cecchin, Prata, & Boscolo, 1978) trace the interaction pattern in a curious, nonblaming manner. The questions start by inquiring about what each person in the system is doing when things are "normal" (no tension) and then traces the interaction pattern as tension rises, climaxes, and most important and most often forgot, the return to "normal" homeostasis (see Chap. 5 for further discussion). Circular questions can also be used with a variation of the narrative technique of mapping in the landscapes of action and consciousness, which separates actions from the mental process, stories, and meanings about those actions (Freedman & Combs, 1996).

Mindful awareness of relational patterns typically involve the following:

- Bringing awareness to the problem interaction patterns (also discussed in Chap. 5)
- Bringing awareness to internal experiences during the interactions
- Bringing mindful, compassionate awareness to interaction patterns
- Reflections for changing interaction patterns

Mindful Reflection on Problem Interaction Cycles

Bringing awareness to problem interactions

- Can you describe how things are going—what each of you is doing—when things are going well or at least are not problematic. When person A does X, how does B (C and D) respond? What does A do in response to that?
- If there are signs that tensions are rising, what are they? Who does what and how does each respond?
- When the problem becomes full force, who does what? How does each person respond—or try not to respond—to others?
- How does this finally resolve and get back to things feeling like "normal"? Does the same person apologize or otherwise facilitate reconciliation or do different people do it at different times?
- How do others experience and/or affect this cycle?

Bringing awareness to internal experiences during the interactions

- What is going on inside for each person during the various phases of "normal"—tension rising—height of tension—resolution of tension—return to "normal?"
- What happens to a sense of feeling safety for each person at various points? How do they express their sense of not feeling safe: anger, hurt, attacking, avoiding, etc.?
- What is going on for others that may be affected by this cycle?

Bringing compassionate awareness to interaction patterns

- After identifying this cycle, are there elements that are now easier to understand or have compassion for?
- When you step back and begin to understand others' experiences of not feeling safe as well as your own of not feeling safe, can you see the interaction cycle any differently?
- Can you have compassion for each person's experience of feeling that the relationship suddenly seems unsafe or unsupportive?

For many clients, simply bringing awareness to these patterns is helpful in both motivating them to change and helping identifying how best to approach change. Therapists can further this process by inviting specific reflections:

Reflecting on Possibilities for Changing Interaction Patterns

* Now that you can see this pattern more clearly, do you have any thoughts about how to interrupt it? Is there a point early in the cycle where you could do something different, such as take a break, express yourself in a different way, or in some way respond differently?
* Are there any simple things that can be done to interrupt the cycle, such as avoiding a particular context or combination of people altogether?
* What can be done to help remind one or both of you that you are entering into the negative cycle the next time it happens?
* What are the most obvious signs that the pattern is starting up—signs that even when you are upset you are likely to notice—that you can use to signal that you are about to enter into the cycle or are in danger of starting it if evasive action is not taken?
* What can you learn from times when you were able to either stop or reduce the intensity of the interaction pattern? What can be used from this and applied more broadly?

Mindful Enactment with Problem Interactions

Whereas an individual's anxiety and depression may not be readily evident in a one-on-one therapy, in couples and family therapy their problem—generally conflictual interactions—often show up "in vivo" during the session: arguments break out and people are screaming, crying, or dead silent. Salvador Minuchin first described how to use the technique of enactment to manage such situations, and they have become a central feature in several evidence-based approaches, including emotionally focused therapy (Johnson, 2004), brief strategic therapy (Szapocznik & Williams, 2000), and multisystemic family therapy (Henggeler, 1998). Even if you would prefer not to have in-session enactment of the problem, they typically happen anyway (Gehart, 2010). In these moments, therapists can use mindfulness to help draw clients' awareness to these patterns in such a way that they are able to respond differently in the future.

Whether spontaneously acted out or politely being asked to do so, therapists can help clients learn to alter their problematic relational patterns by helping them more effectively talk through their most difficult conversations. Typically, therapists start an enactment by asking clients to "show" the therapist how the typical argument or problem interaction goes. Alternatively, therapists can take a more collaborative approach and invite clients to do an enactment, respecting their decision to decline. Based on the case conceptualization, the therapist can then help the couple or family alter their interactions to improve the outcome, actively coaching each member in the process and stopping interactions when they go off course. A mindful approach to enactments builds on this tradition, adding an emphasis on inviting each person to mindfully experience the interaction and their internal processes as part of the enactment. By increasing clients' awareness of the interaction and the internal experiences of each person in dialogue, new options for relating become quickly evident.

Guiding Mindful Enactments

Therapists may either start by asking the couple or family to enact a specific or general problem interaction or take advantage of a problematic set of interactions that naturally arises in session. Then as tensions rise, the therapist invites clients to do the following:

- *Reflect on inner process*: Before you respond, I want each of you to take a few moments in silence to check in with yourselves and notice what thoughts and feelings are going on. Optional: Can you please briefly share what you are experiencing.
- *Reflect on interactional patterns*: I want to pause right here and invite each of you to take a step back and look at the dance or interaction pattern that is emerging. How is each person moving the conversation forward with his or her particular response? How does each response make sense in the context of the prior one? What things are you willing to do to make things move in a new direction? Let's try it.
- *Fly on the wall*: I want to pause the conversation right here, and I want each of you to pretend that you are a fly on the wall that can only see what is going on but does not quite understand the more subtle dynamics. Can you tell me what the fly is seeing? What thoughts do you have about this? Let's put that into action right now.
- *In the moment*: Can you take a pause from the conversation to just describe to us what is going on in the moment for you right now?
- *Mindful restatement*: Please take a moment to consider how your partner/ family member may have heard what you just said. Really try to get into his/her reality. Then try again to say what you want to say but say it in a way that respects his/her reality.
- *Attempts at connection vs. defensive maneuvers*: I want to pause and invite each of you to consider your last response. In what way was it an attempt at connection? To what extent was it a defensive maneuver to protect yourself? Given this reflection, let's go back and try to communicate the same thing again.
- *Reflections on safety*: Let's pause for a moment. I want each of you to check in on how safe you feel in this relationship right now. Notice what you are doing in response to your perceived level of safety. What can you say right now that might help your partner/family member feel greater safety with you?

Just a Beginning

The above practices should not be viewed as complete and final list of mindfulness-informed practices. Instead, they are examples of the many and diverse ways that mindfulness and acceptance can be used to transform dialogues in the therapy process. I invite you to expand upon and create new ways of using mindfulness and acceptance to help clients achieve their goals.

Chapter 8
Mindfulness and Acceptance Interventions for Couples and Families

Mindfulness and Acceptance in Relationships

Couple and family relationships—our most intense and intimate relationships—are where we feel most safe but also the most vulnerable at times. So, when things go wrong in these relationships, we become desperate to "fix" the situation, either by frantically pursuing the reestablishment of connection or by withdrawing to protect ourselves. Neither response actually helps the situation, but instead pushes the relationship into a downward spiral that brings out the worst in each person involved. When this goes on so long that the couple or family can no longer stop the spiraling, they call a therapist for assistance. This chapter will describe some options for helping couples and families develop more satisfying relationships using a model of mindful relating.

Toward a Model of Mindful Relating

As first introduced in Chap. 4, mindfulness and acceptance practices inform a specific model of healthy relational functioning.

Model of Mindful Relating Processes

From a mindfulness perspective, relationships work best when each person demonstrates the following balance of relational and personal process:

Relational processes

- *Emotional presence*: Being emotionally present and available to the other
- *Compassion and acceptance*: Experiencing and expressing compassion for and acceptance of the other

---

(continued)

D.R. Gehart, *Mindfulness and Acceptance in Couple and Family Therapy*,
DOI 10.1007/978-1-4614-3033-9_8, © Springer Science+Business Media New York 2012

(continued)

> *Personal processes*
>
> • *Self-regulation*: Regulating one's own emotions
> • *Self-acceptance*: Practicing acceptance of and compassion for the self

In couple relationships, both parties develop their abilities in these two areas. In parent–child relationships, parents are responsible for teaching and developing these qualities in their children as they grow.

This mindfulness-informed model of relating combines elements of two well-known relationship theories: *attachment theory* and *differentiation*. Widely accepted for decades as a seminal theory for understanding infant–caregiver relationships, attachment theory has more recently been explored across the lifespan. Adult attachment theory proposes that adults need to feel safe and secure in intimate relationships in order to experience emotional and physical wellbeing, and there is a quickly growing research foundation to support this (Gottman, 2011; Johnson, 2004, 2008; Siegel, 1999, 2010b). A leading advocate of attachment theory, Johnson (2008) suggests that this need is as much of a survival need in adults as it is in infants, which explains not only the "primal panic" that couples exhibit when the safety in the relationship is threatened but also the often desperate and cruel behaviors seen in romantic relationships. Johnson's *emotionally focused therapy*, widely regarded as the best researched couples therapy approach, focuses on reestablishing this bond of safety in relationships. Similarly, Gottman (2011) has recently updated his couple's theory to include *trust* in addition to communication and relational skills. Although mindfulness and Buddhist traditions do not have a theory that is equivalent to attachment theory (as noted in Chap. 2, they use the term attachment to apply to an entirely different psychological process), they do emphasize being (a) emotionally present, (b) compassionate, and (c) accepting in relationships. These three elements describe key features of secure attachment as envisioned by attachment theorists.

Mindfulness and acceptance theories emphasize emotional self-regulation and self-acceptance, which correlate with the Bowenian concept of differentiation and self-soothing (Bowen, 1985; Schnarch, 1991). Differentiation involves both the ability to maintain a sense of self in the face of relational pressures for togetherness and the ability to form close, intimate relationships. According to this theory, in order to experience intimacy, a person must be able to *self-sooth*, managing the intense emotions, such as vulnerability and disappointment, that inevitably occur in such relationships (Schnarch, 1991). The ability to self-soothe enables one to more readily create secure relationships as well as recover from ruptures in secure relationships. The practice of mindfulness is one of the most direct means of improving one's ability to self-soothe.

Thus, taken as a whole, a mindful model for relationships involves increasing a person's ability to self-regulate while being emotionally present to and compassion with a significant other: partner, child, parent, close friend, etc. The interventive practices described in this chapter are designed to help couples and families improve their abilities in these two areas.

Mindfulness Applications with Couples

Therapists have numerous options for helping couples manage conflict and building a safer, more intimate relationship. Depending on the needs of a couple, one or more of the following may be useful:

- Facilitated mindful communication
- Mindful pause and reflection
- Listening deeply to what lies beneath
- Loving-kindness meditation
- Compassionate life review
- Love dialogues
- Nonviolent speech
- Practicing together
- Mindful sex and intimacy

Facilitated Mindful Communication for Couples

Most couples present for therapy with the complaint: "we can't communicate." However, as early couple and family therapists were quick to clarify, "one cannot communicate"; communication is happening, but the participants just don't like the message or how it is communicated (Watzlawick, Bavelas, & Jackson, 1967). Mindfulness and acceptance practices provide nonthreatening, easily implemented options for reestablishing more satisfying communication by rebuilding safety and trust and creating opportunities for couples to practice self-soothing during difficult conversations.

Therapists can use mindful communication skills to help couples increase their awareness of what they say and how they say it. Mindful communication strategies generally involve:

- *Presence*: By being emotionally present in conversation with loved ones, it is more likely that a person will bring warmth and sincerity to the conversation and that the other will experience a sense of safety and trust. Something as simple as taking a moment to soulfully look into another's eyes may be all that is needed to bring about a softened tone and attitude.
- *Slowing down*: The conversation generally slows down significantly to allow parties to have time to mindfully experience what the other says and how they receive the message as well as reflect upon their options for responding.

- *Reflection*: Mindful communication encourages reflection before speaking, a pause that allows for internal dialogue and choice in formulating a response rather than reacting out of habit.
- *Carefully chosen words*: Mindful conversation enables and encourages partners to choose their words more carefully when talking with loved ones so that painful emotions are not triggered.

Facilitating Mindful Communication in Session

Therapists can help couples develop mindful communication habits by using some or all of the following practices:

1. *Mindfulness*: Guide the couple in 2–5 minutes of mindful breathing at the beginning to help them enter a calm and more relaxed state.
2. *Loving kindness*: Then guide them through a brief loving-kindness meditation that includes each other, a neutral other, and self.
3. *Invite one partner to speak*: Invite one partner to begin the conversation; Johnson (2004) has found that engaging the most withdrawn partner typically has the best outcomes in couples work.
4. *Guided mindful reflection of communication*: After the one partner is done speaking, ask both to turn their attention inward, allowing them to close their eyes, and do one or more of the following:

   - *Present-moment emotions*: Notice what emotions and thoughts you are feeling in this moment. Avoid becoming fused or overly attached to the emotions, but instead allow them to float through your mind like clouds in the sky. Know that we are working on reducing the painful emotions and increasing the positive emotions through this process.
   - *Sense of safety*: Now I want you to take a moment and get even quieter. Notice whether you are feeling safe right now. Whether you feel safe with your partner, in this session, even with yourself. Just notice and try not to judge or worry too much. We are going to work at creating more safety here.
   - *Present-moment thoughts*: Notice what thoughts are going through your head. Know that you do not have to believe every thought or define yourself with every thought you have. Allow them to float in and out of the mind without becoming overly invested in them. Just notice what arises without judgment.
   - *Bodily sensations*: Notice what is going on in your body right now. Is there tension anywhere? Do you feel okay in any areas? Just notice what is going on.

(continued)

(continued)

- *Acceptance*: Take a moment to simply acknowledge all that is going on in your mind and body, knowing that these are here for the moment but that they need not remain.
- *Compassion*: Take a moment to experience compassion for yourself and all that is going on inside at the moment.
- *Partner's emotions*: Now I want you to imagine as best you can what your partner may be feeling right now—regardless of whether you believe they should feel it or not—simply try to imagine what he/she is feeling. See if you notice even a small amount of compassion for the painful emotions he/she may be experiencing, even if you don't believe they are based on a clear understanding of what you meant.
- *Partner's sense of safety*: Now imagine to what degree your partner is feeling safe right now and what it is like to feel that way.
- *Partner's thoughts*: Take a moment to imagine the many and likely contradictory thoughts that might be going through your partner's mind right now—whether or not you agree with them. Try to accept that this may be your partner's reality for the moment and that this reality is likely to change through this process.
- *Partner's bodily sensations*: Take a moment to imagine what may be going on in your partner's body right now. Is there a place where he/she habitually holds stress? Hands, face, jaw, neck, back. Imagine this and send healing thoughts their way if that feels right to you.
- *Appreciation*: Finally, I want you to take a moment and appreciate what you and your partner are doing: you are both willing to work on the relationship by delving to the root of difficult issues with me. Be thankful that you both care about your relationship enough to go through this process. If it feels right to you, you may send well wishes and thanks to your partner, yourself, and your relationship.
- *Mindful response*: Now I want you to think about what you can do in the next few minutes as you switch listening and speaking roles to make this conversation go well. Either imagining what you might say or how you might listen.
- Now open your eyes if they were closed and we are going to continue the conversation with you (the other partner). Please start when you are ready.

The couple continues to take turns speaking with the therapist guiding a pause between turns that encourages mindful experiencing, compassion, and acceptance, varying the reflections based on the content of the conversation and the couple's emotional process.

Facilitated mindful communication is a bit slow and awkward at first, but the deliberate attention to internal and relational processes greatly promote all elements of the mindful communication: emotional presence, compassion for others, self-regulation, and self-acceptance. Because it is immediate and activates in-the-moment emotions, most couples need only a few practice sessions to significantly shift how they view the relationship and choose to respond in future conversations without such prompting. For example, when working with a lesbian couple struggling with a difference in willingness to "come out" with their respective families, this exercise enabled each to better respect the worries and concerns of the other and resolve to make their relationship a shelter where each felt safe and accepted for where they were in this difficult process.

Mindful Pause and Reflection

After two to three practices with facilitated mindful communication, couples are often ready to practice the mindful pause at home. A natural next step from the longer facilitated process, the *mindful pause* involves either intentionally pausing a few seconds than seems natural in everyday conversation before responding during a conversation or asking for a longer pause or break. The exact "best" timing varies with each couple and is often affected by gender, cultural background, and trauma history. In most cases of mild to moderate non-abusive conflict, this pause can significantly reduce the hurtfulness of responses.

The mindful pause has many practical uses:

- *Relaxation response*: Clients can use the mindful pause to briefly practice mind-fulness with a single breath. For clients who maintain a regular mindfulness meditation practice, taking even 1–10 second to focus on the breath can quickly invoke the relaxation response, enabling them to draw upon the more "reason-able" parts of their brain.
- *Awareness of inner processes*: Much like the guided version, the pause can also be used to bring awareness to the emotions, sense of safety, thoughts, and bodily sensations one is experiencing in the moment. By taking an observer perspective, a person can quietly survey what emotions are rising and fading after words are spoken. This mindful observation of emotions in the moment quickly brings not only obvious emotions—such as anger and hurt—to the surface but also more subtle and vulnerable feelings related to a sense of safety (i.e., secondary and primary emotions in emotionally focused therapy; Johnson, 2004). These emotions can then be fully experienced in the moment when they are most vivid.
- *Attunement with and compassion for partner's experience*: Especially when pause follows listening to one's partner, the time can be used to accept "what is" for one's partner and become attuned to that reality whether or not one agrees with it. With practice, partners can also learn to use the pause to practice loving

kindness and compassion for one's partner. Although difficult in an exceptionally heated argument, when used in slower, mindful conversations, most people can access a sense of attunement with and compassion for their partners.

- *Better responses*: The pause enables most people to consciously choose a better way of responding.

Introducing the Pause

Therapists can introduce the pause once couples have had several good experiences with facilitated mindful communication in session. The pause can be introduced with some variation of the following:

- *Introduction*: Now that you two have had several successful experiences with mindful communication with me, would you be interested in trying a less awkward version for use at home? (If they say yes, proceed; if they say no, explore why but do not force the practice if they are not interested).
- *Basic instructions*: When you find you are having a potentially difficult or tense conversation, and I want you to try inserting a mindful pause between talk turns, a much shorter version of what we have done here. The pause may be only seconds within a conversation or it may be a more formal break lasting several minutes, hours, or days. During this pause, you can take a moment to tune into:
  - Your emotions, sense of safety, thoughts, and bodily sensations in the moment
  - Imagining what your partner might be experiencing in each of these areas
  - Acceptance and compassion for where each is in the moment, knowing that these thoughts and feelings will change
  - How you might better respond in the next moments of the conversation

- *Initiating and ending the pause*: Unless the pause is to be less than 30 seconds within a conversation, rarely will both partners eager to take a mindful pause at the same time. So, you will need to come up with a friendly means to request such a pause. Some couples simply say, "I would like to take a mindful pause for 5 minutes," close their eyes, and then use a timer to signal when to resume. You may also choose a code word or other signal. Sometimes each partner has a different signal they prefer to receive from the other when they feel upset. What do you think might work for you two when one of you wants to take a mindful pause?
- *Preparing for mismatched motivation*: We should take some time to discuss the likely situation that one of you asks to take a break and the other does not want to and may even feel the other is using this pause as a power move of some kind. How do you think you two can best handle this?

(continued)

(continued)

> • *Practice in session*: Before I send you home with this task, I want you to
>   practice. So, I am going to ask you to briefly go back to a difficult conver-
>   sation you had last week and practice and have each of you practice asking
>   for a pause.
> • *Allow practice*: Allow the couple to practice for several talk turns.
> • *Debrief on process*: Then debrief with the couple on the process of taking
>   the pause: Was each able to use the pause constructively? Did they know
>   how to resume?
> • *Debrief on preparing to trip-ups*: Then discuss the issue identified related
>   to best ways to handle trip-ups and come up with a plan for such
>   situations.

With high conflict couples, even a mindful pause can quickly become a weapon used to hurt the other in order to win an argument, thus therapists should be careful recommending the pause in such situations.

Listening Deeply

Hahn (1997) encourages couples to *listen deeply* to one another from a position of love and compassion and *only* in moments when they are calm, waiting for the heat of the moment to pass and both to return to a peaceful state of being. Gottman (1999) similarly recommends listening deeply: listening for the *dreams within* a partner's desire or stance in a stalemate and to do so when couples are calm, specifi- cally when heartbeats are well under 100. In both practices, the focus is on under- standing the often unspoken motivations for why each partner has taken their particular stance. In addition to being a very useful in-session exercise, this is an even more important life skill for anyone wanting to create a satisfying long-term relationship.

The basic formula is illustrated in Fig. 8.1.

Inevitably, couples will take different positions on numerous issues over the course of a relationships simply because they are two separate beings with their own preferences, needs, and desires. Virtually all couples will have differences that lead to gridlock: neither is able or willing to give in and they don't know how to move forward together. Such gridlock is best approached by shifting the conversation away from surface level differences in terms of opinions, requests, and demands and instead shifting to a discussion of the aspirations, hopes, and dreams that are behind each person's position in the stalemate: *this shift changes the topic of discussion*. The focus of the conversation instead becomes how can the couple move forward in such a way that both parties are able to pursue the aspirations and hopes that are

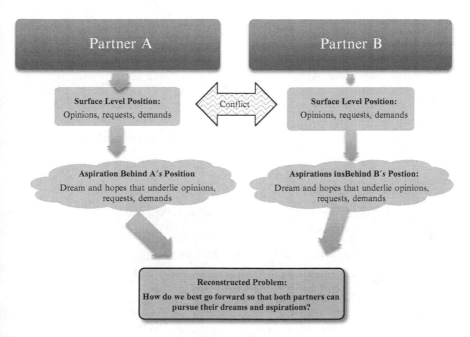

Fig. 8.1 Listening deeply

behind their position. The more couples learn to move to the aspirational level
when they have a disagreement, the faster they can resolve issues in ways that are
mutually satisfying.

	Partner A	Partner B
Surface level position: Stated request, opinion, demand, need, etc.	Wants bonus money to upgrade house	Wants to spend bonus money for vacation
Aspiration behind position: The motivation, hope, dream that lie beneath	Create a beautiful home where friends and family can gather; sense of community	Feeling a sense of relief from pressures at work; give full attention to family

Arguing a matter at the surface level sets couples up for a zero-sum game—one
winner and one loser—or compromise, where both feel as though they have lost
something. In contrast, if the disagreement is moved to the aspirational level, the
problem can then be framed in such a way that the couple is most likely to enable
both partners to pursue the hopes and dreams that motivated their original position.
From the aspirational level, the couple can take in the "big picture" and have the
flexibility of many options, whereas if a couple stays at the surface level, very few
options seem possible because the context is too narrow. In the example above, if
the couple stayed at the surface level, they would argue about how to spend their

bonus money, with each trying to convince the other by making a case for their position. In contrast, if they move to the aspirational level, they have many more options for working collaboratively to handle the situation because they will work with this fundamental question: How do we best proceed to help partner A have a home that builds community and for partner B to rejuvenate from the stress of work? When framed this way, the couple has many more possibilities for working *together* to resolve the issue, while showing respect and concern for the other's needs and desires.

Facilitating Deep Listening

When couples report gridlock conversations, the therapist can help them as follows:

- *Surface level position*: Allow each a turn to share their current position while their partner listens.
- *Aspiration behind level*: Then ask each to answer the following: "What is the hope, dream, or aspiration that motivates your position?"
- *Redefine the problem*: "How do you best move forward enabling both partners to fulfill their dreams and aspirations?"
- The remainder of the conversation involves answering the redefined problem question.

Loving-Kindness Meditation

As described in Chap. 3, one of the distinguishing features of mindfulness work with couples and families is an emphasis on loving kindness or *metta* (from Pali) meditation in addition to mindfulness breath meditation (Salzburg, 1995). Loving-kindness meditation comes from Tibetan and Mahayana traditions (primarily in East Asia) and is a practice that involves more visualization and language than traditional mindfulness practices. Loving-kindness meditation employs repetitive phrases and visualizations of sending positive, loving energy and intentions to a variety of people, including loved ones, acquaintances, strangers, neutral others, oneself, and "enemies," persons with whom one has a strained or difficult relationship.

In mindfulness-based relationship enhancement, loving-kindness meditation is taught before mindfulness because it more directly addresses the goals of couple and family therapy: to improve interpersonal relationships (Carson, Carson, Gil, & Baucom, 2004). As the benefits of loving-kindness meditation are directly applicable to their relationship problems and because the results tend to be dramatic and immediate, clients typically are more motivated to practice loving kindness regularly than mindfulness.

There are several variations of loving-kindness meditation, and I encourage my clients to develop wording that has personal significance for them. If they are associated with a specific religious or spiritual tradition, I encourage them to use language that reflects their beliefs. Although I teach a traditional ordering of the exercise—loved one, acquaintance, self, enemy—I also encourage them to play with the ordering to discover what works best for them. I have found that the more a person can personalize the practice, the more likely they are to do it regularly.

The Makings of Loving-Kindness Meditation

Potential phrases for loving-kindness meditation

- May X be happy (joyful, mentally happy, loving, etc.).
- May X be free from suffering (pain, harm, illness, etc.).
- May X be physically well (healthy, in radiant health, healed, etc.).
- May X have ease of well-being (a sense of well-being, live with ease, etc.).
- May X be deeply at peace (dwell in peace, live with peace, etc.).
- May X be at peace with people in his/her life.

X = Potential persons to whom to direct loving kindness

- A neutral other (e.g., acquaintance, coworker)
- Significant others (e.g., partner, family)
- Difficult other (e.g., someone with whom there is conflict)
- Self
- All beings (e.g., everyone)

Putting it all together: Beginning with the first person, send each loving-kindness thoughts to that person; then continue doing the same for each subsequent person.

Therapists can introduce loving-kindness meditation to couples, families, or anyone struggling with a relationship in the early sessions of therapy, and in some cases even the first. Compared to mindfulness, less instruction and motivation development are needed when introducing clients to loving-kindness meditation because its purpose is clear whereas the link between watching yourself breathe to reduce depression is less intuitive. Therapists should first guide clients through the meditation in session and leave ample time to discuss the exercise and how to apply it at home. Clients generally benefit from a handout with at-home instructions and/or a guided audio recording of the meditation (available www.dianegehart.com).

When using this meditation with couples and families, therapists discuss if they will do the meditation together or if each person will do it separately. If the couple (or family) is equally motivated and is still able to be cooperative with one another, it generally works best to have them practice together at clearly defined times and with clear procedures to avoid generating new conflict about the issue. I always take time to problem solve issues such as one partner not wanting to practice on a given day, another feeling the burden to always remind the other, changes in schedule, etc. Simply having the discussion around these common problems greatly helps to prevent conflict and enables them to better benefit from the practice.

Common areas of conflict around jointly practicing loving-kindness meditation:

- One partner has to remember and "nag" the other to do it (in families, parents will typically take the lead but should avoid making it a chore).
- One person is "not in the mood" to mediate at the designated time.
- Schedule changes in other areas of life conflict with set time to practice.
- One person says he/she does not experience benefits.
- One person begins to feel superior in some way related to the practice (e.g., I am more dedicated than you).

Ideally, therapists work with couples *prior* to starting their practice as well as in the early weeks following assignment to identify and remedy such problems.

Compassionate Life Review

I was first introduced to a meditation that I refer to as the "compassionate life review" at a retreat with Kornfield (1993) many years ago. I use it to help train new therapists (Gehart & McCollum, 2008) and have more recently begun using it with couples to help them increase their sense of compassion for each other. This is the most emotionally intense mindfulness practice I have experienced, so I use it with caution and only with clients whom I believe can benefit from it.

The exercise entails gazing into your partner's eyes while listening to a guided visualization that covers the span of the other's life, beginning with their parent's anticipation of your partner's birth and then continuing through childhood, adolescence, adulthood, and death. During the exercise, partners are asked to reflect upon the events, joys, and sorrows that characterized each period. Most people who do this exercise experience tears and a wide range of emotions, including a sense of loss and grief during the visualizations of the end of life. If couples are unstable for any reason, either individually or as a couple, I would be reluctant to try this. I also think it is best if the practitioners using this exercise experience it themselves first (as a participant) before trying to use it on others.

The Compassionate Life Review

Set up the exercise by having the couple sit facing each other and instruct them to gaze into each other's eyes for as long as they can without staring. Give them permission to look away when they need to periodically but try to return the gaze when they can.

- Begin by guiding them through imagining the potential joys and sorrows of their time in utero, birth, and childhood: "Imagine what your partner's mother and father might have been feeling when they learned about the pregnancy: there may have been great joy of knowing that a dream is coming true, worry about how to support the child, concern about their job, relationship or families. Just imagine the many possible thoughts and emotions your partner's parents may have experienced as they anticipated the birth."

- "Imagine what it was like after hours of labor your partner's mother finally held her newborn infant. There were surely tears of joy in her eyes. It's likely that the father and family were also overjoyed at the miracle of your partner's birth. Also imagine the long, sleepless nights the parents had taking care of this new infant; their fears as new parents; their worries, hopes, and dreams. Also, imagine what it might have been like for this new infant to come into the world and try to make sense of the many sights and sounds. Imagine what it might have been like if a parent was not there or not supportive."

- "Next, imagine what childhood might have been like: the first ice cream, playing in parks, blowing bubbles, riding a bike alone for the first time, etc. Also imagine that your partner was at times likely to have been left out of a game by other children, frightened when lost in a mall, scared by the first day of school. Spend some time imagining some of the possible joys and trials of your partner's childhood."

- "Now, imagine what your partner may have experienced in adolescence: going out with friends for the first time, learning how to drive, a sense of accomplishment at finishing a major project, and falling in love for the first time. Also imagine the more difficult times your partner may have experienced in his/her teen years: feeling misunderstood and fighting with parents, feeling left out of a group of friends, feeling rejected by a person he/she had a crush on, feeling all alone in a meaningless world, etc. Spend some time just imagining what these years may have been like for your partner: both the good times and the difficult times."

- "Next, imagine what early adulthood may have been like for your partner: possibly going away to college or moving out of the house and feeling the exhilaration and fear that comes with moving out of the family home. Imagine the excitement of the first job and/or first college classes and the

(continued)

(continued)

many challenges that come from being out on your own for the first time. Imagine the excitement of falling in love and the heartbreak that comes when things do not work out. Spend some time imagining the possible ups and downs of your partner's early adult years."

- "Now, imagine your partner in his/her adult years: the years that have gone and years yet to come. Be aware that if your partner works, there is the excitement and hope that comes with starting a new job and the sense of pride at a job well done. There are also the inevitable and ongoing challenges of job interviews, working with difficult bosses and coworkers, and having to leave a position. Also, imagine the time when your partner first started dating you—there was likely hope and excitement. Imagine the joys and challenges of your relationship from your partner's point of view. If your partner has children, you can imagine how exciting the arrival of a child was for your partner and also imagine the struggles that come with being a parent. If your partner has not had kids or chosen not to have kids, call to mind the emotions that may be involved with that: possible anticipation or loss. Spend some time imagining the many joys and sorrows of your partner's adult years, both those that you are aware of and those that you may not know about."
- "Now, imagine your partner at the end of his/her life: Imagine your partner is surrounded by the people who care most about him or her. Imagine that your partner knows that his/her time here is almost at its end and is reviewing his/her life, choices, moments of achievement, moments of shame, moments of joy, and moments of sadness. In this process, your partner feels deep gratitude for the love, beauty, and great experiences in life and also regret for poor decisions, hurting others, and missed opportunities. Take a moment to imagine what this process might be like for your partner and have great compassion for this deeper human experience that we must all ultimately face. Imagine the moment when your partner leaves this earth and how your partner will be missed."
- "Finally, take a step back and take in the fullness of your partner's life— from beginning to end. Reflect on its exciting beginning, the joys and sorrows along the way, and how it ends. Take a moment to reflect on how your partner's life has touched you and countless others, and how he/she has been touched by others and how the world was different because of your partner's presence. Take a moment to be thankful for the gift of your partner's presence in this world."

After this intense exercise, allow each person to take some time to turn their gaze away and experience their emotions related to this experience. Then invite each to share what this experience was like for them or if they have new way of perceiving their relationship and partner.

Love Dialogues

Over the past century, couples in Western civilization have come to expect love relationships to provide fulfillment in virtually all areas of life: emotional, psychological, sexual, financial, familial, social, and basic survival. Although these have become "normal" elements of a "good relationship," at no time in history has it been the norm that marriage has fulfilled these many and diverse needs (Schnarch, 1991). Furthermore, research in the twenty-first century indicates our circle of confidants and intimate others continues to decline, leaving us with little choice but to turn to our romantic partners for the nurturing and sense of belonging that our grandparents received from an entire village of concerned and involved others (Johnson, 2008). These sociological shifts put a tremendous pressure on love relationships and beg for reevaluation of what should be expected of them in the first place.

Mindfulness and acceptance practices provide therapists a foundation for helping clients to have productive discussions about more realistic and meaningful definitions and expectations of love and love relationships. A mindfulness perspective emphasizes that love involves fully being present with another in a spirit of compassion and acceptance. Once couples have become more stable, therapists can invite couples to explore how they want to define and "practice" love in their relationship.

Love Dialogues

Therapists can invite couples to have reflective dialogues on how they want to define and "practice" love using some or all of the following:

1. *In-session loving-kindness meditation*: Guide the couple in loving-kindness meditation in session (see above).
2. *Reflective dialogues on love*: After the meditation, invite the couple to explore how their experiences in the exercise can inform their understanding of love and how to love each other.

   - What is it like to "practice" sending loving kindness to your partner and others in this exercise? Does it change how you think about love to see it as a "practice?"
   - What was the quality of your presence like in this exercise and how does that compare with your everyday interactions with those you love? Are there ways to bring more of this sense of presence into your daily interactions?
   - How does your experience of sending love in this exercise compare to how you share love in your normal, daily life? Are there ways to do more of this in your daily interactions?

(continued)

(continued)

> • How do the compassion and kind thoughts you send in this exercise typically get expressed in everyday contexts? Are there ways you can express this more often or in other ways?
> • How does acceptance of who a person is relate to your understanding of love?
> • Do you believe is love more an emotion you feel or an action you decide to take? Or how do these two forms of love interrelate?
> • How can you bring more of the love, warmth, and compassion you experience in this exercise into your daily lives?
> • Moving forward, how do you want to define and practice love on a daily basis in your relationship?

Nonviolent Speech

Buddhism has cultivated a fierce commitment to peacemaking. Whether ordained or lay, devout Buddhist practitioners take multiple vows of nonviolence: they commit to not killing other beings, to not causing others pain, and to acting and speaking without violence (Hahn, 1997). They consider violent words and acts as similar, both needing to be diligently avoided. Rather than an idealist goal, they take this vow seriously and use mindfulness and acceptance practices to work daily on improving their ability to refrain from violent speech and action.

As couples make progress in therapy, introducing the concept of committing to—as individuals and as a couple—nonviolent speech may be helpful in having them redefine the expectations and culture of their relationship. *The key to nonviolent words is nonviolent thoughts.* Often, the tools that they used to help resolve initial conflict—mindfulness, loving-kindness meditation, listening deeply—can be repurposed for helping them to stop the rehearsal of negative interpretations of one's partner and instead generate a more compassionate and accepting view.

The primary mechanism most couples use for promoting nonviolent speech is to allow for pausing difficult conversations (see section "Mindful Pause and Reflection") and returning to them with a commitment to having a conversation that is respectful and loving. Each couple needs to examine their particular conflict patterns to determine how and where are the best pauses and "exits" from tense conversations as well as the best way to return to the subject from a loving attitude. Committing to nonviolent communication is a personal and lifelong practice that no one should feel forced into by either a therapist or a partner but one that is freely chosen and desired.

Options for Nonviolent Communication

Some options couples commonly use for nonviolent communication include:

- *Take a break*: When one feels anger or hurt rising, ask for a break from the conversation; the couple must agree to taking such a break before a heated moment.
- *Ask for a break*: If you are on the receiving end of a harsh comment, then gently ask for a break and return to the discussion at a later time.
- *Wait*: Wait to return to the discussion until both are calm and have reconnected with the commitment to nonviolent speech.
- *Silently reflect*: Rather than rehearse negative thoughts, a commitment to nonviolence involves shifting one's focus to compassion for and acceptance of the other by trying to imagine possible reasons and motivations for the other's actions or words; mindfulness and loving-kindness meditations can help shift gears.
- *Practice, practice*: Commit to the *practice* of nonviolent speech; know that it is a lifetime practice and that both will continue to develop and deepen over the years.

Practicing Together

As discussed in Chap. 6, couples experience many benefits from developing a regular practice together. Couples with such a practice in place can use it to help them when experiencing difficult times or conversations, often with benefits similar to being in a couples therapy session. In cases where such couples know that they are going to have a difficult conversation, they may find it helpful to practice mindfulness or loving-kindness meditations together, such as sitting and doing mindfulness meditation for 5–20 minutes before the conversation. In addition to the obvious benefits of calming themselves down, such practice has the effect of several other well-known strategies for reducing conflict:

- *"Do something different"*: As described classic family systemic approaches, inserting mindfulness prior to an anticipated argument is a form of "doing something different" and serves to interrupt the problem interaction pattern and creates opportunities for each person to alter their thoughts, behaviors, and feelings (Watzlawick, Weakland, & Fisch, 1974). Simply by interrupting the problem interaction pattern, new and better outcomes are more likely; the mindful pause (see above) can also work in this manner.
- *Relaxation response*: Because mindfulness invokes the relaxation response, practicing it before difficult conversations can be helpful in creating better outcomes and avoiding unproductive arguments. As noted earlier, Gottman (1999)

has identified that when one or both partner's stress response is triggered in during an argument and the pulse exceeds 100 beats per minute that the conversation is not likely to be productive. One reason for this is that the middle regions of the brain that specialize in identifying threats and danger are overactive and the higher centers of the brain that enable logical thought and empathy are less active. As you can imagine, the chances of a positive outcome are far less likely. Couples can therefore use mindfulness to get each person into a relaxed state, which will make it less likely—or at least take longer—to excite the stress response, which is known to not be a productive state for resolving couple conflict.

- *Greater awareness of emotion*: Mindful meditation before a difficult conversation can help couples gain greater awareness and insight into their emotional processes before engaging in a difficult topic and therefore may help them better express themselves. Such awareness can help them raise the issue in such a way that is more likely to resolve the conflict. For example, if a couple has had conflict over spending a large sum of money on a vacation, mindfulness practice before returning to discuss this issue could help the partners identify the less obvious meanings and motivations related to the trip and spending money, such as fulfilling a lifelong dream to see a particular spiritual place or feeling obligated to take the family on extravagant vacations as a way of being a "good provider."
- *Acceptance and compassion*: Mindfulness practices are grounded in a fundamental practice of acceptance of and compassion for what is. Thus, mindfulness practice can help couples connect with the deep sense of acceptance that is the heart of mindful practice. Such an acceptance practice is likely to soften the person in relation to the subject and be more willing to see it in a broader context. For example, if a couple has been struggling around in-law issues, mindfulness practice beforehand would likely help put the situation into the broader context—such as he wants to spend more time with his family because his parents' health is quickly going downhill—rather than fixate on the immediate struggle.

Mindful Sex and Intimacy

Mindful experience and sex therapy share a surprising parallel: although both on the surface appear to focus on immediate physical sensations, that is not the heart of the matter for either. In the case of mindfulness, the true focus is acceptance of one's experience; in sex, the key is the emotional and relational context. Thus, although mindfulness lends itself well to classic sex therapy exercises such as sensate focus techniques (Masters & Johnson, 1974), and mindful sensation exercises can be used to help couples with physical sexual concerns, a mindful perspective would instead concur with contemporary sex therapy approaches that emphasize the relational context as determining the conditions for sexual functioning (Gottman, 2011; Schnarch, 1991).

The typical approach to helping couples with sexual difficulties, such as low libido, premature ejaculation, or simply differences in sexual style would involve the following process:

1. *Acceptance*: As with everything else in life, a mindful first-step to sexual difficulties is to non-judgmentally accept what is: a difference in libido or sexual preferences, the body not responding as one would expect, etc. Because sexual issues are laden with intense shame in modern culture and confused with hyperbolic media images, cultivating acceptance can be extraordinarily difficult. Thus acceptance of sexual issues should be approached gently and with realistic expectations. The more frank and open a therapist can discuss sexual concerns, the easier it is for couples to accept where they are.

2. *Compassion*: After or along with acceptance, therapists can help couples work toward generating and expressing compassion for each person's unique form of suffering related to the sexual concerns. Heterosexual couples may have greater difficulty empathizing with their partners' struggles because each has different physiological experiences and gender role perspective. In contrast, same-sex couples who have a better understanding of the physical experience of their partner struggle instead with ill-defined roles, fluctuating acceptance of one's own sexuality, disapproval from significant others and religious institutions, as well as numerous other issues related to being a sexual minority. Slowing down these conversations and identifying the pertinent issues can help build compassion for the many of forms of suffering related to sex, sexual identity, and gender roles.

3. *Safety and trust*: As compassion is shared, couples experience and increase in safety and trust. For many couples, thoughtfully discussing sexual preferences, concerns, and desires is new territory; therapists can help them do so in a way that builds each partners sense of safety and trust.

4. *Collaboratively define the problem*: Ideally, without the use of modern diagnostic categories, therapists help couples to define the sexual issue(s) within the larger relational and emotional context. Common definitional concerns include the following themes:

   (a) *Emotional connection*: One or both not feeling emotionally safe and connected in the relationship.
   (b) *Anxiety*: One or both is anxious about needing to perform in a certain way to meet personal or partner expectations (real or imaginary).
   (c) *Avoiding communication*: One or both have been afraid to clearly communicate sexual needs or expectations
   (d) *External distractions*: Children, work, or other stressors leave one or both partners from putting energy into their relationship.
   (e) *Social norms*: Perceived social, gender, or sexual norms create anxiety or unrealistic expectations.
   (f) *Medical issues*: Medications or medical conditions that affect sexual functioning.

5. *Collaboratively develop a plan*: Once couples have discussed their sexual concerns and developed an understanding of what might motivate them, they can then develop a plan for how to address them. Mindfulness and acceptance practice offer some excellent options:

- *Mindful holding*: Hugging or holding each other mindfully with compassion and acceptance for several minutes allows both to feel physically and emotionally safe and physically relaxed.
- *Mindful sensing*: Either individually or together, mindful attention can be paid to any of the senses—touch, taste, smell, sound, or sight—allowing the mind to become fully absorbed in the present moment with the sensation; this practice can then be transferred to sexual encounters.
- *Mindful touching*: Similar to sensate focus exercises, couples can spend time touching each other, either with their hands or with tactile objects such as a feather or silk scarf. Depending on the nature of their concerns, couples can do this with their clothes on in a nonsexual environment or without clothes as a form of foreplay.
- *Mindful sex*: Finally, mindful attention can be used during sex encounters to enhance the experience of pleasure and emotional connection during sex.
- *Paradox*: Sexual function and expectation often respond well to paradoxical injunctions, such as "we are not going to have intercourse, just foreplay," especially if performance anxiety is an issue.

Mindfulness Applications with Families

I have found that mindfulness is particularly elegant when used with families because the basic practices of being present and acceptance quickly remedy many of the common issues of families who seek professional assistance. Mindfulness provides a nonthreatening approach that relatively quickly reestablishes an emotional connection between parents and child without making parents feel judged by the therapist as "bad." Some of the options therapists have for working with families include:

- Mindful parent–child attunement
- Slowing to the present moment
- Out-the-door mindfulness
- Mindful puppet enactments
- Narrating *what is*
- "Rocking" mindfulness
- Mini-mindfulness and acceptance moments

In addition, many of the practices described for couples above can also be used with families, notably:

- Loving-kindness meditation
- The mindful pause

Therapists wanting to work more extensively with young children may enjoy reading more about the work of Greenland (2010) and Willard (2010).

Parent–Child Attunement

Interpersonal neurobiology researchers and theorists emphasize the importance of secure parent–child relationships, not only in the first 3 years of a child's life but throughout childhood and into adulthood (Schore, 1994; Siegel, 1999). We now know that not only is a secure parent–child bond essential emotionally for a child, but it is also required for optimal development of the brain, sense of self, and the ability to regulate emotion. To put it in bare-bones terminology, a parent must establish a secure attachment with their child for that child to develop well at all levels: physical, emotional, and psychological. Unfortunately, contemporary living makes this challenging. Furthermore, in contrast to couple relationships, the parent has most of the burden for establishing a safe bond with the child. By enhancing a person's ability to be emotionally present with the self and in relationships, mindfulness provides an invaluable tool for parents needing to improve their abilities to become consistently emotionally available and attuned to their children.

Mindfulness practices such as the ones described below provide parents with a wealth of options for learning how to slow themselves down enough to become more emotionally attuned with their child. Many parents do this naturally with young children because interacting with infants and toddlers routinely demands it. But, as children become better able to conceptualize and "live apart" from their experiences, being present is not as effortless. Mindfulness can play a key role in helping parents remain emotionally available to their children either through more formal or informal practices.

Therapists can use all of the practices described in this section as well as elements of *facilitated mindful communication* and *listening deeply* above to help parents attune to their young children and help parents with older children to become more attuned to each other. With children, attunement often takes a more nonverbal form. To help parents become more comfortable with less verbal forms of attunements, therapists can encourage parents to "follow their child's lead," by simply noticing what the child is doing and joining in (Wieder & Greenspan, 2003); this can happen in action or in words. When parents allow themselves to be led by the child's thoughts, interests, and impulses, this enables them to mindfully experience their child's inner world and attunement naturally follows. Although following the child's lead has a more verbal form with adolescents, it is an equally valuable relational practice during typically turbulent years.

Slowing to the Present Moment

If you really want to upset the applecart of contemporary families with school-aged children, suggest they do *less*: fewer music lessons, sports teams, play dates, tutoring sessions, volunteer activities, movies, gadgets, games, etc. Most parents act as though you have asked them to permanently maim their children, if not physically, at least in terms of their changes of going to a decent college. But *doing* less and *being* more is often the key to helping families that come to therapy. Many of whom—with the absolute best of intentions—have fallen prey to the modern parenting trap of doing, doing, doing—always on the go—with little time to actually *be* together, to be emotionally present with one another. Many believe that if they do not sign their child up for tons of activities the child's future will be in jeopardy. Alternatively, others feel great pressure to work—with some having more real survival pressures than others—leaving little energy or time to be with their children. In either case, helping families slow down enough to be present with one another can be a powerful first step to reconnecting as a family. Often, I start this process of reconnecting even before trying to "address" the presenting problem because this more general change can dramatically reduce the severity of many problems families experience.

Slowing Down to the Present Moment

Therapists can help families to be more present with one another using a two-step process:

1. *Map the day*: Begin by having the family describe their typical school day, from the early morning routine to the afternoon and evening routine. Identify the typical points of conflict and connection.
2. *One small change*: As family routines can be difficult to change due to the number of moving parts, I recommend families start with one small change, such as saying grace or out-the-door mindfulness (see below). Continue working with the family each week to find ways to make these moments work and to expand the time they are emotionally present with each other during the week. Common examples include:

   - Saying grace before dinner (1–2 minutes)
   - Ritualized sharing about the day at dinner (5–10 minutes)
   - Bedtime routine that is calm and relaxing for all (20–30 minutes)
   - A sit-down breakfast (20–30 minutes)
   - Taking a walk (10–20 minutes)
   - Playing with a pet (2–10 minutes)
   - Playing a game or sport together (10–30 minutes)
   - Dancing, singing, or making music together (2–30 minutes)
   - Out-the-door mindfulness (1–5 minutes; see below)

How slow does a family need to go? I believe families should work at slowing down until each member feels safely connected with the others and does not feel overwhelmed most of the time. In some cases, once relational bonds have healed and conflict has subsided, they may be able to add more activities into their schedule. In other cases, families were living in overdrive and find that a slower pace was most of what they needed in the first place.

Out-the-Door Mindfulness

A 2–5-minutes practice before leaving the house, *out-the-door mindfulness* evolved from my work with families who had a child diagnosed with ADHD and wanted to use mindfulness to increase the child's focus at school and reduce or avoid the use of medication. This practice involves mindfulness as a family and is an elegant example of real-world mindfulness.

For most families, trying to get out the door is a trial on everybody: parents are barking orders at kids who seem less than interested. At the very end, everyone is in a mad rush to brush teeth, find homework, grab their bags, sneak a bite, and jump in the car. Somewhere between the front door and the stepping on the gas pedal is an ideal moment for practicing mindfulness together to quiet the stress response and get everyone in the right frame of mind for learning, working, and enjoying their day. I have families pick a place and time in the routine and commit to doing it even if they will be 2–5 minutes late to wherever they are going; it is hardest to get the parents' agreement, but most will agree to being 2 minute late, especially if they believe it will help their child focus more in school, at practice, or other lesson.

I have frequently seen this seemingly simple shift in the routine dramatically transform a family's interactions not only in their morning routine but throughout the week. Both children and parents report that this practice clams everybody so that not only the ride to school but the minutes and hours before it also become peaceful and harmonious. Apparently, the anticipation of practicing mindfulness helps many families change their tenor and, in fact, the culture of the family changes after several weeks. Parents find it easier to get out of the panicky rush mode, and children find it easier to calm themselves and center. As one child summed it up when I asked him if he noticed any difference with this practice, "Yes. My mom is in a much better mood, which makes me enjoy talking with her on the way to school." Most families report that conflict almost effortlessly ends because "we are all in a good mood." I have personally found that this works for me as a professional too and is a great addition to self-care (see Chap. 10).

Mindful Puppet Enactments

An intervention originally developed with inspiration from Andersen's (1991) reflecting team practices, puppet enactments offer an excellent opportunity for reflecting on a situation from multiple perspectives (Gehart, 2007). These creative enactments allow children tell their stories in a medium that is familiar to them: play. Many children actually seem to find it easier to discuss emotional difficulties with puppets or figures that enable them to "see" the story rather than having to imagine it in their minds. If the puppets in a therapist's office are enticing enough, many teens and adults also enjoy telling their stories in a more playful way, often helping to engage more reluctant participants. Additionally, puppets allow for the unusual option of having family members to "switch" roles in the problem scenario, offering an excellent opportunity to develop greater compassion and acceptance of another's perspective.

Mindful Puppet Enactments

Puppet enactments can be used in numerous ways to share a problem story, develop compassion for others' experiences, and identify new ways of relating. Therapists can select from the options below based on client need and interest. Each of the options below begins by identifying the cast of characters by having each person choose a puppet to represent himself or herself. If necessary, include additional puppets to represent key players, such as a teacher or friend and assign a person to play that role.

Options

- *Mindful replay*: Invite the family to replay a particular incident or demonstrate a typical relational pattern. Pause them while telling the story to have them mindfully reflect upon and share their experiences:

    - What is your puppet thinking and feeling in this moment?
    - Is your puppet feeling safe in this situation right now?

- *Switch roles*: An excellent option for increasing compassion and acceptance of others, the family can then be invited to switch roles and go through the role play again, this time reflecting on the experience of another person.
- *Worse ending*: Counterintuitive to most therapists, having the family role play how it could have gone worse is a powerful intervention, especially if members are feeling hopeless or critical. This worse example helps cultivate a sense of appreciation for what is going right.
- *Better ending*: A more conventional approach, having the family act out preferred endings provides exploration and practice of new responses, which is critical for young children but is surprisingly helpful for parents who often have entrenched patterns of interacting with their children.

For example, one mother I worked with complained that she and her son fought every morning before school and that she had to nag him every step of the way—not an uncommon problem. The 7-year-old son, Danny, insisted that he was tired and couldn't move as fast as his mother wanted. So, I invited Danny and his mother, Susan, to show me what happens using the puppets in my office. They took some time to pick out the right ones—actually had a few giggles with various options— and then I directed them to put their puppets in their beds asleep. Since the mother was always up first, I had her wake up her puppet, a butterfly, and do her whole routine that she typically does before Danny got up. Danny was a little surprised to learn about all the things she did: take a shower, get dressed, put on her makeup, let the dog out, feed the dog, start coffee, and make breakfast. Meanwhile, Danny's dragon was snoring away: I made sure we checked in with him while mom's butterfly was getting ready. Throughout the enactment, I had them take a moment to pause and reflect upon the thoughts, feelings, and sensations each was experiencing in the enactment to encourage a mindful perspective.

Then, it was time for the butterfly to wake the dragon. The dragon definitely resisted, and the butterfly became more and more persistent. The tug-of-war continued the entire time until they got into the car. I had them stop at several points in this interaction to describe the repetitive interaction pattern and to reflect up on the in-moment experiencing of each in the drama.

Then, I suggested that they *reverse* roles, so that the son was the butterfly and the mother was the dragon. I had Danny wake the butterfly and do its morning rituals. When it came time to wake the dragon, the dragon really, really didn't want to get up. Danny became quite frustrated, and I reminded him that he knew a lot about how dragons think and like, so maybe he could come up with some other ideas for how to help him enjoy waking up. Danny became creative, turning on the dragon's favorite cartoons downstairs to lure him down and cooking eggs, which he knew he could not resist. At the end, I had each reflect on the inner relational experiences from the new roles, which they used in the following weeks to change their morning routine.

Narrating What Is: Narrating the Self

A rare point of agreement between philosophers and scientists, our sense of self is created through *narratives*, the stories we tell ourselves about who we are (Gergen, 1991, 1999; Siegel, 1999). This process begins in the first years of life with parents and caregivers who narrate and describe for children their own and others mental experiences, such as intention, emotion, thought, and inner dialogue (Siegel, 1999). For example, "Michael is feeling sad right now because he does not want his friend to leave. Luis is also sad right now because he has to leave. But, both Michael and Luis will have fun tonight eating dinner with their families and telling them about what they did while playing together today. Both will also look forward to each other next time to play together."

Like it or not, aware of it or not, parents profoundly shape their children's sense of self and understanding of their inner worlds by how they relate to their children's and their own emotion and thought processes. Recently, psychologists such as John Gottman and others have emphasized the importance of teaching parents emotional coaching skills (Gottman, 1999) to promote their children's emotional intelligence (Goleman, 2005). The key to successfully coaching or guiding their child's inner dialogue is parents' ability to calmly observe their own internal processes, which is facilitated through mindfulness and acceptance practices that parents can do formally through regular practice or with the help of a therapist using facilitated mindful communication and similar interventions that help children and their parents make coherent sense of their inner lives.

Expanding upon the practice of emotional coaching, the process of *narrating what is* not only helps children become more aware of their emotions but also helps them to see that from one's interpretation of and relation to emotions, thoughts, motivations, expectations, relationships, and actions the "self" emerges. Young children developmentally require someone to help them do this, while older children and adults generally benefit from someone to help them bring greater coherence to their stories about what just happened and, more specifically, their identity as it emerges from their narratives. This process begins in therapy but should ideally continue at home, with parents helping children to narrate what is in their daily lives.

The key to this process is *narrative coherence*: coherently putting the story together from the perspective of the person speaking in such a way that his/her emotions, actions, thoughts, decisions, and plot development make sense to the others who are listening (Anderson, 1997). This practice is grounded on the assumption that *everyone's internal world makes sense to them*, even if they cannot quickly put it into words. Even a person diagnosed with schizophrenia "makes sense," but it is a reality that is only shared by one. In contrast, most people share *elements*—but only elements—of their definition of what makes "sense" with persons from their family (a micro-culture) and from the ethnic, national, gender, sexual, religious, social, linguistic, occupational, and other cultural groups of which they are a part. Although we may have many similar ways of interpreting the world with these others, each person's particular system for making meaning is unique.

Narrating *What Is*

Therapists can use the following steps to help each family member narrate "what is" for them related to a problem interaction. Parents can use this same process at home for daily interactions.

- *Take a not knowing position*: Narrating what is begins by not knowing and not assuming anything because it is based on the premise that each person constructs his/her own reality and thus has their own unique interpretational logic.
- *Listen curiously*: As the speaker shares his/her story, the listener attends curiously to "interpretations" and "internal logic" that link together each element of the story.
- *Ask questions to "make sense" from the speaker's perspective*: As the story unfolds, ask to clarify the meanings and internal logic that make the story

---

(continued)

(continued)

"make sense" in the speaker's world, not by any external source of reason. For example, if the speak starts by saying, "I went to the park today," the curious listener asks about the motivation for going to the park, the person's expectations for what would happen, who was involved to make it happen, etc.

• *Put it together*: At the end, the listener can help retell the story with the internal logic, assumptions, meanings, and interpretations added to link each element together so that the story "makes sense" to others, even if they do not agree with it.

• *Reflect*: Finally, take some time to reflect and talk about the speaker's and other's thoughts about how the story "makes sense" from the speaker's position.

   – What stands out the most in the story?
   – What has the most meaning to you in this story? What has the least?
   – What was most surprising (often the speaker has not put the internal logic of their world into words)?
   – Are there parts you wish were different? How?
   – Are there other ways you might interpret the situation? Do others have a different perspective that you are already aware of? What are some of the other possible ways of looking at the situation?

So often what happens in families is that the parents have already decided that the child's approach to making sense of their world is "wrong" or "unrealistic" (which it often is from an adult's perspective), and so they do not even try to understand from the child's vantage point. However, such understanding is prerequisite to helping children make coherent sense of their worlds and selves. As any parent knows, simply giving children or teens a more "reasonable" way to make sense of what is happening rarely helps. Nonetheless, many parents continue trying because they do not know another way. What children need is assistance in interpreting their world, and in cases, a bridge from where they are to more useful ways of interpreting what is happening. Therapists can help parents to use the above process at home to more successfully communicate with their children.

"Rocking" Mindfulness Practice for Children

Teaching young children mindfulness practices requires a bit of creativity. In many ways, children enter into a mindful state much easier than adults because they don't have the intellectual capacity to live entirely separate from the present moment. As they grow though, learning mindfulness techniques can help them consciously maintain their natural abilities to live in the moment. This also creates a great opportunity for parents and children to meditate together.

My favorite mindfulness meditation for children involves "rocking" a stuffed animal to sleep and was developed by Greenland (2010) and her associates at Inner Kids Foundation, an organization dedicated to teaching mindfulness practices to children. A simple yet effective approach that allows children to practice mindfulness to help center and calm themselves, "rocking" mindfulness meditation involves lying down and putting a stuffed animal on the belly and then mindfully watching as the animal is gently rocked as the belly rises and falls with the breath. For most kids, this is a fun and familiar task: to finally have the chance to rock someone else to sleep. It also naturally invites a quiet and calm demeanor, especially if the child has a well-established bedtime routine that helps him/her wind down.

To do this, the child and parent(s) should lie on their backs with a beanbag or stuffed animal that will stay in place for this "rocking" meditation. The therapist can guide them with the following words or their own preferred narration:

Rocking Meditation

- *Positioning*: Lie on your back in a comfortable position, using pillows if they help. Take a moment to feel what the floor feels like under your body. Now notice how your belly rises and falls as you breathe. It does this naturally, without you doing anything at all.
- *Placement of the animal*: When you are ready, put the stuffed animal in the middle of your belly (note: beanbag animals work best because they are least likely to slip).
- *Notice*: Notice how your animal rises and falls with your natural breath. You do not need to change your breath at all. It happens all by itself. And your little friend is now being rocked gently to sleep by the natural rise-and-fall of your breath.
- *Narrate*: As you breathe in, your belly fills with air, and your animal rocks up; as you breath out, your belly empties and your animal rocks down. You don't need to do anything extra; it all happens naturally.
- *Rock to sleep*: Take a few moments to simply observe your animal as it is rocked to sleep, watching it rise and fall with your natural breath.
- *Closing observations*: Before we finish up, I invite you to take a moment to notice how your breathing is now. Is it the same or different from when you started—is there more space between breaths or are the breaths deeper? Notice your body. Is it the same or is something different—do you feel more relaxed, achy, or tired? Notice your mind. Is it the same or different— is it calmer, clearer, or more relaxed? Note to what has happened in the room. Are people the same or different—quieter or calmer? Just notice what you are experiencing right now.

Rocking meditation is a great option for family practice because both parents and young children can meaningfully participate in mindfulness together.

Mini-mindfulness and Acceptance Moments

More than techniques, mindfulness and acceptance are *attitudes* and *values* that shape how families relate to their daily life and experiences. Once families have made progress with mindful communication and other practices, they can begin to identify possibilities to putting mini-mindfulness and acceptance moments in to their everyday routines. More so than individuals or couples, families with children are a tightly scheduled lot: school, soccer practice, music lessons, homework, and bedtime tend to set the rhythm in most homes. Scheduling small moments of mindfulness and acceptance into this well-orchestrated routine can have a profound effect on a family because it engages all members in a consistent practice, thus dramatically redefining the micro-culture that families establish through their regular routines.

Identifying ways to integrate mindfulness and acceptance into the family routine is usually a fun process in which all members take an active role. Ideally, families come up with their own unique ideas based on what is learned in session. Mindful moments are most easily integrated into activities the family is already doing: getting up, going to school, eating dinner, and preparing for bed. For these to be successful, they need to be short or, better yet, not take longer than what they are already doing.

Some common ones involve:

- *Mindful weather check*: Standing outside (or put your hand out the window in northern climes) for a few moments to mindfully experience the sensations of air temperature, the breeze, the sun, or the rain; a fun way to start the day as a family and, more practically, decide what to wear.
- *Ride or walk to school*: On the way to school, each person can identify one thing he/she can do to make the day better for themselves AND for someone else as a compassion practice.
- *Ride or walk from school*: Narrating "what was" (see above) and make coherent sense of the day, practicing compassion and acceptance for self and others.
- *Mindful grace*: Saying grace or a prayer before dinner that invites mindful experience, compassion, and/or acceptance.
- *Mindful bites*: Spending the first 2 minute of dinner mindfully eating in silence.
- *Dinner conversation*: Begin dinner conversation by having each member identifying 1–3 moments of mindfulness, compassion, acceptance, or other positive experiences during the day.
- *Gratitude practice*: Bringing mindful attention to the things that were enriching during the day, which can happen at dinner or bedtime; practicing gratitude has been correlated with greater levels of happiness (Seligman, 2002).

- *Mindful bath time*: Taking the first few minutes of bath time to feel the water, bubbles, and other sensations of being in the tub.
- *Bedtime story telling*: Retelling the stories of the day in ways that practice acceptance, mindfulness, and compassion for self and others.
- *Bedtime blessings or prayers*: Using a religious prayer or mindful gratitude and compassion, families can end the day taking a mindful moment to appreciate the good that happened, have compassion for the challenges, and accept that all of those things together constitute the beauty and preciousness of life.

Respecting Their Ways

I find it helpful to think of each couple or family as a unique mini-culture, with its own set of values and "goods" to which they aspire. As excited as I am about mindfulness, acceptance, and compassion practices, I am careful not to force these ideas on people but instead invite them to see if these have meaning for them. Most find at least some of these practices very useful and, quite frankly, more engaging than what they have experienced in therapy before because they allow for a more proactive and engaged approach to problems. Most likely due to the speed of modern life, many couples and families find these practices quite relevant and immediately helpful in relieving the stress and pressures they are experiencing for long enough to have hope that things indeed can and will be better.

Part III
Training and Self-Care

Chapter 9
Training and Supervision

A Better Way

One of my more puzzling experiences as a new supervisor doing live supervision involved watching trainees—whom I knew were bright and competent and therefore had fully understood what I just explained to them—return to session after a midsession break and fail to remember anything I had said or even to recall the basic skills demonstrated numerous other times in class. The trainees were intelligent, knew what to do, had exhibited the exact skill in class role-plays, but went "blank" when in front of a client. Over time I realized what was happening: these trainees became anxious, their stress responses kicked in, and they could no longer access the things they "knew" because that information was stored in the higher regions of their prefrontal cortexes, which are nearly inaccessible under high stress.

Unaware of this dynamic, many trainees initially complain that they do not learn enough in class to prepare them for seeing clients. In response, I now explain how the anxiety of seeing clients for the first time affects their abilities to use what they learn in class; thus, even 240 units of classes would not prepare them to see clients without anxiety. Furthermore, I have observed another dynamic as well. Even if a trainee were to remain calm, many clinical skills can only be learned in real world settings. I compare this to learning how to swimming: even if you had an Olympic coach explain to you in a dry classroom how to swim, you would still do most of your learning in the pool. The same seems to be true of therapy: educators can lecture ad nauseam (and many do), but the pivotal learning moments happen with actual clients in the therapy room.

Because it directly affects the stress response, mindfulness holds the potential to enable trainees to manage their anxiety so they can use more of what they learned in class as well as learn more quickly in vivo with clients. This chapter will briefly review how educators in several health fields have begun using mindfulness to train professionals. Then, the majority of the chapter will provide a detailed curriculum for teaching mindfulness as part of clinical preparation and training, including specific meditation exercises and assignments.

D.R. Gehart, *Mindfulness and Acceptance in Couple and Family Therapy*,
DOI 10.1007/978-1-4614-3033-9_9, © Springer Science+Business Media New York 2012

Why Teach Professionals-in-Training Mindfulness?

Educators consistently identify two distinct premises for teaching mindfulness to professionals-in-training:

1. *Reducing trainees' personal stress* that hinders performance and overall well-being (Bruce, Manber, Shapiro, & Constantino, 2010; Rimes & Wingrove, 2011).
2. *Teaching core relational and therapeutic skills*, including the following:

   - *Paying attention*: Helping trainees stay focused during session even when anxiety is provoked (Fulton, 2005).
   - *Attentive listening*: Improving trainee's ability to listen to what clients are saying from a not-knowing, nonassuming position (Shafir, 2008).
   - *Attunement and empathy*: Increasing trainees' abilities to become empathically attuned with clients by developing self-attunement (Bruce et al., 2010; Rimes & Wingrove, 2011; Shapiro & Izett, 2008).
   - *Therapeutic presence*: Providing a means to help trainees develop therapeutic presence more directly and quickly (Gehart & McCollum, 2008).
   - *Affect tolerance*: Enabling trainees to remain emotionally present and nonanxious when clients express strong emotion and when they themselves begin to feel anxious in session (Fulton, 2005; Rimes & Wingrove, 2011).
   - *Practicing acceptance*: Reducing the natural tendency to judge others or circumstances and instead accept and have compassion for what is (Fulton, 2005; Rimes & Wingrove, 2011).
   - *Equanimity and the limits of helpfulness*: Developing an ability to move with the ups and downs of life and therapy and to also accept that therapy is not a panacea for the many forms of suffering that are inherent to living (Fulton, 2005).
   - *Learning to see the process of construction*: Understanding how the mind "constructs" the problems it sees and knowing how to interact with this natural process to help resolve client concerns (Fulton, 2005).
   - *Exposing inappropriate personal needs*: Increasing awareness of how the therapist's mind can become overly and inappropriately attached to the process and outcome of therapy as way to boost self-esteem and self-image (Fulton, 2005; Rimes & Wingrove, 2011).

To support the proposition that mindfulness can meaningfully contribute to the training of health professionals, educators have conducted several pilot and controlled studies with a range of health professionals-in-training, including physicians, therapists, and nurses (Bruce et al., 2010; Cohen-Katz, Wiley, Capuano, Baker, & Shapiro, 2005; Epstein, 2003a, 2003b; Jain et al., 2007; Shapiro, Astin, Bishop, & Cordova, 2005; Shapiro, Brown, & Biegel, 2007; Shapiro & Carlson, 2009; Shapiro, Schwartz, & Bonner, 1998). These studies consistently support the effectiveness of mindfulness to (a) reduce stress, depression, anxiety, rumination etc. and (b) increase compassion, empathy, self-compassion, and positive affect experiences. Furthermore, Rimes and Wingrove (2011) found that although all trainees benefited in terms of less rumination and greater empathy, only first-year trainees had significant decreases in stress, underscoring the potential additional benefit for practicing mindfulness in the first year of clinical training.

Additionally, preliminary research has begun to link therapist mindfulness training to measurable client outcomes. In a double-blind study conducted in Germany, therapists-in-training were randomly assigned to either the treatment group that was instructed to practice mindfulness Zen meditation regularly or to a control group for a 9-week period. The clients of therapists practicing mindfulness reported greater improvement on Symptom Checklist (SCL-90-R) as well as other measures of clinical change (Grepmair et al., 2007). Similarly, in a study that examined therapist *trait* mindfulness, Padilla (2011) found that clients of therapists who scored higher on the Kentucky Inventory of Mindfulness Skills reported better therapeutic alliance and had better therapeutic outcomes on most measures. These studies on client outcome—in addition to the well-documented effects of stress reduction and increased compassion for self and others—provide empirical support for the growing interest in teaching mindfulness practices to professionals-in-training.

Contemplative and Mindfulness Pedagogy

Teaching mindfulness fits with newer contemplative and mindful pedagogical paradigms (Bush, 2010; Lief, 2007; Shapiro, Warren, & Astin, 2008; Siegel, 2007). Rather than teach critical thinking based on logic and analysis, contemplative pedagogy focuses on teaching *reflective thinking*, a second-order or meta-cognitive process that involves thinking about thinking, learning, emotion, and related processes. Mindful pedagogical paradigms emphasize the openness to novelty (not knowing), implicit awareness of more than one perspective (a constructivist position), alertness to distinction (mindful awareness), context sensitivity (mindful observation), and present-moment orientation.

Contemplative teaching strategies use mindfulness and other present-moment awareness practices to help students observe their mental and/or emotional processes *during* the learning process. There are several contemplative pedagogy strategies that can be integrated into all types of courses in mental health training programs:

- *Randomly ringing a bell*: A signal such as a bell can be randomly rung or rung on a schedule to signal a time for everyone in the class to spend a minute or so to simply become mindful of what they are experiencing in mind, heart, and body. Then, the class conversation resumes, generally without a need to comment upon the pause. Obviously, to the person speaking—often the instructor—the interruption can be abrupt and even challenging—but it generally enhances the quality of the learning experience.
- *Instructor mindfulness*: Instructors can bring mindfulness to the room by doing a brief moment of mindfulness practice prior to entering the classroom, beginning class, and/or at opportune moments throughout the class. Much like the impact

that the therapist's presence in therapy sessions, the quality of presence that the instructor brings to class can dramatically change the class climate, quality of student participation, and the flow of class.

- *Contemplative assignments*: In addition to or instead of assigning critiques of research or analysis of theories, instructors can create assignments designed to guide students in meaningful contemplative reflection on their readings, class dialogues, or online postings. For example, the assignment might involve mindfully describing their internal dialogues about a particular lesson and identifying the source of the various perspectives, opinions, and arguments that were part of their thinking process.
- *Ethical or other dilemmas*: Inviting students to reflect on ethical or other challenging dilemmas provides fertile ground for engaging in contemplation. Such exercises are easily integrated into courses on professional ethics; for example, students can be asked to silently contemplate and write about a particular dilemma in class before discussing it with others to ensure that each takes time in the contemplative process.
- *Reflecting on the learning process*: Assigning students to reflect on their personal learning process, how they respond to specific learning activities, and how they learn best can also increase their capacity for personal reflection and awareness related to learning and relational interactions.

Mindfulness in Clinical Training

Also described elsewhere (Gehart & McCollum, 2008; McCollum & Gehart, 2010), Eric McCollum and I teach mindfulness as part of our clinical training of master's level therapists and counselors with the intention of helping them develop therapeutic presence (also see Chap. 4). We have been requiring regular mindfulness and contemplative practices of our students for almost a decade, refining our teaching methods and studying outcomes along the way (McCollum & Gehart, 2010). Students report numerous personal, clinical, and relational benefits from the curriculum, including increased ability to be present with clients, less inner chatter in session, increased compassion for clients and self, improved sleep, and increased sense of calm in session.

Below, I will outline key elements of the curriculum:

- Overview: when, where, who, and how of the curriculum
- Readings and resources
- In-class lecture and discussion
- In-class meditations
- Online modules
- Mindfulness practice
- Journals and logs
- Building community
- Walking the talk

Curriculum Overview

When: Timing the Introduction to Mindfulness

Ideally, therapists-in-training can be introduced to mindfulness prior to or simultaneously with seeing clients for the first time, generally early in training; preliminary research indicates there may be additional benefits of reducing stress at this time (Rimes & Wingrove, 2011). If possible, including mindfulness in a two-semester course with the same teacher and students can significantly deepen the learning and practice. However, most students who have begun applied training in the field are generally eager to learn mindfulness at any point in their training.

Where: Class Choice and Size

Although it can also be taught in larger lecture classes, the opportunity for more direct instructor-student contact and intimate settings in supervision or other small class allows for more individualized mentoring and guidance. A minimum of 10–15 hours of class should be dedicated to mindfulness training.

Who: Instructor Experience

Much like learning how to do therapy, learning to practice mindfulness requires a certain amount of mentoring and guidance from a more experienced practitioner. Thus, the instructor wanting to teach mindfulness in class should have a well-established meditation practice for at least a year, ideally much longer. The instructor can then provide meaningful guidance in the numerous struggles that come with learning to practice mindfulness regularly.

How to Introduce Mindfulness

As mindfulness can be taught and practiced in many ways, the "how" of introducing mindfulness depends greatly on the learning context. Some important issues to consider:

- *Making it relevant*: Students are more motivated to explore and practice mindfulness if the instructor makes it highly relevant in their everyday clinical work and personal lives. Thus, when introducing mindfulness practice to students, instructors can emphasize that it will help them become better therapists in several ways:
  - Improve their ability to cope with the stress of seeing new clients
  - Enable them to develop a sense of therapeutic presence
  - Increase their sense of compassion and empathy

- Deepen their understanding of how the human mind works (and more importantly how it does *not*)
- Prepare them to be able to develop mindfulness as an area of specialty
- Improve their abilities to focus and retain information in session and while studying
- Enable them to be more present in their personal relationships
- Increase self-awareness and insight in clinical and personal situations
- Deepen their spiritual or religious practice (see "Cultural and Religious" section below)

Because mindfulness has the potential to help new professionals in numerous ways, most students are greatly motivated to give it a serious try for at least one semester. For the few who do not, instructors can collaboratively discuss other contemplate practices and additional options to find activities that help achieve the same or similar ends. The main goal is to help them develop a sense of therapeutic presence and successfully manage stress, and when instructors emphasize the ends more than the means, students are generally willing to find ways that work for them and to add such practices to their lives.

- *Cultural and religious/spiritual context*: When introducing mindfulness to an entire class of students, instructors need to carefully consider the cultural, religious, and spiritual dimensions of students' lives and strive to ensure that space is created to respect these. I have found that how a student perceives mindfulness fitting with their religious or spiritual traditions often predicts whether a student is highly motivated or resistant to the practice. For example, when teaching a traditional student body, more time needs to be spent addressing traditional forms of contemplative practice and how these compare with contemporary forms of mindfulness. In contrast, in programs attracting a more liberal students, instructors may find that the majority of their students have some form of contemplative training and that they can build upon the existing foundation.

When working with students who are closely affiliated with a religious tradition, such as Christianity, Judaism, or Islam, I encourage them to find the contemplative traditions within their faiths and draw upon these. For example, Catholic monks and nuns have had a long tradition of contemplative prayer based on the teachings of St. John of the Cross and Teresa Avila, both of whom were Christian mystics who used mindfulness techniques to directly encounter God (Keating, 2006). Similarly, Jewish contemplative traditions are regaining popularity with many synagogues now offering meditation and contemplative groups (Roth, 2009). Many religious students integrate mindfulness practice with their regular prayer time (either before or after) to deepen their religious practice. Additionally, many students who see themselves as more spiritual than religious have found mindfulness practice as a helpful means to deepen these practices. Thus, encouraging dialogue about integrating mindfulness with students' existing religious and spiritual traditions enables them to more firmly root mindfulness practice in their lives in ways that are likely to endure once class has ended.

- *Required or optional*: Mindfulness can be introduced as either a required or optional class activity. Because of the quickly growing research support for using mindfulness to develop skills necessary to be an effective therapist, I have university support when requiring mindfulness practice in clinical training courses. In contrast, in more traditional style "lecture" style classes, I typically make mindfulness practice optional for "extra credit" as a way to support students in deepening their practice and/or making it more widely available in our program because not all practicum or fieldwork instructors teach it. In such courses, I offer extra meetings and online modules on the mindfulness training, have students maintain weekly logs of their practice, and provide a final summary report.

Much to my own surprise, when I have allowed classes to collaboratively create the syllabus, something I do for advanced courses using a social constructionist pedagogy (Gehart, 2007), students have frequently insisted I make mindfulness a "required" assignment. They state that when practice is a class requirement, they are more likely to be consistent with their practice because they are accountable for it in a concrete way. Many report that they *want* to do it, but too often other priorities get in the way. Having it be an assignment enables them to keep it as a high priority.

Readings and Resources

Instructors have numerous readings to choose from to support students in developing their mindfulness practices. Rather than teach a single approach, I assign one or two required readings and then encourage students to explore variations that might be of particular interest to them, such as Christian contemplative prayer or Jewish meditation. Some of the many excellent resources available for consideration are:

- *A Mindfulness-Based Stress Reduction Workbook* (Stahl & Goldstein, 2010): A comprehensive workbook for the MBSR curriculum; includes a meditation CD.
- *Meditation for Dummies, 2nd edition* (Bodin, 2006): Although other academics may raise an eyebrow at the title, it provides a well-rounded approach to meditation that includes a wide range of religious and nonreligious meditation practices; includes a meditation CD.
- *Get Out of Your Mind and into Your Life: The New Acceptance and Commitment Therapy* (Hayes & Smith, 2005): This ACT workbook provides students with numerous written exercises that complement a mindfulness practice.
- *The Zen of Listening* (Shafir, 2000): A practical approach to using mindfulness listening in a wide range of business and professional contexts, including therapy.
- *The Mindful Therapist* (Siegel, 2010b): A thoughtful description of how therapists can use mindfulness and interpersonal neurobiology to inform their practice and intervene with clients.
- *Fully Present: The Science, Art, and Practice of Mindfulness* (Smalley & Winston, 2010): An engaging introduction to mindfulness based on UCLA's mindfulness program.

- *Peace is every step* (Hahn, 1992): A delightful and down-to-earth introduction to Buddhist mindfulness in everyday activity.
- *When Things Fall Apart* (Chödrön, 1997): An excellent introduction to a Buddhist approach to suffering.

Typically, I do not provide comprehensive lectures on these assigned readings, but instead have them reflect upon the readings in their online or other journal. The readings are there to support their practice and development of contemplative and mindfulness practices and used as each sees fit.

In-Class Lectures and Discussions

Approximately 10–60 minutes of each 3-hour class is devoted to lecture and discussion, with increasingly more time devoted to student–student and student–teacher dialogue as the semester progress. During this time, key points of the readings are explored and students are encouraged to actively discuss the personal and clinical applications. Often students share insights from the readings and examples of how mindful practice enabled them to better connect with or otherwise serve their clients. Additionally, each week time is devoted to discussing experiences and struggles with at-home practice. This time is used to not only impart information, but also create a sense of engaged community and unity in the learning process.

In-Class Meditations

Length of In-Class Practice

When teaching mindfulness, some form of mindful activity should be incorporated into each class meeting as part of the regular class time. Depending on the class, I include 10–60 minutes of time devoted to discussion and activities, with an average of 10–20 minutes of that time used for practice. During the first 6–8 classes when I first introduce the practice, I spend more time on mindfulness, allowing time for lecture, practice, and discussion. As students become more skilled, the practice time consists of 5–20 minutes of activity with less discussion.

Timing of Practice

Mindfulness can be successfully practiced at the beginning, middle, or end of class. The benefits of beginning a class with practice is that it is easiest to ensure class time is set aside; many students find that meditating at the beginning of class helps them transition from a hectic commute or work day and enable them to better focus in class. Ending a class with mindfulness works especially well when it is the last class of the night, enabling students to more fully relax (they don't have to worry about the upcoming class) and transition to their evening routine. Practicing in the middle of class is a good option if the time is divided into two separate lessons with mindfulness and an *intermezzo*.

Guided Meditations for In-Class

My colleague Eric McCollum and I (Gehart & McCollum, 2008) have used a wide variety of mindfulness and related contemplative practices in class to introduce students to a range of practices that they can use at home and/or to deepen their general understanding of mindfulness. These include (note: detailed instructions for each can be found at the end of this chapter or in the chapters designated below):

- *Mindfulness breath meditation* (see Chap. 6): Mindfulness meditation on the breath, the most common form of mindfulness; both guided and unguided versions are used in class.
- *Compassion meditation* (see Chaps. 8 and 10): Compassion meditation for self, intimate other, neutral other, enemy or difficult other, clients, and classmates.
- *Compassionate life review* (see Chap. 8): A partner meditation in which they imagine the beginning, current, and future life of their partners with its joys and sorrows.
- *Mindful eating*: A guided meditation in mindfully eating a raisin, grape, or chocolate that includes attention to all senses (see end of this chapter).
- *Mindful standing/walking*: A guided experience of bodily sensations while standing and walking (see Chap. 6).
- *Mindful yoga stretching*: A guided mindful practice on bodily sensations while doing very basic yoga stretching while in class chairs or in open space if it is available (see end of this chapter).
- *Mindful body scan*: Mindful attention to each part of the body without trying to relax or change anything (see Chap. 6).
- *Ice meditation* (on painful sensations): A guided mindful experience of holding ice and mindfully watching the mind respond to mild pain sensations (see end of this chapter).
- *Mindful listening*: An outdoor exercise to encourage mindfully noticing the noise in our everyday environment (see end of this chapter).
- *"Being seen" contemplative drama exercise*: An exercise in which each member of the class takes turns allowing themselves to be seen by the group (see end of this chapter).
- *Mindful daily activities*: Mindfully engaging in ordinary daily activities (Chap. 6).
- *Three-minute breathing space*: A brief meditation from MBCT that uses mindfulness to help a person regain their sense of focus and center during an otherwise hectic day (Chap. 6).
- *Stress reduction visualization*: A visualization exercise in which stressful situations are shrunk to a manageable size (see end of this chapter).

In many of the mindfulness-based group curricula, mindful eating and/or body scan are used to introduce the mindfulness before providing instruction in the more disciplined practice of breath meditation.

At-Home Mindfulness Practice

In addition to participating in classroom exercises, students are required to practice some form of regular mindfulness or contemplative practice at home to fully benefit from mindfulness training. Having instructed students and clients in mindfulness for almost a decade, I have had the most success starting with a minimal requirement of 2–5 minutes of practice 5 days per week based on the premise (that is now supported in emerging research; Rimes & Wingrove, 2011) that more frequent practice vs. fewer long sessions is better for long-term outcomes. Many of my students who had a practice at one time have reported that giving themselves permission to practice for only 5 minutes has made their practice far more regular than when they believed they had to practice for 20 minutes for them to meditate at all.

I encourage students to increase the length of practice once they feel motivated and ready to do so. The majority of students average 10 minutes or more per day within the first couple of months. Some students struggle with trying to maintain a regular 5-minutes practice, and I encourage them to explore the reasons and possible remedies. Although it is a course requirement, students do not lose points for not practicing regularly, only for not completing mediation journals and logs (see below).

Many students report that it helps to use a mantra, counting, or image to get started, and so I increasingly introduced breath meditation with greater discussion of such options:

- *Counting*: Counting each breath, beginning with one, going up to ten, and then beginning again with one; this is more effective than counting the total number of breaths, which can distract from the mindfulness practice itself.
- *Mantra*: Choosing a word or phrase that is repeated with each breath, such as "peace in/peace out," "Amen," or other phrase the practitioner finds calming.
- *Image*: Imagining oneself as either a solid mountain or lake that is calm beneath a busy surface or simply imaging one's thoughts to be bubbles that float away once attention is placed on them.

Mindfulness Journals, Blogs, and Logs

Journals

After surveying students and refining my teaching approach over the years, I have found that most students report that a reflective journal for the first 8 weeks of practice increases their awareness of what is and is not working for them and motivates them to find effective ways integrate mindfulness into their daily routines. Students turn in their journals and/or post their journals at regular intervals so that I can monitor their progress and adjust the class discussions and lectures as necessary. I use the following prompt for their journaling:

Each week during the first half of the semester you will complete a one-page journal entry (or blog) reflecting on your mindfulness or contemplative practice for the week. The journal must be typed and should address the following:

- Were you able to practice for at least 5 minutes five times in the week? If so, what helped you achieve this goal? If not, what were the impediments?
- Describe your mindfulness or contemplative practice: focus, timing, place, etc.
- Describe strategies you used for returning to your focus? Were you able to be patient with yourself during the practice?
- Describe any insights you may have gained from observing your mind.
- Describe any differences in your daily life that may have resulted from this practice.
- Describe any differences in your professional practice that may have resulted from this practice.
- Describe new insights, practices, or experiences related to developing therapeutic presence (Gehart & McCollum, 2008, p. 184).

Having experimented with both private pen-and-paper versions and online blog versions, I generally prefer the online journaling because of how it builds a sense of community and support for what is otherwise an isolating activity. Online blog journaling creates a sense of excitement and momentum as people share their successes and struggles with learning to practice regularly. These online journals provide a vivid sense of how very differently the same practice affects different people, even those who are in relatively similar situations in life (e.g., therapists in training). For example, some students journal about how their practice helps them improve their marriage or parenting, while others describe how they drive differently, and still others describe how chronic illnesses get better. It is also fascinating to learn about how each student finds very different strategies for practicing—some in the morning, others in their cars, some at work, and others at night. Furthermore, in the online forum students learn about many different barriers to practicing besides the ones with which they are personally struggling, providing a great learning experience for those who go on to use mindfulness with clients. By having access to intimate reports of how others successfully overcome barriers to mindfulness practices, trainees are better prepared to help future clients work through a wide variety of common issues in mindfulness practice.

Logs

Once students have finished the 8-week journaling process, we switch to doing weekly logs that are designed using solution-focused (i.e., no guilt) approach (see Chap. 6 for a copy of a sample log; download from www.dianegehart.com).

The logs include the 7 days of the week with boxes for noting length of practice or "day off" (rather than none), to honor the choice to not practice without judgment. The reflection questions for each are designed to help them set useful practice goals for the next week; these questions include:

- What strategies (i.e., time of day, place, timers, etc.) made it easiest to practice this week?
- What strategies (i.e., type of focus, refocus technique, etc.) helped to improve the quality of practice?
- Did I notice any benefits in daily life (patience, calmness, etc.) that seemed to come from my practice?
- What is one thing I can do next week to improve practice and maximize these benefits?

Online Modules

In addition to the in-class lectures and assigned readings, instructors may also provide students access to online modules that review the theory and practice of mindfulness for students to use at home to support their practices. When class time is tight, I use these modules to cover parts of the lecture (posted at www.dianegehart. com). A recent randomized control study conducted at the University of Vienna by Tobias Glück and his colleague in Zurich Maercker (2011) found that mindfulness practices can be successfully taught in a web-based format with gains maintained at the 3-month follow-up.

Building Community

When introducing mindfulness and contemplative practice into a curriculum, the most important element to cultivate is a sense of community that supports the practice. Education has historically been focused on the individual: learning is viewed as a personal endeavor rather than a community event. Although this pedagogical model dominates most universities and may still be an excellent choice for learning academic knowledge, a quick review of the mindfulness literature reveals that most evidence-based treatments are *group* treatments. Ironically—or perhaps because— it is one of the most solitary of human activities, meditation seems to be best learned in group settings. The sense of having community when practicing such a private activity provides encouragement and support that many new practitioners find invaluable when trying to find the motivation to practice and work through the associated challenges.

Ideally, a program can offer an entire class on mindfulness to create a strong sense of a practice community. However, many programs (including mine) are not in a position to add such a class and therefore mindfulness must be integrated into another class, such as fieldwork or practicum, requiring that class's sense of community related to mindfulness is developed in brief segments of face-to-face meeting time or online communities. The regularity of the in-class discussion— even if brief—is vital to generating a sense of continuity, especially in the early weeks. Additionally, online journals, blogs, and discussion forums are excellent ways for students to share more intimate experiences and exchange other resources to further these practices, adding the critical dimension of community in classes with limited time for mindfulness.

Walking the Talk

Perhaps the most challenging element of teaching mindfulness is walking the talk: consistently engaging students from a place of mindfulness and acceptance. I don't believe this means being a flawless icon of anxiety-free living each moment of each day or exuding Mother-Teresa-like compassion for all living beings. Instead, walking the talk requires that as you move through life, mindfulness is an ongoing part of the journey to find greater balance, heart, and insight. Personally, I find that it is an ebb and flow between times when mindfulness comes effortlessly and periods where it is a struggle to remember to practice, leave alone doing it. I share with students the ups and downs of a mindful lifestyle and explain that a lifetime of practice does not guarantee happily-ever-after tranquility and calm—because life continues to happen even if you practice regularly: there are losses, health problems, long hours at work, and difficult relationship periods. By demystifying how mindfulness is a lifestyle rather than a cure-all—because it does not stop suffering from coming into one's life—students can then approach mindfulness with greater commitment and more realistic expectations.

Detailed Description of In-Class Exercises

Mindful Eating: Chocolate Meditation

Mindfulness eating is typically introduced using raisins (Stahl & Goldstein, 2010), which is an excellent choice, along with grapes or almonds. Being a devotee of chocolate, however, I prefer to teach it with chocolate, which I find a more fun and engaging medium than raisins (Gehart & McCollum, 2008). Chocolates also have the significant advantage to having a wrapper, which I find allows for a richer experience that includes mindfully experiencing sound, sights, smells, taste, and tactile sensations. That said, having a no-chocolate option, such as almonds in a bag or raisins in a box, is often appreciated by at least one member of the audience.

Most mindfulness-based programs include a guided eating meditation in the first session to introduce the practice because it is one of the best easiest ways to demonstrate the principles of being present and how it can transform common, everyday experiences. There are many variations (also see Stahl & Goldstein, 2010), but I generally use the following outline:

Guided Eating Meditation

- Begin by picking up the object with your nondominant hand (note: generally easier to perceive things differently with this hand).
- Take a moment to observe this object as if you have never seen anything like it before. If it helps, you may want to imagine that you are an archeologist from the future or from an alien culture (mindful observation).
  - Notice its colors and how the light reflects off the object.
  - Notice its shape and contours and how the lines come together.
  - If there happen to be letters, try to observe them as if they were only shapes, simply noticing the lines and shapes of the letters without reading the word. Do the same with any images you may see.
  - Notice its texture and firmness: Is it hard or soft? (tactile mindfulness).
- Now take a moment to move it toward your nose and notice if you can perceive any scent. You may or may not. Try not to judge the sense as good or bad or let your mind wander to a memory associated with the scent, simply try and notice the scent as it is (olfactory mindfulness).
- Try moving the object from hand to hand and notice if it feels lighter or heavier in either hand. Just notice. There may or may not be a difference.
- In a moment, I am going to ask you to unwrap the object in your hand. As you do so, I want you to simply notice the sound that is made when you do. So please go ahead and unwrap the object now (allow for silence; mindful silence).
- Again, I want you to take some time to observe the object in your hand, noticing its color, how the light reflects off it, its shape, texture, and contours. Spend a few moments observing this object as if you had never seen anything like it before. Simply noticing what is there without judging it as beautiful or ugly; interesting or uninteresting, simply noticing.
- Again, move the object towards your nose and notice if you detect a scent. You may or may not. Simply notice without judging if it as good or bad; pleasant or unpleasant.
- In a moment, I am going to ask you to move the object toward your mouth, but I do not want you to take a bite yet. I want you to simply observe how your body, mind, and emotions react as you move it toward your lips.

(continued)

(continued)

- So, go ahead and move the object right up toward your lips. Notice how the body responds: Do you experience salivating or other bodily responses? What types of thoughts start to go through your head? What types of emotions or desires do you experience? Are you frustrated, excited, anticipating, dreading? Simply notice all of the thoughts, feelings, and bodily sensations that are arising in you right now? (Extra long pause).
- Go ahead and take a small bite, but try not to chew the object immediately. Allow it to roll around on your tongue, noticing if it tastes or feels different in different areas of your mouth. Simply notice the experience of having the object in your mouth.
- When you are ready, go ahead and slowly, mindfully chew the object, paying attention to the experience of doing so. Noticing the tastes, sensations, and flavors without trying to judge them as good or bad. Simply noticing.
- Now go ahead and continue to mindfully chew the rest of the object you are eating.

After the exercise, I allow time for class discussion and reflection and link their experiences to mindfulness practice.

Mindful Yoga

A seminal practice in mindfulness-based stress reduction (Kabat-Zinn, 1990; Stahl & Goldstein, 2010), mindful yoga involves mindful awareness of bodily sensations while doing basic yoga stretching. When done in a classroom setting, students can either remain in chairs or move to an open space if it is available. For most people, mindful yoga is a relatively enjoyable and easy mindfulness practice because it is often easier to focus on large, observable bodily movements than the more subtle focus of breath. Furthermore, the physical relief that comes from stretching also makes this a class favorite. I have also found that many of my students (actually the majority—I teach in Los Angeles) have experience with yoga, so this practice is a familiar to them. I have also found that yoga mindfulness is particularly refreshing between sessions on a long day of therapy to get me up and out of my seat and get the blood flowing while calming the mind.

Similar to other forms of mindfulness, mindful yoga involves quieting the mind while focusing one's attention on a singular phenomenon: in this case it is the physical sensations in the body while stretching. Thus, complex yoga positions are not recommended or necessary for this practice: although experienced yogis generally bring mindfulness easily to more complex poses, for the purposes of a class exercise this should be very simple and, above all, safe. Some common classroom poses are:

- Stretching arms overhead.
- Sweeping arms from the side up over the head and then bringing them back around (or down; may also bring into prayer position over the heart).
- Forward bend.
- Seated twist to left and right side.
- Stretching the neck right, left, forward, and back.
- Rolling the neck: circle to the left and right.
- Shrugging the shoulders up and down.
- Rolling the shoulders: circle forward and back.
- Leg stretches and lunges with the room available.
- Feet stretches: front, back, and in circular motions.

Ice Meditation

Certainly the messiest meditation, ice meditation often provides the most insight in a single sitting because it brings the practitioner face-to-face with pain and how they relate to it. Ice meditation involves holding a piece of ice and mindfully experiencing the pain of holding it. Although it is not one that a person is likely to practice regularly, it is an outstanding choice for a classroom filled with therapists-in-training wanting to help others cope with many forms of pain. For most people, it is quite eye opening to mindfully experience pain and how it evolves and moves. It is particularly good for helping people learn to develop a different relationship to chronic pain. It is also helpful for learning how to understand how the mind responds to pain and how it is experienced. If you haven't tried it, I recommend you do it a few times before trying to lead the class in such an exercise.

Ice Meditation

Set up: This meditation requires several items for set up:

- A bucket of ice cubes
- Paper towels
- A floor that can tolerate water being dripped on it
- If possible, several assistants to pass out ice quickly when working with a large group (1 per 10 people is ideal)

Introduction: In just a minute, you will be handed an ice cube. I will then lead you in an exercise to mindfully notice the sensations of holding a piece of ice. It will likely be uncomfortable and you will likely experience physical sensations you would prefer not to experience. I invite you to explore this experience to learn more about how your mind and body respond to pain. Of course, feel

---

(continued)

(continued)

free to stop or alter the exercise if you become overwhelmed or believe you are being hurt in any way. The purpose is to explore how the mind and body respond to pain so that you may be better able to handle it in other situations, but it is not to cause bodily or other harm. So, please feel free to pause or stop at any time.

Exercise: Please take a piece of ice and hold it in one hand. To begin with, just let it sit in one place in your open hand. Notice what it feels like in your hand: notice the physical sensations as well as what thoughts or emotions go through your head. You may feel sensations of cold, heat, burning, tingling, moisture, and/or numbness. The sensations may change slightly or significantly from moment to moment. Just notice what is there. Become an intensely curious observer of the discomfort (pause for five sections). Also notice what is going through your mind: thoughts, emotions, fear, anticipation. Notice these thoughts and then let them drift away, returning your focus to the sensation of ice in your hand. When you are ready, allow the ice to move around slightly in your hand. Simply notice what you experience. Try to not to move or adjust yourself otherwise. Notice the sensations in your hand while quieting the mind (pause for another 5–10 sections). Notice what is happening to the size and shape of the ice. If there is water now, simply notice it, how it moves, and how it feels in your hand. Simply notice without trying to change anything. Without trying to judge anything as good or bad. Just notice the experience. Notice how your mind, body, and emotions want to react. Take a few more moments to simply notice in silence.

End: We are going to come around and pass out paper towels and a bucket to put any remaining ice into.

Discussion (for partners or whole group):

- Describe the process of holding ice cube?
- What were the physical sensations like?
- What types of thoughts or emotions did you notice?
- What was the most difficult part?
- What was your response to the water dripping?
- What did you learn about your response to pain?

Mindful Listening

Mindfulness listening practice can be conducted either inside or outside, with a natural outside environment being the ideal. In this exercise, participants are invited to mindfully experience the many sounds in their natural environment.

Mindful Listening

In a few moments, we are going to sit in silence and listen to the sounds in our environment. I want you to begin with eyes closed, but you may experiment with them open and closed. And I want you to notice the sounds you hear. Do you hear sounds that are far in the distance? A car, a plane, a lawn mower, or a person shouting? Do year hear sounds that are close by? Your watch, a person speaking, the sound of the heater or air conditioner? Do you hear any sounds from your body? Your breathing or heart beating? As you listen, try not to judge sounds or the things that make them as good or bad, but just notice what you hear. The mind routinely screens out background noise, but for the next few minutes I want you to tune into it. At the end, we will discuss your experiences.

"Being Seen": Contemplative Drama Exercise

This contemplative drama exercise is an excellent option for therapists-in-training who are learning to develop intimate relationships with strangers. In the exercise, each person in the group takes a turn with "being seen" on an imaginary stage with the others mindfully observing them. This seemingly simple exercise can be powerfully moving.

Being Seen

Set up: An imaginary stage needs to be set up that is ideally 10–15 ft long with a depth of at least 6 ft. Tape, books, or other objects may be used to mark the stage boundaries and the center of the stage where each person is to stand (optional). Have the entire group stand facing the stage, taking the position of the audience.

Instructions: Provide the following verbal instructions: "We are each going to take two turns 'being seen.' For this exercise, each of us will enter stage left, slowly walk to the center of the stage and pause. The person on stage will mindfully stand and allow themselves to be seen in silence by the audience. When it is your turn to be on stage, mindfully experience what it is like to be seen. After 60 seconds or so of standing, the person on stage exits stage right. Then another member of the audience will enter from the left after a brief pause. We will all go through once (specify if there is a particular order or if each should move forward spontaneously; spontaneously is generally preferred), and then we will go through a second time. We will all be silent the entire time. I will go first to demonstrate."

(continued)

(continued)

Exercise: The exercise then continues in silence until all members have gone through twice.

Discussion: Afterward allow for reflection and discussion about the exercise:

- What was it like to be seen the first time? The second time? To what do you attribute any difference?
- What was it like to observe others in the class?
- Describe the relational experience you had with others in the group during this exercise.
- Were there elements of the group dynamics or process that made you feel more safe and/or vulnerable?
- How might what you learned from this exercise translate to "seeing" clients and "being seen" by clients?

Stress Reduction Visualization

A visualization exercise in which stressful situations are shrunk to a manageable size, the stress shrinking visualization is not a formal mindfulness mediation but a useful visualization for students, who are often experiencing high levels of stress (note: if you want to have a formal mindfulness class, you should not include this exercise). Instructors can use many variations, but the key element is to develop a visual picture or symbol of the stressful situation and shrink it down to a manageable size and to experience the self in relation to this smaller image. Visualizing the alternative, preferred ending can also be added:

Stress-Reducing Visualization

- Allow a currently stressful event or situation to come to mind. If many come to mind, simply choose one knowing you can go back and do this exercise with the others later. Choose whichever seems to ask for the most attention in this moment.
- Allow an image or symbol of this stressful situation to come to mind. For example, if it is a paper you need to write, allow the image of the paper or writing process come to mind. If it is a client, you may want to imagine a picture of their face. The image does not need to be logical and clear to others, simply to have meaning and significance for you.

(continued)

(continued)

- Spend some time taking a closer look at this image. Notice the colors, shapes, and contours. And now, I want you to start shrinking the image, down, down, down. If it seems to get stuck at points, that is fine, just wait and gently allow it to shrink down, down, down (pause for several seconds). Continue shrinking the image until it is the size of pea or small seed. Down, down, down.
- Notice how you feel now in relation to the situation. Does it seem more manageable or the same? Do you feel different in your capacity to handle it or not? Just notice what it is like to experience the problem image now that it is smaller.
- Now take this seed and plant it in the ground. Imagine rain falling and the sun heating the earth to nurture it. Allow time to pass for the sun and rain to nurture it.
- Now imagine that spring has arrived and the image reemerges from the ground, but this time it is different. The situation is transformed so that you respond in such a way that you feel good about yourself and your response. As the image grows to life size, notice how you feel about yourself in relation to the new, reemerging situation in which you feel good about your response. Notice if you happen to experience a greater sense of integrity, hope, inner calm, even pride in how you are handling the situation. Notice how others may be responding. Take one last moment to experience how the transformed situation feels.

Chapter 10
Therapist Self-Care and Style of Life

An Honest Dialogue

In this chapter, I hope to invite you into a more reflective dialogue with me about how to live well as a therapist. I am going to make myself more transparent in this chapter, because I want it to be from Diane the person, not the professional. I hope the personal tone of the chapter inspires you to use the ideas in your private life as well.

Although I have never heard it said or read it anywhere, my experience has been that therapists have to live life a bit differently: our personal relationships, relationship to the media, responsibilities at the mall, choices of entertainment, and stress management techniques all can be affected by our professional role and our professional role affects how we engage these and many other facets of life. Mindfulness and acceptance practices enter this equation on the right side: as part of the answer for how to live well as a therapist. For those wanting to teach mindfulness to clients, establishing a regular mindfulness practice is an ethical necessity (Kabat-Zinn, 1990). I would add that I have difficulty imagining doing clinical work without some form of practice that regularly cultivates compassion, acceptance, and inner peace. If you are reading this book, I guess you agree with me too.

This chapter explores mindfulness and acceptance practices that can help renew therapists in their professional lives as well as enhance their overall well-being and quality of life. I will outline a specific suggested plan for integrating mindfulness and acceptance practices into your personal and professional life in such a way that they are easily sustained. Finally, I offer reflections on how to better engage the process of living well as mental health professionals.

D.R. Gehart, *Mindfulness and Acceptance in Couple and Family Therapy*,
DOI 10.1007/978-1-4614-3033-9_10, © Springer Science+Business Media New York 2012

Mindfulness and You

Having been a therapist for nearly 20 years, I can say that I have found mindfulness to be one of the most practical and powerful tools for being effective in this profession because it provides unparalleled resources for handling the often unspoken realities of the job, which includes balancing personal and clinical worlds. Although it goes against popular myth, life happens to therapists too: people die, relationships have their seasons, and children do what children do. I think many who enter the profession secretly hope—at least now and again—that all of the training in how to help others will make one's own life measurably better. And, to a certain extent, it does: it is easier to identify abusive relationships, bad habits, and ineffective patterns. But, in so many ways it does not. And, for many, being a professional actually creates more stress and demands *because of* the professional knowledge and intense personal demands of daily work.

As already discussed, there are numerous physical, mental, and relational benefits to practicing mindfulness for the average practitioner (Chap. 1) and numerous benefits for using mindfulness to improving a therapist's quality of presence in the therapy room (Chap. 9). In addition to these, mindfulness and acceptance practices have multiple other benefits to the professional. The lists below summarize these benefits.

Direct benefits of mindfulness to professional work

- Stronger sense of therapeutic presence and "being there" for clients
- More sincere and effective therapeutic relationship
- Better understanding of how the human mind works
- More acceptance and compassion for the human condition
- Greater self-awareness in relation to client issues and relationships with clients
- Increased capacity for empathy and acceptance with clients
- Improved ability to focus in session
- Better able to access and use professional knowledge
- Method for "rebooting" between sessions and/or before or after work
- Reduced burnout

Benefits in personal life

- Greater overall sense of well-being
- Increased capacity to quickly calm and soothe oneself
- Greater self-awareness, self-acceptance, and self-compassion
- Increased intimacy and compassion in personal relationships
- Greater physical and psychological health
- Reduced stress
- Better sleep

With so many commonly experienced benefits, it seems that taking 10–20 minutes/day would not be an issue for most professionals. A no-brainer! Ah, but there is the issue: the brain and its ingrained habits. Similar to their clients, for most therapists, the question is not whether they think it is a good idea to practice mindfulness, but rather how to fit it into busy modern life.

The key challenge with using mindfulness for therapist self-care is *consistency*: maintaining some form of practice year in and year out. In short, mindfulness and acceptance must become an approach to life. Because, as Siegel explains, "Mindful awareness over time may become a way of being or a trait of the individual, not just a practice initiating a temporary state of mind" (2007, p. 118). When mindfulness becomes a default or at least frequent way of being in the world, a person's sense of personal and relational well-being shifts in measurable ways: more resilience, more integration, and more adaptability to the ever-changing flow of life.

The Therapist's Personal Mindfulness Practice

Therapists have many resources for learning mindfulness practices, with Jon Kabat-Zinn's mindfulness-based stress reduction perhaps the oldest and most recognized approach. With most communities having numerous organizations, hospitals, yoga studios, and religious groups offering training in mindfulness, interested clinicians should not have great difficulty finding a reputable program for formal training. Additionally, after formal training, therapists should ideally attend a regular mindfulness practice group with a teacher to support them for at least the initial 6 months to firmly establish a regular and well-developed practice. A skilled instructor can help practitioners navigate the typical problems that arise when learning mindfulness, such as not having time to practice, feeling stuck, feeling like nothing is happening, feeling like you aren't good at it, distractions, schedule changes, mental chatter, expectations, etc. Formal training and having a sense of community are crucial to making mindfulness a lifelong practice rather than a one-time intensive learning experience. Receiving a certificate in mindfulness is just the beginning of the journey. Over the years, mindfulness and meditation practice has taken many forms in my life, ranging from long practice sessions with retreats when I was single to shorter, "daily living" practices as a wife and new mother. I suspect that your practice will have similar seasons too.

A Mindful Self-Care Plan for Therapists

The remainder of this chapter outlines specific ways that therapists can use mindfulness and acceptance practices to develop an integrated self-care approach. The plan involves formal and informal practices at home, at the office, and in the community. You may choose to integrate and/or adapt any of the elements to create a sustainable approach that works for you. The elements of the plan are as follows:

Overview: Mindful Self-Care Plan

- Formal meditation practice

  - Compassion
  - Vipassana meditations
  - Strategies for ensuring regular practice

- Informal at-work practice

  - Mindfulness Breath Meditation
  - Mindful daily activity
  - Mindful yoga

- Community and relational practices

  - Couple and family practice
  - Community groups

Meditations for Therapists

I recommend two meditations in particular for therapists to practice as part of their formal practice:

- Loving-kindness meditation
- *Vipassana* or insight meditation

Loving-Kindness Meditation

Already introduced in Chaps. 6 and 8, loving-kindness or *metta* meditation involves sending wishes of peace, happiness, and well-being to self and others. As *compassion fatigue* is considered a risk and precursor to burnout in the mental health professions, loving-kindness meditation has particular relevance for therapists. Although I have not seen it discussed in the literature, I would also add that, at least for me ($n = 1$), loving-kindness meditation seems to promote almost an immediate sense of happiness and well-being in ways that I experience less consistently in more traditional forms of mindfulness meditation. Furthermore, this practice can quickly improve one's perspective and resourcefulness in difficult relationship situation, an invaluable resource in an intensely relational profession.

Therapists have two basic options for practicing loving kindness: the traditional version or a version that is more directly related to their clinical practice.

Loving-Kindness Meditation for Therapists

Phrases for loving-kindness meditation
- May X be happy and joyful.
- May X be free from suffering.
- May X be healthy and in radiant health.
- May X have a sense of well-being and live with ease.
- May X be at peace with people in his/her life.
- May X dwell in peace.

X = Persons to whom to direct loving kindness
Version 1: practice enhancing
- Clients (either individually or as a whole)
- Colleagues
- Self
- All beings (e.g., everyone)

OR
Version 2: traditional loving-kindness practice (see Chap. 8)
- A neutral other (e.g., acquaintance, coworker)
- Significant others (e.g., partner, family)
- Difficult other (e.g., someone with whom there is conflict)
- Self
- All beings (e.g., everyone)

Vipassana or Insight Meditation

Vipassana, or Insight Meditation, is a more advanced form of mindfulness meditation (*samatha* or single-pointed meditation) and is taught as *choiceless awareness* in the mindfulness-based stress reduction program (Stahl & Goldstein, 2010). Rather than having a single object of focus, such as the mindfulness of the breath, in the practice of vipassana *whatever arises in one's consciousness in the present moment* is the object of focus (Goleman, 1997). Significant competence in traditional mindfulness meditation on the breath or other single object of attention is essential before beginning vipassana practice. Requiring a steady observer perspective, the practitioner watches thoughts, feeling, sensations, and any other mental phenomena emerge, rise, and dissolve in consciousness from a curious, compassionate yet distinct witnessing position. The practice is analogous to watching the clouds pass by in the sky or watching a river float by: simply noticing as things pass through without attempting to stop or change the flow. As the translation implies, this practice is designed to promote insight into profound spiritual truths, most notably the illusionary nature of selfhood and reality and the interdependent nature of all things.

The practice of vipassana has many interesting parallels to a meditation technique developed in Western research labs called *open focus brain*. Fehmi experimented with numerous visualizations and experiences to help people enter into a synchronous alpha brain wave state, a pattern associated with relaxation and a heightened sense of overall well-being (Fehmi & Robbins, 2007). Of all of the relaxing images and sensations—imagining a peaceful scene, listening to one's favorite music, smelling beautiful fragrances, or seeing colorful lights—only one thing consistently helped research participants enter synchronous alpha: imagining *nothing*. When Fehmi asked subjects to imagine the space between one's eyes or between their ears, they quickly entered into brain wave patterns associated with a deep sense of well-being. Fehmi has developed this into a meditation technique that has practitioners visualize space and nothingness. Arguably the oldest practice of this is vipassana meditation, and research has shown that veteran meditators spend more time in synchronous alpha than the rest of us.

For therapists, vipassana practice greatly deepens their understanding of how the human mind works and does not work. Although we conventionally speak as though a person "makes up her mind" or "sets his mind to it," such descriptions are meaningless after carefully observing how the mind actually works. The constant fluctuation and contradiction that more accurately describes the flow of information through the mind inspires humility as well as great compassion for the confusion, "stuckness," inconsistency, and lack of peace clients frequently report. To meaningfully be a "therapist" of the psyche—the mind—I believe such intense experiential knowledge of the mind and ultimately the reality it creates is essential and transforms one's practice immeasurably.

Make It Happen

The easy part is knowing how to meditate; the challenge is making the time to do it. Even when aiming for only 2–5 minutes of practice five times per week, the majority of people I have worked with—myself included—struggle to set the time aside due to the fast-pace of our society and its numerous demands. Most of us have few cultural or social reinforcements for spending time "doing nothing"—let alone "observing nothing"—and instead have strong pressures in the opposite direction: to do, produce, and do some more. Fast and faster are the two allowable speeds. Often, the 5 minutes is not the real issue: slowing down and losing momentum from the rest of the day is. The truth is that taking the 5, 10, and 20 minutes to practice mindfulness *does* slow you down afterward. It changes you so that the standard pace of modern society is not as comfortable. You will *be* different (and that's why you want to do it).

In the beginning, it never feels like the "right" or "natural" time to do it. That's why I recommend using basic behavioral conditioning so that taking time to practice and slow down begins to feel normal and desirable. Surely, you remember how Pavlov got his dogs to salivate with the ringing of the bell; he consistently paired the bell with dinner. Over time, the dogs learned to start salivating because the bell consistently predicted that food was coming. Similarly, you can get your mind to salivate—get primed—to meditate simply by practicing at the same time everyday (or at least the 5 workdays/week when you have a regular schedule). I have trained my brain to expect and look forward to mindfulness at some point in my morning routine, generally after my shower. By consciously creating this association, my mind and body expect and crave this each day, which greatly increases the chances that I will actually practice. When I try to squeeze it in when I "happen" to have a moment to practice, it rarely happens.

The other behavioral tactic I use is positive reinforcement. I am one of those people who derives great pleasure from checking items off of my to do list, and admittedly at times put recently completed items that weren't on another list onto the current list I am writing just to give myself credit. Enjoying positive rewards and wanting a "safety net," I have programmed my computer's to-do list software to load with meditation practice on the top of each day's list. I can check it off if I already did it or am otherwise quickly reminded to make time to practice at the beginning of my busy workday. If you do not have a particularly busy life and taking time for practice is easy, then you do not need what follows; otherwise, try the following steps to find time for making mindfulness fit into a busy schedule.

The Busy Therapist's Savvy Steps for Developing a Consistent Practice

Step 1: Pair with another regular activity
Identify another daily activity (getting up, getting dressed, breakfast, arriving at the office, arriving home, etc.) that allows for 5–20 minutes of mindfulness practice either before or after.
I will practice for ___ minutes ❑ before, ❑ after_____ (regular, daily activity).

Step 2: Create a space
Find a proper place to sit and add at least one thing to the space that will help remind you to practice and/or symbolize the benefits of or reasons for practice.
My meditation space:_____; reminder/symbol in that space:_____.

Step 3: Add positive reinforcement
After practicing give yourself a little treat or reward for practicing; this can be as simple as checking practice off your to do list, journaling about your mindfulness practice, or having a favorite cup of tea or piece of chocolate. Whatever it is, it should occur immediately after practice for optimal effectiveness, not later in the day. My chosen reinforcement:_____

(continued)

(continued)

> *Step 4: Create a safety net*
> Create one other reminder for your practice: an alarm on your phone, an entry in your to do list, or a note on your dashboard to gently remind you on the days your routine is a bit off. My backup reminder system:_____
>
> *Step 5: Log or Journal*
> Maintaining a mindfulness log (see Chap. 6) or journal to track your practice and what you learn from it can dramatically improve your motivation and consistency of practice. The journal should be kept in or near the meditation space.
> Where I will keep my log/journal:_____

Mindfulness at Work

Integrating mini-mindfulness meditations and activities into daily routines at the office can dramatically change how therapists function in their clinical roles as well as reduce the overall stress levels at the end of the day, allowing one to return home with more energy and emotional availability. I recommend three variations of mindfulness practices for therapists to use in their work settings, all of which were also introduced in Chap. 6:

- Mindfulness breath meditation
- Mindful daily activity
- Mindful yoga

Bookending the Work Day with Mini-Mindful Breath Meditations

Short mindful breath meditations upon arrival and departure from work have a remarkable affect on preparing for both transitions. When arriving to work and/or just before seeing clients, practicing 2–10 minutes of mindfulness can help clear the mind and center oneself to be more fully present and focused with clients; or to put it into neurological terms, helps therapists enter an integrated neural state (Siegel, 2010b). The shift is palpable to oneself and to clients and is likely to make a significant difference in client outcomes, one that has been measured in recent studies (Grepmair et al., 2007; Padilla, 2011). Practicing mindfulness at the end of the day is a gift to yourself and those you come home to because it allows you to more gracefully transition from work to home life.

Mindful Daily Activities

Mindfulness in daily activities refers to bringing full, present-moment awareness to ordinary activities, such as feeling the sensations of warm water and bubbles while washing one's hands. Selecting one or two innocuous routine activities at the office for mindful practice can also add small moments of mindfulness that instantly invoke the relaxation response due to repeat conditioning. For example, after reading Hahn's (1992) *Peace is Every Step*, I began dishwashing meditation to bring mindfulness to one of my least enjoyable daily chores. Over the years, it has resulted in invoking relaxation whenever I do dishes or wash my hands, which is several times a day on long days at the office. Those brief moments of washing my hands now remind me to be present and just notice how I am doing, what I am feeling, and where my mind is, helping me to clear my mind and prepare myself to be fully present for the next client. Other common therapist activities include:

- Mindfully sipping water
- Mindfully walking down the hall
- Mindfully grabbing the room's door handle
- Mindfully locking and unlocking a file cabinet at the start and end of the day
- Mindfully signing progress notes

Mindful Yoga

Between sessions—especially when a client is running late—I enjoy practicing mindful yoga, which allows me to stretch my body that is otherwise mostly immobile during my hours in therapy. Doing gentle stretching while deeply breathing with the stretch helps relax the body and allows me to bring my full attention and presence into the room.

Community of Support

In addition to practicing regularly and at work, ideally therapists find relationships and communities that support their mindfulness practice as well as support them as a person. Therapists with partners can develop a couple of practice of mindfulness or compassion meditation that integrates mindfulness into home life (see Chap. 8). Similarly, therapist with children can introduce any of many child-friendly mindfulness practices into the regular family routine. Religious or spiritually oriented therapists have many options for participating in meditation groups affiliated with these organizations.

The primary benefit of building a community of support is to reset the norm for how to move through the day and life. For the vast majority of people, the chronic stress levels that characterize modern living simply detract from living a rich, fully satisfying life. I would go so far as to say that being present in one's own life and relationships is countercultural at this time in history when bigger and faster is always better. Thus, finding a community—whether it is your partner or your church—who is committed to living with greater awareness and vitality greatly simplifies doing so yourself. Being with people who rejoice in noticing the quality of the sun, the color of flowers, or the taste of local fruit encourages you and reminds you to do the same. Whereas when your day is spent with people multitasking and rushing from activity to activity and comparing who has the biggest and the best, you slowly begin to also live apart from your experience.

Spiritual Development

I define spirituality as how a person relates to life in its largest sense see discussion in Chap. 5, and thus, I believe even atheists have a form of spirituality. Even when done for practical purposes such as becoming a better therapist or managing stress, regular mindfulness, compassion, and vipassana practice inevitably awaken, reshape, and deepen one's sense of connection to life, and if you construct it so, the divine. These practices open a person to experiencing states of being that are rarely spoken about in modern culture: a palpable sense of being connected to all living beings, of liberation from the cares of worldly life, and of feeling the touch of the divine. Similarly, an unimpeded embrace of suffering irreversibly changes ones working assumptions about life, its purpose, your purpose, and the role of others in our lives and our role in their lives. Suffice it to say, that regular mindfulness practice will sculpt you from the inside out in ways that are difficult to imagine. Although it appears that you are sitting and doing nothing, you are in many ways engaged in life's most profound quest: to understand your role in the mystery of life.

Intersection of Personhood and Professional Life

Many of us were told that we needed to keep "healthy boundaries" between our personal lives and therapeutic work by not thinking about clients at home and not discussing our personal lives at work. Not only does my experience tell me that this guideline misses many core issues, but emerging research also points to more subtle issues as well. Recent studies on therapeutic presence pinpoint the quality of being or the *who* of the therapist being a—if not the most—critical factor that predicts client outcomes (Lambert & Simon, 2008; McDonough-Means, Kreitzer, & Bell, 2004; Miller, Duncan, & Hubble, 1997). Furthermore, research in neuroscience suggests that our mental state significantly impacts our clients and their ability to work through trauma and stabilize emotions (Siegel, 2010b). More specifically, a therapist's ability to enter integrated neural states and develop safe, secure relationships is increasingly considered essential to therapeutic effectiveness. With cumulative evidence pointing to the person of the therapist as a crucial change element, the question becomes can you be one person in therapy and another outside?

Whether you believe we have a singular self, lean more toward postmodern views of multiple selves, or embrace a Buddhist position of "no" or empty self (see Chap. 2 for further discussion), I believe most would agree that the self outside of therapy is closely related to the self inside of therapy. Thus, the things therapists do outside of therapy—how they spend their time, where they direct their attention, how they conduct their relationships—enter the therapy room in some form. For example, if a therapist chooses to stay long-term in a chaotic and unsafe relationship, that quality of relating is likely to affect how he or she relates in session in some form. Similarly, if a therapist lives in a chronically stressed state, the lack of calm, integrated emotional and mental functioning is likely to trickle in to their professional work. Would it also not stand to reason that when therapists work around people with whom they do not have good, safe relationships—perhaps in the office next door or down the hall—that this too might affect who they are in session?

More so than some, therapists need to be thoughtful stewards of their time and energy in personal life to help them maintain emotional balance, optimism, and well-being. Not every form of entertainment, news show, relationship, or hobby may be conducive to supporting a sense of self that enhances therapeutic presence. For example, I have found that unnecessarily violent movies with pessimistic themes about humanity affect me in ways that diminish who I am in session, so I avoid them. The practice of mindfulness can help therapists become much more attuned to the subtle elements in their life that reduce their effectiveness in session and in life.

Permission for Self-Care

Self-care matters. It matters just as much as caring for our clients, if not more. Clinicians who do not take the time for quality self-care reduce their helpfulness to clients (Shapiro & Carlson, 2009). Most of us do an excellent job ensuring we meet ethical mandates to not become impaired by abusing substances or having our personal problems affect our work. But good self-care requires more than that. Meaningful self-care involves mindfully examining how we live and move through our day; how our stress affects our health, happiness, and relationships; how we relate to the significant others in our lives; and what we tell ourselves about the events in our lives mean. It also involves days when you do none of this, and just simply live.

But when faced with our clients' suffering and the needs of our families and friends, many professional helpers have difficulty giving themselves permission to take care of themselves. Not always recognizing the depth of our ultimate interconnectedness, therapists are more likely to wonder how they could do more to help others than they are to take the time they need to cultivate their own well-being. It seems selfish to focus oneself when those we meet day-in and day-out are in such great need. For this same reason, the Federal Aviation Administration has to continually remind parents of the obvious: they must take care of themselves by putting on the gasmask first to be in a position to help their children in an emergency. Similarly, therapists seem to need constant reminders that self-care is a necessity, not a luxury in this line of work. Quite frankly, I find self-care a much greater challenge than stabilizing suicidal crisis or helping couples get back on track. I am well trained in those skills. But there are fewer guidelines and well-worn paths in the area of self-care. It is a journey and task that requires my ongoing attention. Although I have certainly gotten better over the years, I know I have more to learn. I, for one, have found mindfulness and acceptance practices an integral part of that journey. Thus, I enthusiastically suggest it to you.

The Journey Toward Well-Being

A few notable colleagues and mentors I with have had stand out because they possessed *well-being*, radiating a sense of peace with oneself, others, and life. They brought out the best in others by sharing the best in themselves. You would think in the field of mental health we have many examples of living with a deep sense of well-being. Unfortunately, that is not the case. Perhaps, as positive psychologists have pointed out, we have mistakenly equated health—the lack of pathology—for wellness and optimal functioning (Seligman, 2002). Increasingly, I think therapists can do more to promote well-being for our clients and for ourselves. While certainly not the only means, mindfulness and acceptance practices offer a wealth of highly efficient and flexible methods to help create richer and fuller lives.

I hope some part of this book has touched you or inspired you to pursue a life that is full of adventure, love, and laughter—whether or not you need to meditate to achieve these ends. When all is said and done, mindfulness—observing what is—is nothing more than a tool for developing a more effective relationship with life, others, and yourself. There is no particular magic in it—it simply is an option that many find useful in cultivating well-being. The more significant issue is the journey: how you choose to move through your day, treat each person you meet, talk with yourself, and approach the challenges that life presents.

Although the most common English translation for the goal of meditation is "enlightenment," the alternative translation increasingly holds greater meaning for me: "liberation." After years of practice, the idea of enlightened liberation has lost its mystical, semi-magical meaning and instead holds a more dear and precious connotation: liberation from the self-perpetuated suffering I generate day-in and day-out. In truth, we each have the option to create or eliminate the vast majority of suffering in our lives. I cannot say that choosing to eliminate it is easy, but I have found that mindfulness practices make it easier for me. I have found that the more mindful and accepting I am of my life, the less likely I am to create unnecessary suffering and instead know the true taste of freedom and peace: to be well in the world. Such freedom cannot be acquired through money, the right relationships, or special training; it must be consciously chosen each day anew. May we each have the courage to do so again and again.

About the Author

Dr. Diane R. Gehart is a Professor in the Marriage and Family Therapy Program at California State University, Northridge. She has authored numerous books, including *Mastering Competencies in Family Therapy, Theory and Treatment Planning in Counseling and Psychotherapy, The Complete MFT and Counseling Core Competency Assessment Systems,* and she has co-edited *Collaborative Therapy: Relationships and Conversations That Make a Difference.* Her areas of research and specialty include postmodern therapies, mindfulness, Buddhist psychology, sexual abuse, gender, children, relationships, client advocacy, mental health recovery, qualitative research, and education in family therapy and counseling. In addition, she has studied classical Buddhist literature in the original Chinese and Tibetan. She speaks internationally, having given workshops to professional and general audiences in the United States, Canada, Europe, and Mexico. Her research has been featured in newspapers, radio shows, and television worldwide. She is an associate faculty member at the Taos Institute, Houston Galveston Institute, and the Marburg Institute for Collaborative Studies in Germany. She maintains a private practice in Thousand Oaks, California, specializing in couples, families, trauma, life transitions, and difficult-to-treat cases. For fun, she enjoys hiking or going to the beach with her family, trail running, yoga, meditation, cooking, traveling, and dark chocolate in any form. You can learn more about her current work and adventures at www.dianegehart.com.

D.R. Gehart, *Mindfulness and Acceptance in Couple and Family Therapy,*
DOI 10.1007/978-1-4614-3033-9, © Springer Science+Business Media New York 2012

References

Andersen, T. (1991). *The reflecting team: Dialogues and dialogues about the dialogues*. New York: Norton.

Andersen, T. (2007). Human participating. In H. Anderson & D. Gehart (Eds.), *Collaborative therapy* (pp. 81–98). New York: Routledge.

Anderson, H. (1997). *Conversation, language and possibility*. New York: Basic.

Anderson, H., & Gehart, D. R. (Eds.). (2007). *Collaborative therapy: Relationships and conversations that make a difference*. New York: Brunner-Routledge.

Anderson, H., & Goolishian, H. (1992). The client is the expert: A not-knowing approach to therapy. In S. McNamee & K. J. Gergen (Eds.), *Therapy as social construction* (pp. 25–39). Newbury Park, CA: Sage.

Aron, A., & Aron, E. N. (1997). Self-expansion motivation and including other in the self. In S. Duck (Ed.), *Handbook of personal relationships: Theory, research, and interventions* (pp. 251–270). Chichester, UK: Wiley.

Badenoch, B. (2008). *Being a brain-wise therapist: A practical guide to interpersonal neurobiology*. New York: Norton.

Baer, R. A. (2003). Mindfulness training as a clinical intervention: A conceptual and empirical review. *Clinical Psychology: Science and Practice, 10*(2), 125–143. doi:10.1093/clipsy/bpg015.

Baer, R. A. (Ed.). (2006). *Mindfulness-based treatment approaches: Clinician's guide to evidence base and applications*. San Diego, CA: Elsevier Academic Press.

Baer, R. A. (2010). Self-compassion as a mechanism of change in mindfulness- and acceptance-based treatments. In R. A. Baer (Ed.), *Assessing mindfulness and acceptance processes in clients: Illuminating the theory and practice of change* (pp. 135–153). Oakland, CA: Context Press/New Harbinger Publications.

Barks, C. (2003). *Rumi: The book of love*. San Francisco, CA: Harper.

Barnes, S., Brown, K., Krusemark, E., Campbell, W., & Rogge, R. D. (2007). The role of mindfulness in romantic relationship satisfaction and responses to relationship stress. *Journal of Marital and Family Therapy, 33*(4), 482–500. doi:10.1111/j.1752-0606.2007.00033.x.

Bateson, G. (1972). *Steps to an ecology of mind*. New York: Ballentine.

Bateson, G. (1991). *Sacred unity: Further steps in an ecology of mind* (R. Donaldson, Ed.). New York: Corneila and Michael Bessie.

Bateson, G. (1979/2002). *Mind and nature: A necessary unity*. Cresskill, NJ: Hampton.

Birnie, K., Garland, S. N., & Carlson, L. E. (2010). Psychological benefits for cancer patients and their partners participating in mindfulness-based stress reduction (MBSR). *Psycho-Oncology, 19*(9), 1004–1009. doi:10.1002/pon.1651.

Birnie, K., Speca, M., & Carlson, L. E. (2010). Exploring self-compassion and empathy in the context of mindfulness-based stress reduction (MBSR). *Stress and Health, 26*(5), 359–371. doi:10.1002/smi.1305.

Bishop, S. R., Lau, M., Shapiro, S., Carlson, L., Anderson, N. D., Carmody, J., et al. (2004). Mindfulness: A proposed operational definition. *Clinical Psychology: Science and Practice, 11*(3), 230–241. doi:10.1093/clipsy.bph077.

Black, D. S., Milam, J., & Sussman, S. (2009). Sitting meditation interventions with youth: A review of treatment efficacy. *Pediatrics, 124*, e532–e541.

Block-Lerner, J., Adair, C., Plumb, J. C., Rhatigan, D. L., & Orsillo, S. M. (2007). The case for mindfulness-based approaches in the cultivation of empathy: Does nonjudgmental, present-moment awareness increase capacity for perspective-taking and empathic concern? *Journal of Marital and Family Therapy, 33*(4), 501–516. doi:10.1111/j.1752-0606.2007.00034.x.

Bodin, S. (2006). *Meditation for dummies* (2nd ed.). New York, NY: Wiley.

Bögels, S., Hoogstad, B., van Dun, L., de Schutter, S., & Restifo, K. (2008). Mindfulness training for adolescents with externalizing disorders and their parents. *Behavioural and Cognitive Psychotherapy, 36*(2), 193–209. doi:10.1017/S1352465808004190.

Bowen, M. (1985). *Family therapy in clinical practice*. New York: Jason Aronson.

Brown, K., & Ryan, R. M. (2003). The benefits of being present: Mindfulness and its role in psychological well-being. *Journal of Personality and Social Psychology, 84*(4), 822–848. doi:10.1037/0022-3514.84.4.822.

Brown, K., Ryan, R. M., & Creswell, J. (2007). Mindfulness: Theoretical foundations and evidence for its salutary effects. *Psychological Inquiry, 18*(4), 211–237.

Bruce, N. G., Manber, R., Shapiro, S. L., & Constantino, M. J. (2010). Psychotherapist mindfulness and the psychotherapy process. *Psychotherapy: Theory, Research, Practice, Training, 47*(1), 83–97. doi:10.1037/a0018842.

Buber, M. (1958). *I and Thou*. Edinburgh: T & T Clark.

Burke, C. A. (2010). Mindfulness-based approaches with children and adolescents: A preliminary review of current research in an emergent field. *Journal of Child and Family Studies, 19*(2), 133–144. doi:10.1007/s10826-009-9282-x.

Burpee, L. C., & Langer, E. J. (2005). Mindfulness and marital satisfaction. *Journal of Adult Development, 12*(1), 43–51. doi:10.1007/s10804-005-1281-6.

Bush, M. (2010). *Contemplative higher education in contemporary America*. Retrieved from www.acmhe.org

Carmody, J., & Baer, R. A. (2008). Relationships between mindfulness practice and levels of mindfulness, medical and psychological symptoms and well-being in a mindfulness-based stress reduction program. *Journal of Behavioral Medicine, 31*(1), 23–33. doi:10.1007/s10865-007-9130-7.

Carson, J. W., Carson, K. M., Gil, K. M., & Baucom, D. H. (2004). Mindfulness-based relationship enhancement. *Behavior Therapy, 35*(3), 471–494. doi:10.1016/S0005-7894(04)80028-5.

Carson, J. W., Carson, K. M., Gil, K. M., & Baucom, D. H. (2006). Mindfulness-Based Relationship Enhancement (MBRE) in couples. In R. A. Baer (Ed.), *Mindfulness-based treatment approaches: Clinician's guide to evidence base and applications* (pp. 309–331). San Diego, CA: Elsevier Academic Press.

Carson, J. W., Carson, K. M., Gil, K. M., & Baucom, D. H. (2007). Self-expansion as a mediator of relationship improvements in a mindfulness intervention. *Journal of Marital and Family Therapy, 33*(4), 517–528. doi:10.1111/j.1752-0606.2007.00035.x.

Cecchin, G. (1987). Hypothesizing, circularity, and neutrality revisited: An invitation to curiosity. *Family Process, 26*, 405–413.

Chiesa, A. A., & Serretti, A. A. (2010). A systematic review of neurobiological and clinical features of mindfulness meditations. *Psychological Medicine, 40*(8), 1239–1252. doi:10.1017/S0033291709991747.

Chödrön, P. (1997). *When things fall apart: Heart advice for difficult times*. Boston: Shambala.

Christensen, A., & Jacobson, N. (2000). *Reconcilable differences*. New York: Guilford Press.

Christensen, A., Sevier, M., Simpson, L. E., & Gattis, K. S. (2004). Acceptance, mindfulness, and change in couple therapy. In S. C. Hayes, V. M. Follette, & M. M. Linehan (Eds.), *Mindfulness and acceptance: Expanding the cognitive-behavioral tradition* (pp. 288–309). New York, NY: Guilford Press.

Ciarrochi, J., Bilich, L., & Godsell, C. (2010). Psychological flexibility as a mechanism of change in acceptance and commitment therapy. In R. A. Baer (Ed.), *Assessing mindfulness and acceptance processes in clients: Illuminating the theory and practice of change* (pp. 51–75). Oakland, CA: Context Press/New Harbinger Publications.

Coatsworth, J., Duncan, L. G., Greenberg, M. T., & Nix, R. L. (2010). Changing parent's mindfulness, child management skills and relationship quality with their youth: Results from a randomized pilot intervention trial. *Journal of Child and Family Studies, 19*(2), 203–217. doi:10.1007/s10826-009-9304-8.

Cohen-Katz, J., Wiley, S. D., Capuano, T., Baker, D. M., & Shapiro, S. (2005). The effects of mindfulness-based stress education on nurse stress and burnout, part II. A quantitative and qualitative study. *Holistic Nursing Practice, 18*, 302–308.

Dalai Lama. (1996). *The good heart: A Buddhist perspective on the teachings of Jesus* (T. Jinpa, Trans.). Boston: Wisdom.

Dalai Lama, Benson, H., Thurman, R. A. F., Gardner, H. E., & Goleman, D. (1991). *Mind science: An East-West dialogue*. London: Wisdom.

Davidson, R. J., Kabat-Zinn, J., Schumacher, J., Rosenkranz, M., Muller, D., Santorelli, S. F., et al. (2003). Alterations in brain and immune function produced by mindfulness meditation. *Psychosomatic Medicine, 65*, 564–570.

deShazer, S. (1988). *Clues: Investigating solutions in brief therapy*. New York: Norton.

Didonna, F. (Ed.). (2009). *Clinical handbook of mindfulness*. New York, NY: Springer. doi:10.1007/978-0-387-09593-6.

Dumas, J. E. (2005). Mindfulness-based parent training: Strategies to lessen the grip of automaticity in families with disruptive children. *Journal of Clinical Child and Adolescent Psychology, 34*(4), 779–791. doi:10.1207/s15374424jccp3404_20.

Duncan, L. G., & Bardacke, N. (2010). Mindfulness-based childbirth and parenting education: Promoting family mindfulness during the perinatal period. *Journal of Child and Family Studies, 19*(2), 190–202. doi:10.1007/s10826-009-9313-7.

Duncan, L. G., Coatsworth, J., & Greenberg, M. T. (2009a). A model of mindful parenting: Implications for parent–child relationships and prevention research. *Clinical Child and Family Psychology Review, 12*(3), 255–270. doi:10.1007/s10567-009-0046-3.

Duncan, L. G., Coatsworth, J., & Greenberg, M. T. (2009b). Pilot study to gauge acceptability of a mindfulness-based, family-focused preventive intervention. *The Journal of Primary Prevention, 30*(5), 605–618. doi:10.1007/s10935-009-0185-9.

Elkin, I., Shea, M., Watkins, J. T., & Imber, S. D. (1989). National Institute of Mental Health Treatment of Depression Collaborative Research Program: General effectiveness of treatments. *Archives of General Psychiatry, 46*(11), 971–982.

Epstein, M. (1995). *Thoughts without a thinker: Psychotherapy from a Buddhist perspective*. New York: Basic.

Epstein, M. (1999). *Going to pieces without falling apart: A Buddhist perspective on wholeness*. New York: Broadway.

Epstein, R. (2003a). Mindful practice in action I: Technical competence, evidence-based medicine, and relationship-centered care. *Families, Systems & Health, 21*, 1–9.

Epstein, R. (2003b). Mindful practice in action II: Cultivating habits of mind. *Families, Systems & Health, 21*, 11–17.

Fan, Y., Tang, Y., Ma, Y., & Posner, M. I. (2010). Mucosal immunity modulated by integrative meditation in a dose-dependent fashion. *Journal of Alternative and Complementary Medicine, 16*(2), 151–155. doi:10.1089/acm.2009.0234.

Fehmi, L., & Robbins, J. (2007). *The open-focus brain: Harnessing the power of attention to heal mind and body*. Boston: Trumpter Books.

Ferguson, J. K. (2010). Centering prayer: A method of Christian meditation for our time. In T. G. Plante (Ed.), *Contemplative practices in action: Spirituality, meditation, and health* (pp. 60–77). Santa Barbara, CA: Praeger.

Flemons, D. G. (1991). *Completing distinctions: Interweaving the ideas of Gregory Bateson and Taoism into a unique approach to therapy*. Boston: Shambhala.

Follette, V. M., & Vijay, A. (2009). Mindfulness for trauma and posttraumatic stress disorder. In F. Didonna (Ed.), *Clinical handbook of mindfulness* (pp. 299–317). New York, NY: Springer. doi:10.1007/978-0-387-09593-6_17.

Fredrickson, B. L., Cohn, M. A., Coffey, K. A., Pek, J., & Finkel, S. M. (2008). Open hearts build lives: Positive emotions, induced through loving-kindness meditation, build consequential personal resources. *Journal of Personality and Social Psychology, 95*(5), 1045–1062. doi:10.1037/a0013262.

Freedman, J., & Combs, G. (1996). *Narrative therapy: The social construction of preferred realities.* New York: Norton.

Fulton, P. R. (2005). Mindfulness as clinical training. In C. K. Germer, R. D. Siegel, & P. R. Fulton (Eds.), *Mindfulness and psychotherapy* (pp. 55–72). New York, NY: Guilford Press.

Gale, J. (2009). Meditation and relational connectedness: Practices for couples and families. In F. Walsh & F. Walsh (Eds.), *Spiritual resources in family therapy* (2nd ed., pp. 247–266). New York, NY: Guilford Press.

Gambrel, L., & Keeling, M. L. (2010). Relational aspects of mindfulness: Implications for the practice of marriage and family therapy. *Contemporary Family Therapy, 32*(4), 412–426. doi:10.1007/s10591-010-9129-z.

Gehart, D. (2004). Achtsamkeit in der therapie: Buddhistische Philosophie im postmoderner Praxis [Mindfulness in therapy: Buddhist philosophy in postmodern practice]. *Zeitschrift für Systemische Therapie [Journal for Systemic Therapy], 22,* 5–14.

Gehart, D. (2007). Process-as-content: Teaching postmodern therapy in a university context. *Journal of Systemic Therapies, 26,* 15–28.

Gehart, D. (2010). *Mastering competencies in family therapy: A practical approach to theory and clinical case documentation.* Pacific Grove, CA: Brooks/Cole.

Gehart, D. (2012). *Counseling and psychotherapy theories and treatment planning.* Pacific Grove, CA: Brooks/Cole.

Gehart, D., & Coffey, A. (2004). *Love in couple's therapy: A Buddhist approach.* In Workshop (2 hour) presented at the Texas Association for Marriage and Family Therapy annual conference, Houston, TX, January 2004.

Gehart, D., & McCollum, E. (2007). Engaging suffering: Towards a mindful re-visioning of marriage and family therapy practice. *Journal of Marital and Family Therapy, 33,* 214–226.

Gehart, D., & McCollum, E. (2008). Inviting therapeutic presence: A mindfulness-based approach. In S. Hick & T. Bien (Eds.), *Mindfulness and the healing relationship* (pp. 176–194). New York: Guilford.

Gehart, D., & Pare, D. (2009). Suffering and the relationship with the problem in postmodern therapies: A Buddhist re-visioning. *Journal of Family Psychotherapy, 19,* 299–319.

Gehart, D. R., & Lyle, R. R. (1999). Client and therapist perspectives of change in collaborative language systems: An interpretive ethnography. *Journal of Systemic Therapy, 18*(4), 78–97.

Gergen, K. (1991). *The saturated self.* New York: Basic Books.

Gergen, K. J. (1999). *An invitation to social construction.* Thousand Oaks, CA: Sage.

Glück, T., & Maercker, A. (2011). A randomized controlled pilot study of a brief, web-based mindfulness training [Abstract]. *International Journal of Integrated Care, 11.* Retrieved from http://www.ijic.org/index.php/ijic/article/viewArticle/701/1281

Goleman, D. (1997). *Healing emotions: Conversations with the Dalai Lama on mindfulness, emotions, and health.* Boston: Shambala.

Goleman, D. (2003). *Destructive emotions: How can we overcome them?* New York: Bantam.

Goleman, D. (2005). *Emotional intelligence* (10th ed.). New York: Bantam Books.

Goleman, D. J., & Schwartz, G. E. (1976). Meditation as an intervention in stress reactivity. *Journal of Consulting and Clinical Psychology, 44*(3), 456–466. doi:10.1037/0022-006X.44.3.456.

Goodman, T. A. (2005). Working with Children: Beginners mind. In C. K. Germer, R. D. Siegel, & P. R. Fulton (Eds.), *Mindfulness and psychotherapy* (pp. 197–219). New York, NY: Guilford Press.

Goodman, T. A., & Greenland, S. (2009). Mindfulness with children: Working with difficult emotions. In F. Didonna (Ed.), *Clinical handbook of mindfulness* (pp. 417–429). New York, NY: Springer. doi:10.1007/978-0-387-09593-6_23.

Gottman, J. M. (1999). *The marriage clinic: A scientifically based marital therapy.* New York: Norton.

Gottman, J. M. (2011). *The science of trust: Emotional attunement for couples.* New York: Norton.

Gratz, K. L., & Tull, M. T. (2010). Emotion regulation as a mechanism of change in acceptance- and mindfulness-based treatments. In R. A. Baer (Ed.), *Assessing mindfulness and acceptance processes in clients: Illuminating the theory and practice of change* (pp. 107–133). Oakland, CA: Context Press/New Harbinger Publications.

Greco, L. A., & Hayes, S. C. (Eds.). (2008). *Acceptance and mindfulness treatments for children and adolescents: A practitioner's guide.* Oakland, CA: New Harbinger Press.

Greenan, D. E. (2010). Therapy with a gay male couple: An unlikely multisystemic integration. In A. S. Gurman (Ed.), *Clinical casebook of couple therapy* (pp. 90–111). New York, NY: Guilford Press.

Greenland, S. K. (2010). *The mindful child.* New York: Free Press.

Greeson, J., & Brantley, J. (2009). Mindfulness and anxiety disorders: Developing a wise relationship with the inner experience of fear. In F. Didonna (Ed.), *Clinical handbook of mindfulness* (pp. 171–188). New York, NY: Springer. doi:10.1007/978-0-387-09593-6_11.

Grepmair, L., Mitterlehner, F., Loew, T., Bachler, E., Rother, W., & Nickel, M. (2007). Promoting mindfulness in psychotherapists in training influences the treatment results of their patients: A randomized, double-blind, controlled study. *Psychotherapy and Psychosomatics, 76*(6), 332–338. doi:10.1159/000107560.

Grossman, P., Niemann, L., Schmidt, S., & Walach, H. (2004). Mindfulness-based stress reduction and health benefits: A meta-analysis. *Journal of Psychosomatic Research, 57*(1), 35–43. doi:10.1016/S0022-3999(03)00573-7.

Gudmunsen, C. (1977). *Wittgenstein and Buddhism.* New York: Harper Row.

Gyeltsen, T. (2000). *Mirror of wisdom: Teachings on emptiness.* Boston, MA: Thubten Dhargye Ling Publications.

Hahn, T. N. (1992). *Peace is every step: The path of mindfulness in everyday life.* New York: Bantam.

Hahn, T. N. (1997). *Teachings on love.* Berkeley, CA: Parallax.

Hahn, T. N. (1998). *The heart of Buddha's teaching: Transforming suffering into peace, joy & liberation.* Berkeley, CA: Parallax.

Haley, J. (1987). *Problem-solving therapy* (2nd ed.). San Francisco: Jossey-Bass.

Halford, W. K., Markman, H. J., Kline, G. H., & Stanley, S. M. (2002). Best practices in couple relationship education. *Journal of Marital and Family Therapy, 29,* 385–406.

Hamdan, A. (2010). A comprehensive contemplative approach from the Islamic tradition. In T. G. Plante (Ed.), *Contemplative practices in action: Spirituality, meditation, and health* (pp. 122–142). Santa Barbara, CA: Praeger.

Hamilton, N. A., Kitzman, H., & Guyotte, S. (2006). Enhancing health and emotion: Mindfulness as a missing link between cognitive therapy and positive psychology. *Journal of Cognitive Psychotherapy, 20*(2), 123–134. doi:10.1891/jcop. 20.2.123.

Hanson, R. (2009). *The Buddha's brain: The practical neuroscience of happiness, love, and wisdom.* Oakland, CA: New Harbinger.

Harris, R. (2009). *ACT with love: Stop struggling, reconcile your differences, and strengthen your relationship.* New York: New Harbinger.

Hayes, S. C. (2004). Acceptance and commitment therapy, relational frame theory, and the third wave of behavior therapy. *Behavior Therapeutic, 35,* 639–666.

Hayes, S. C., & Smith, S. (2005). *Get out of your mind and into your life.* Oakland, CA: New Harbinger.

Hayes, S. C., Strosahl, K. D., & Wilson, K. G. (1999). *Acceptance and commitment therapy: An experiential approach to behavior change.* New York: Guilford.

Hayward, J. W., & Varela, F. J. (1992). *Gentle bridges: Conversations with the Dali Lama on the sciences of the mind.* Boston: Shambhala.

Henggeler, S. W. (1998). *Multisystemic therapy.* Charleston, NC: Targeted Publications Group. Retrieved from www.addictionrecov.org/paradigm/P_PR_W99/mutisys_therapy.html

Hick, S., & Bien, T. (Eds.). (2008). *Mindfulness and the healing relationship.* New York: Guilford.
Hofmann, S. G., Sawyer, A. T., Witt, A. A., & Oh, D. (2010). The effect of mindfulness-based therapy on anxiety and depression: A meta-analytic review. *Journal of Consulting and Clinical Psychology, 78*(2), 169–183. doi:10.1037/a0018555.
Hölzel, B. K., Carmody, J., Evans, K. C., Hoge, E. A., Dusek, J. A., Morgan, L., et al. (2010). Stress reduction correlates with structural changes in the amygdala. *Social Cognitive and Affective Neuroscience, 5*(1), 11–17. doi:10.1093/scan/nsp034.
Hölzel, B. K., Carmody, J., Vangel, M., Congleton, C., Yerramsetti, S. M., Gard, T., et al. (2011). Mindfulness practice leads to increases in regional brain gray matter density. *Psychiatry Research: Neuroimaging, 191*(1), 36–43. doi:10.1016/j.pscychresns.2010.08.006.
Imel, Z., Baldwin, S., Bonus, K., & MacCoon, D. (2008). Beyond the individual: Group effects in mindfulness-based stress reduction. *Psychotherapy Research, 18*(6), 735–742. doi:10.1080/10503300802326038.
Jain, S., Shapiro, S. L., Swanick, S., Roesch, S. C., Mills, P. J., Bell, I., et al. (2007). A randomized controlled trial of mindfulness meditation versus relaxation training: Effects on distress, positive states of mind, rumination, and distraction. *Annals of Behavioral Medicine, 33*(1), 11–21. doi:10.1207/s15324796abm3301_2.
Jha, A. P., Stanley, E. A., & Baime, M. J. (2010). What does mindfulness training strengthen? Working memory capacity as a functional marker of training success. In R. A. Baer (Ed.), *Assessing mindfulness and acceptance processes in clients: Illuminating the theory and practice of change* (pp. 207–221). Oakland, CA: Context Press/New Harbinger Publications.
Johnson, S. M. (2002). The revolution in couple therapy: A practitioner-scientist perspective. *Journal of Marital and Family Therapy, 29*, 365–384.
Johnson, S. M. (2004). *The practice of emotionally focused marital therapy: Creating connection* (2nd ed.). New York: Brunner-Routledge.
Johnson, S. M. (2008). *Hold me tight.* New York: Little, Brown, and Co.
Johnson, S. M., Hunsley, J., Greenberg, L., & Schindler, D. (1999). Emotionally focused couples therapy: Status and challenges. *Clinical Psychology: Science and Practice, 6*(1), 67–79. doi:10.1093/clipsy/6.1.67.
Jung, C. G. (1927/1960). The Tibetan book of the dead: Psychological commentary (R. F. C. Hull, Trans.). In W. Y. Evans-Wentz (Eds.), *The Tibetan book of the dead* (pp. xxxv–lii). New York: Oxford University Press.
Kabat-Zinn, J. (1990). *Full catastrophe living: Using the wisdom of your body and mind to face stress, pain, and illness.* New York: Delta.
Kabat-Zinn, J. (2003). Mindfulness-based interventions in context: Past, present, and future. *Clinical Psychology: Science and Practice, 10*(2), 144–156. doi:10.1093/clipsy/bpg016.
Kabat-Zinn, M., & Kabat-Zinn, J. (1997). *Everyday blessings: The inner work of mindful parenting.* New York: Hyperion.
Keating, T. (2006). *Open mind open heart: The contemplative dimension of the gospel.* New York: Continuum International Publishing Group.
Keeney, B. (1996). *Everyday soul: Awakening the spirit in daily life.* New York: Riverhead.
Keeney, B. P. (1983). *Aesthetics of change.* New York: Guilford.
Kimbrough, E., Magyari, T., Langenberg, P., Chesney, M., & Berman, B. (2010). Mindfulness intervention for child abuse survivors. *Journal of Clinical Psychology, 66*(1), 17–33.
Kocovski, N. L., Segal, Z. V., & Battista, S. R. (2009). Mindfulness and psychopathology: Problem formulation. In F. Didonna (Ed.), *Clinical handbook of mindfulness* (pp. 85–98). New York, NY: Springer. doi:10.1007/978-0-387-09593-6_6.
Kornfield, J. (1993). *A path with heart: A guide through the perils and promises of spiritual life.* New York: Bantam.
Kristeller, J. L. (2010). Spiritual engagement as a mechanism of change in mindfulness- and acceptance-based therapies. In R. A. Baer (Ed.), *Assessing mindfulness and acceptance processes in clients: Illuminating the theory and practice of change* (pp. 155–184). Oakland, CA: Context Press/New Harbinger Publications.

Kristeller, J. L., Baer, R. A., & Quillian-Wolever, R. (2006). Mindfulness-based approaches to eating disorders. In R. A. Baer (Ed.), *Mindfulness-based treatment approaches: Clinician's guide to evidence base and applications* (pp. 75–91). San Diego, CA: Elsevier Academic Press.

Kristeller, J. L., & Wolever, R. Q. (2011). Mindfulness-based eating awareness training for treating binge eating disorder: The conceptual foundation. *Eating Disorders, 19*(1), 49–61. doi:10.108 0/10640266.2011.533605.

Labbre, E. E. (2011). *Psychology moment by moment: A guide to enhancing your clinical practice with mindfulness and meditation*. Oakland, CA: New Harbinger.

Lambert, M. J., & Simon, W. (2008). The therapeutic relationship: Central and essential in psychotherapy outcome. In S. F. Hick & T. Bien (Eds.), *Mindfulness and the therapeutic relationship* (pp. 19–33). New York: Guilford.

Lax, W. D. (1996). Narrative, social constructionism, and Buddhism. In H. Rosen (Ed.), *Constructing realities: Meaning-making perspectives for psychotherapists* (pp. 195–220). San Francisco: Jossey-Bass.

Lee, J., Semple, R. J., Rosa, D., & Miller, L. (2008). Mindfulness-based cognitive therapy for children: Results of a pilot study. *Journal of Cognitive Psychotherapy, 22*(1), 15–28. doi:10.1891/ 0889.8391.22.1.15.

Levine, M. (2000). *The positive psychology of Buddhism and yoga: Paths to a mature happiness, with a special application to handling anger* (2nd ed.). New York, NY: Routledge/Taylor & Francis Group.

Lief, J. (2007). *Contemplative education: The spark of East and West working within*. Retrieved from http://www.naropa.edu/conted/conted_primer.cfm

Liehr, P., & Diaz, N. (2010). A pilot study examining the effect of mindfulness on depression and anxiety for minority children. *Archives of Psychiatric Nursing, 24*(1), 69–71. doi:10.1016/j. apnu.2009.10.001.

Linehan, M. M. (1993). *Cognitive-behavioral treatment of borderline personality disorder*. New York: Guilford.

Ma, S., & Teasdale, J. D. (2004). Mindfulness-based cognitive therapy for depression: Replication and exploration of differential relapse prevention effects. *Journal of Consulting and Clinical Psychology, 72*(1), 31–40. doi:10.1037/0022-006X.72.1.31.

Macy, J. (1991). *Mutual causality in Buddhism and general systems theory*. Albany: SUNY.

Masters, W. H., & Johnson, V. E. (1974). *The pleasure bond*. New York: Bantam Books.

McCollum, E., & Gehart, D. (2010). Using mindfulness to teach therapeutic presence: A qualitative outcome study of a mindfulness-based curriculum for teaching therapeutic presence to master's level marriage and family therapy trainees. *Journal of Marital and Family Therapy, 36*, 347–360. doi:10.1111/j.1752-0606.2010.00214.x.

McDonough-Means, S. I., Kreitzer, M. J., & Bell, I. R. (2004). Fostering a healing presence and investigating its mediators. *Journal of Alternative and Complementary Medicine, 10*, S25–S41.

McWilliams, S. A. (2010). Inherent self, invented self, empty self: Constructivism, Buddhism, and psychotherapy. *Counseling and Values, 55*(1), 79–100.

Meckel, D. J., & Moore, R. L. (1992). *Self and liberation: The Jung/Buddhism dialogue*. New York: Paulist Press.

Mendelson, T., Greenberg, M. T., Dariotis, J. K., Gould, L., Rhoades, B. L., & Leaf, P. J. (2010). Feasibility and preliminary outcomes of a school based mindfulness intervention for urban youth. *Journal of Abnormal Child Psychology, 38*(7), 985–994. doi:10.1007/s10802-010-9418-x.

Miller, S. D., Duncan, B. L., & Hubble, M. (1997). *Escape from Babel: Toward a unifying language for psychotherapy practice*. New York: Norton.

Minor, H. G., Carlson, L. E., Mackenzie, M. J., Zernicke, K., & Jones, L. (2006). Evaluation of a Mindfulness-Based Stress Reduction (MBSR) program for caregivers of children with chronic conditions. *Social Work in Health Care, 43*(1), 91–109. doi:10.1300/J010v43n01_06.

Moacanin, R. (1988). *Jung's psychology and Tibetan Buddhism*. London: Wisdom.

Modinos, G., Ormel, J., & Aleman, A. (2010). Individual differences in dispositional mindfulness and brain activity involved in reappraisal of emotion. *Social Cognitive and Affective Neuroscience, 5*(4), 369–377. doi:10.1093/scan/nsq006.

Monk, G., & Gehart, D. R. (2003). Conversational partner or socio-political activist: Distinguishing the position of the therapist in collaborative and narrative therapies. *Family Process, 42*, 19–30.

Müller, F. M. (Trans.). (1898). *The sacred books of the East: Vol. 10, Part 1. The Dhammapada: A collection of verses* (2nd ed.). Oxford, England: Clarendon Press.

Northey, W. F., Wells, K. C., Silverman, W. K., & Bailey, C. E. (2002). Childhood behavioral and emotional disorders. *Journal of Marital and Family Therapy, 29*, 523–546.

O'Hanlon, W. H., & Weiner-Davis, M. (1989). *In search of solutions: A new direction in psychotherapy*. New York: Norton.

Padilla, A. (2011). Mindfulness in therapeutic presence: How mindfulness of therapist impacts treatment outcome. *Dissertation Abstracts International, 71*(9), 5801.

Patterson, J. E., Miller, R. B., Carnes, S., & Wilson, S. (2004). Evidence-based practice for marriage and family therapists. *Journal of Marital and Family Therapy, 30*, 183–195.

Percy, I. (2008). Awareness and authoring: The idea of self in mindfulness and narrative therapy. *European Journal of Psychotherapy and Counselling, 10*(4), 355–367. doi:10.1080/13642530802577109.

Peterson, B. D., Eifert, G. H., Feingold, T., & Davidson, S. (2009). Using acceptance and commitment therapy to treat distressed couples: A case study with two couples. *Cognitive and Behavioral Practice, 16*(4), 430–442. doi:10.1016/j.cbpra.2008.12.009.

Philipsen, A., Richter, H., Peters, J., Alm, B., Sobanski, E., Colla, M., et al. (2007). Structured group psychotherapy in adults with attention deficit hyperactivity disorder: Results of an open multicentre study. *The Journal of Nervous and Mental Disease, 195*(12), 1013–1019. doi:10.1097/NMD.0b013e31815c088b.

Pinto, A. (2009). Mindfulness and psychosis. In F. Didonna (Ed.), *Clinical handbook of mindfulness* (pp. 339–368). New York, NY: Springer. doi:10.1007/978-0-387-09593-6_19.

Pruitt, I. T., & McCollum, E. E. (2010). Voices of experienced meditators: The impact of meditation practice on intimate relationships. *Contemporary Family Therapy, 32*(2), 135–154. doi:10.1007/s10591-009-9112-8.

Rimes, K. A., & Wingrove, J. (2011). Pilot study of mindfulness-based cognitive therapy for trainee clinical psychologists. *Behavioral and Cognitive Psychotherapy, 39*, 235–241.

Rogers, C. (1961). *Onbecoming a person: A counselor's view of psychocounseling*. London: Constable.

Rogers, C. (1981). *Way of being*. Boston: Houghton Mifflin.

Rosenbaum, R., & Dyckman, J. (1996). No self? No problem!: Actualizing empty self in psychotherapy. In M. Hoyt (Ed.), *Constructive therapies, Vol. 2* (pp. 238–274). New York: Guilford.

Roth, B., & Calle-Mesa, L. (2006). Mindfulness-Based Stress Reduction (MBSR) with Spanish- and English-speaking inner-city medical patients. In R. A. Baer (Ed.), *Mindfulness-based treatment approaches: Clinician's guide to evidence base and applications* (pp. 263–284). San Diego, CA: Elsevier Academic Press.

Roth, J. (2009). *Jewish meditation practices for everyday life: Awakening your heart, connecting with God*. Woodstock, VT: Jewish Lights Publications.

Saavedra, M. C., Chapman, K. E., & Rogge, R. D. (2010). Clarifying links between attachment and relationship quality: Hostile conflict and mindfulness as moderators. *Journal of Family Psychology, 24*(4), 380–390. doi:10.1037/a0019872.

Sagamura, G., Haruki, Y., & Koshikawa, F. (2007). Building more soild bridges between Buddhism and Western psychology. *American Psychologist, 62*(9), 1080–1081. doi:10.1037/0003-066X.62.9.1080.

Salzburg, S. (1995). *Loving kindness: The revolutionary art of happiness*. Boston: Shambala.

Satir, V., Banmen, J., Gerber, J., & Gomori, M. (1991). *The Satir model: Family therapy and beyond*. Palo Alto, CA: Science and Behavior Books.

Sauer, S., & Baer, R. A. (2010). Mindfulness and decentering as mechanisms of change in mindfulness- and acceptance-based interventions. In R. A. Baer (Ed.), *Assessing mindfulness and acceptance processes in clients: Illuminating the theory and practice of change* (pp. 25–50). Oakland, CA: Context Press/New Harbinger Publications.

Schnarch, D. M. (1991). *Constructing the sexual crucible: An integration of sexual and marital therapy*. New York: Norton.

Schore, A. N. (1994). *Affect regulation and the origin of the self: The neurobiology of emotional development*. Hillsdale, NJ: Lawrence Erlbaum Associates.

Schwartz, R. C. (1995). *Internal family systems therapy*. New York, NY: Guilford Press.

Segal, L. (1991). Brief therapy: The MRI approach. In A. S. Gurman & D. P. Kniskern (Eds.), *Handbook of family therapy* (pp. 171–199). New York: Brunner/Mazel.

Segal, Z. V., Williams, J. G., & Teasdale, J. D. (2002). *Mindfulness-based cognitive therapy for depression: A new approach to preventing relapse*. New York, NY: Guilford.

Selekman, M. D. (1997). *Solution-focused therapy with children: Harnessing family strengths for systemic change*. New York: Guilford.

Seligman, M. E. P. (2002). *Authentic happiness*. New York: Free Press.

Selvini Palazzoli, M., Boscolo, L., Cecchin, G., & Prata, G. (1978). *Paradox and counterparadox: A new model in the therapy of the family in schizophrenic transaction*. New York: Jason Aronson.

Semple, R. J., Lee, J., & Miller, L. F. (2006). Mindfulness-based cognitive therapy for children. In R. A. Baer (Ed.), *Mindfulness-based treatment approaches: Clinician's guide to evidence base and applications* (pp. 143–166). San Diego, CA: Elsevier Academic Press.

Semple, R. J., Lee, J., Rosa, D., & Miller, L. F. (2010). A randomized trial of mindfulness-based cognitive therapy for children: Promoting mindful attention to enhance social-emotional resiliency in children. *Journal of Child and Family Studies, 19*(2), 218–229. doi:10.1007/s10826-009-9301-y.

Shafir, R. Z. (2000). *The Zen of listening*. Wheaton, IL: Quest Books.

Shafir, R. Z. (2008). Mindful listening for better outcomes. In S. F. Hick & T. Bien (Eds.), *Mindfulness and the therapeutic relationships* (pp. 215–231). New York: Guilford.

Shapiro, S. L., Astin, J. A., Bishop, S. R., & Cordova, M. (2005). Mindfulness-based stress reduction for health care professionals: Results from a randomized trial. *International Journal of Stress Management, 12*(2), 164–176. doi:10.1037/1072-5245.12.2.164.

Shapiro, S. L., Brown, K., & Biegel, G. M. (2007). Teaching self-care to caregivers: Effects of mindfulness-based stress reduction on the mental health of therapists in training. *Training and Education in Professional Psychology, 1*(2), 105–115. doi:10.1037/1931-3918.1.2.105.

Shapiro, S. L., & Carlson, L. E. (2009). *The art and science of mindfulness: Integrating mindfulness into psychology and the helping professions*. Washington, DC: American Psychological Association.

Shapiro, S. L., & Izett, C. D. (2008). Meditation: A universal tool for cultivating empathy. In S. F. Hick & T. Bien (Eds.), *Mindfulness and the therapeutic relationships* (pp. 161–165). New York: Guilford.

Shapiro, S. L., Schwartz, G. E., & Bonner, G. (1998). Effects of mindfulness-based stress reduction on medical and premedical students. *Journal of Behavioral Medicine, 21*(6), 581–599. doi:10.1023/A:1018700829825.

Shapiro, S. L., Warren, K., & Astin, J. (2008). *Toward the integration of meditation into higher education: A review of research*. Retrieved from www.acmhe.org

Shaver, P. R., Lavy, S., Saron, C. D., & Mikulincer, M. (2007). Social foundations of the capacity for mindfulness: An attachment perspective. *Psychological Inquiry, 18*(4), 264–271.

Siegel, D. J. (1999). *The developing mind: How relationships and the brain interact to shape who we are*. New York: Guilford.

Siegel, D. J. (2006). An interpersonal neurobiology approach to psychotherapy: Awareness, mirror neurons, and neural plasticity in the development of well-being. *Psychiatric Annals, 36*(4), 248–256.

Siegel, D. J. (2007). *The mindful brain*. New York: Norton.

Siegel, D. J. (2009). Mindful awareness, mindsight, and neural integration. *Humanistic Psychologist, 37*(2), 137–158. doi:10.1080/08873260902892220.

Siegel, D. J. (2010a). *Mindsight: The new science of personal transformation.* New York, NY: Bantam Books.

Siegel, D. J. (2010b). *The mindful therapist: A clinician's guide to mindsight and neural integration.* New York, NY: Norton.

Singh, N. N., Lancioni, G. E., Joy, S., Winton, A. W., Sabaawi, M., Wahler, R. G., et al. (2007a). Adolescents with conduct disorder can be mindful of their aggressive behavior. *Journal of Emotional and Behavioral Disorders, 15*(1), 56–63. doi:10.1177/10634266070150010601.

Singh, N. N., Lancioni, G. E., Winton, A. W., Singh, J., Curtis, W., Wahler, R. G., et al. (2007b). Mindful parenting decreases aggression and increases social behavior in children with developmental disabilities. *Behavior Modification, 31*(6), 749–771. doi:10.1177/014544550 7300924.

Singh, N. N., Singh, A. N., Lancioni, G. E., Singh, J., Winton, A. W., & Adkins, A. D. (2010). Mindfulness training for parents and their children with ADHD increases the children's compliance. *Journal of Child and Family Studies, 19*(2), 157–166. doi:10.1007/s10826-009-9272-z.

Smalley, S. L., Loo, S. K., Hale, T., Shrestha, A., McGough, J., Flook, L., et al. (2009). Mindfulness and attention deficit hyperactivity disorder. *Journal of Clinical Psychology, 65*(10), 1087–1098. doi:10.1002/jclp.20618.

Smalley, S. L., & Winston, D. (2010). *Fully present: The science, art, and practice of mindfulness.* Philadelphia, PA: Life Long Books.

South, S. C., Doss, B. D., & Christensen, A. (2010). Through the eyes of the beholder: The mediating role of relationship acceptance in the impact of partner behavior. *Family Relations, 59*(5), 611–622. doi:10.1111/j.1741-3729.2010.00627.x.

Sprenkle, D. H., Davis, S. D., & Lebow, J. L. (2009). *Common factors in couple and family therapy: The overlooked foundation for effective practice.* New York: Guilford.

Stahl, B., & Goldstein, E. (2010). *A mindfulness-based stress reduction workbook.* Oakland, CA: New Harbinger.

Szapocznik, J., & Williams, R. A. (2000). Brief Strategic Family Therapy: Twenty-five years of interplay among theory, research and practice in adolescent behavior problems and drug abuse. *Clinical Child and Family Psychology Review, 3*(2), 117–134.

Tang, Y., Lu, Q., Geng, X., Stein, E. A., Yang, Y., & Posner, M. I. (2010). Short-term meditation induces white matter changes in the anterior cingulate. *PNAS Proceedings of the National Academy of Sciences of the United States of America, 107*(35), 15649–15652. doi:10.1073/pnas.1011043107.

Tang, Y., Ma, Y., Fan, Y., Feng, H., Wang, J., Feng, S., et al. (2009). Central and autonomic nervous system interaction is altered by short-term meditation. *PNAS Proceedings of the National Academy of Sciences of the United States of America, 106*(22), 8865–8870. doi:10.1073/pnas.0904031106.

Tang, Y., Ma, Y., Wang, J., Fan, Y., Feng, S., Lu, Q., et al. (2007). Short-term meditation training improves attention and self-regulation. *PNAS Proceedings of the National Academy of Sciences of the United States of America, 104*(43), 17152–17156. doi:10.1073/pnas.0707678104.

Thompson, M., & Gauntlett-Gilbert, J. (2008). Mindfulness with children and adolescents: Effective clinical application. *Clinical Child Psychology and Psychiatry, 13*(3), 395–407. doi:10.1177/1359104508090603.

Ting-Toomey, S. (2009). A mindful approach to managing conflict in intercultural intimate couples. In T. A. Karis & K. D. Killian (Eds.), *Intercultural couples: Exploring diversity in intimate relationships* (pp. 31–49). New York, NY: Routledge/Taylor & Francis Group.

Treadway, M. T., & Lazar, S. W. (2010). Meditation and neuroplasticity: Using mindfulness to change the brain. In R. A. Baer (Ed.), *Assessing mindfulness and acceptance processes in clients: Illuminating the theory and practice of change* (pp. 186–205). Oakland, CA: Context Press/New Harbinger Publications.

Trungpa, C. (1991). *Crazy wisdom.* Boston: Shambala.

Twohig, M. P., Hayes, S. C., & Berlin, K. S. (2008). Acceptance and commitment therapy for childhood externalizing disorders. In L. A. Greco & S. C. Hayes (Eds.), *Acceptance and mindfulness treatments for children and adolescents: A practitioner's guide* (pp. 163–186). Oakland, CA: New Harbinger Publications.

van den Hurk, P. M., Giommi, F., Gielen, S. C., Speckens, A. M., & Barendregt, H. P. (2010). Greater efficiency in attentional processing related to mindfulness meditation. *The Quarterly Journal of Experimental Psychology, 63*(6), 1168–1180. doi:10.1080/17470210903249365.

Vestergaard-Poulsen, P., van Beek, M., Skewes, J., Bjarkam, C. R., Stubberup, M., Bertelsen, J., et al. (2009). Long-term meditation is associated with increased gray matter density in the brain stem. *NeuroReport: For Rapid Communication of Neuroscience Research, 20*(2), 170–174. doi:10.1097/WNR.0b013e328320012a.

Wachs, K., & Cordova, J. V. (2007). Mindful relating: Exploring mindfulness and emotion repertoires in intimate relationships. *Journal of Marital and Family Therapy, 33*(4), 464–481. doi:10.1111/j.1752-0606.2007.00032.x.

Walsh, J. J., Balint, M. G., Smolira SJ, D. R., Fredricksen, L., & Madsen, S. (2009). Predicting individual differences in mindfulness: The role of trait anxiety, attachment anxiety and attentional control. *Personality and Individual Differences, 46*(2), 94–99. doi:10.1016/j.paid.2008.09.008.

Watts, A. (1961). *Psychotherapy East and West*. New York: Vintage.

Watzlawick, P. (Ed.). (1984). *The invented reality: How do we know what we believe we know?* New York: Norton.

Watzlawick, P., Bavelas, J. B., & Jackson, D. D. (1967). *Pragmatics of human communication: A study of interactional patterns, pathologies, and paradoxes*. New York: Norton.

Watzlawick, P., Weakland, J., & Fisch, R. (1974). *Change: Principles of problem formation and problem resolution*. New York: Norton.

Weber, B. B., Jermann, F. F., Gex-Fabry, M. M., Nallet, A. A., Bondolfi, G. G., & Aubry, J. M. (2010). Mindfulness-based cognitive therapy for bipolar disorder: A feasibility trial. *European Psychiatry, 25*(6), 334–337. doi:10.1016/j.eurpsy.2010.03.007.

Weiss, Z., & Levy, D. (2010). 'The eternal is with me, I shall not fear': Jewish contemplative practices and well-being. In T. G. Plante (Ed.), *Contemplative practices in action: Spirituality, meditation, and health* (pp. 103–121). Santa Barbara, CA: Praeger.

White, M. (2007). *Maps of narrative practice*. New York: Norton.

White, M., & Epston, D. (1990). *Narrative means to therapeutic ends*. New York: Norton.

Wieder, S., & Greenspan, S. I. (2003). Climbing the symbolic ladder in the DIR model through floor time/interactive play. *Autism, 7*(4), 425–435. doi:10.1177/1362361303007004008.

Willard, C. (2010). *Child's mindfulness: Mindfulness practices to help our children be more focused, calm, and relaxed*. Berkeley, CA: Parallax Press.

Wilson, K., Sandoz, E. K., Flynn, M. K., Slater, R. M., & DuFrene, T. (2010). Understanding, assessing, and treating values processes in mindfulness- and acceptance-based therapies. In R. A. Baer (Ed.), *Assessing mindfulness and acceptance processes in clients: Illuminating the theory and practice of change* (pp. 77–106). Oakland, CA: Context Press/New Harbinger Publications.

Witkiewitz, K., Marlatt, G., & Walker, D. (2005). Mindfulness-based relapse prevention for alcohol and substance use disorders. *Journal of Cognitive Psychotherapy, 19*(3), 211–228. doi:10.1891/jcop. 2005.19.3.211.

Wolever, R. Q., & Best, J. L. (2009). Mindfulness-based approaches to eating disorders. In F. Didonna (Ed.), *Clinical handbook of mindfulness* (pp. 259–287). New York, NY: Springer. doi:10.1007/978-0-387-09593-6_15.

York, M. M. (2007). A qualitative study into the experience of individuals involved in a mindfulness group within an acute inpatient mental health unit. *Journal of Psychiatric and Mental Health Nursing, 14*(6), 603–608. doi:10.1111/j.1365-2850.2007.01148.x.

Young, M. (2005). *Learning the art of helping: Building blocks and techniques* (3rd ed.). Upper Saddle River, NJ: Pearson.

Zylowska, L., Ackerman, D. L., Yang, M. H., Futrell, J. L., Horton, N. L., Hale, T., et al. (2008). Mindfulness meditation training in adults and adolescents with ADHD: A feasibility study. *Journal of Attention Disorders, 11*(6), 737–746. doi:10.1177/1087054707308502.

Zylowska, L. L., Smalley, S. L., & Schwartz, J. M. (2009). Mindful awareness and ADHD. In F. Didonna (Ed.), *Clinical handbook of mindfulness* (pp. 319–338). New York, NY: Springer. doi:10.1007/978-0-387-09593-6_18.

Index